Birding South Carolina

D1057793

Help Us Keep This Guide Up to Date

Every effort has been made by the author and editors to make this guide as accurate and useful as possible. However, many things can change after a guide is published—trails are rerouted, regulations change, facilities come under new management, and so forth.

We would love to hear from you concerning your experiences with this guide and how you feel it could be improved and kept up to date. While we may not be able to respond to all comments and suggestions, we'll take them to heart, and we'll also make certain to share them with the author. Please send your comments and suggestions to the following address:

The Globe Pequot Press
Reader Response/Editorial Department
P.O. Box 480
Guilford, CT 06437

Or you may e-mail us at:

editorial@GlobePequot.com

Thanks for your input, and happy birding!

Birding South Carolina

A Guide to 40 Premier Birding Sites

Jeff Mollenhauer

GUILFORD, CONNECTICUT
HELENA, MONTANA

AN IMPRINT OF THE GLOBE PEQUOT PRESS

To buy books in quantity for corporate use
or incentives, call **(800) 962–0973**
or e-mail **premiums@GlobePequot.com.**

FALCONGUIDES®

Copyright © 2009 by Morris Book Publishing, LLC

ALL RIGHTS RESERVED. No part of this book
may be reproduced or transmitted in any form by
any means, electronic or mechanical, including pho-
tocopying and recording, or by any information storage and retrieval system, except as may be expressly
permitted in writing by the publisher. Requests for
permission should be addressed to The Globe Pequot
Press, Attn: Rights and Permissions Department,
P.O. Box 480, Guilford, CT 06437.

Falcon, FalconGuides, and Outfit Your Mind are
registered trademarks of Morris Book Publishing,
LLC.

All interior photos by Jeff Mollenhauer unless other-
wise credited
Project manager: Jessica Haberman
Text design: Eileen Hine
Layout: Melissa Evarts
Maps: Daniel Lloyd © Morris Book Publishing, LLC

Library of Congress Cataloging-in-Publication Data
    Mollenhauer, Jeff.
    Birding South Carolina : a guide to 40 premier
birding sites / Jeff Mollenhauer.
        p. cm.
    Includes bibliographical references and index.
    ISBN 978-0-7627-4579-1
    1. Bird watching—South Carolina—Guidebooks.
2. South Carolina—Guidebooks. 3. Birds—South
Carolina. I. Title.
    QL684.S6M65 2009
    598.072'34757—dc22
                                    2008046128

Printed in the United States of America
10 9 8 7 6 5 4 3 2 1

The author and The Globe Pequot Press assume no liability for accidents happening
to, or injuries sustained by, readers who engage in the activities described in this book.

Contents

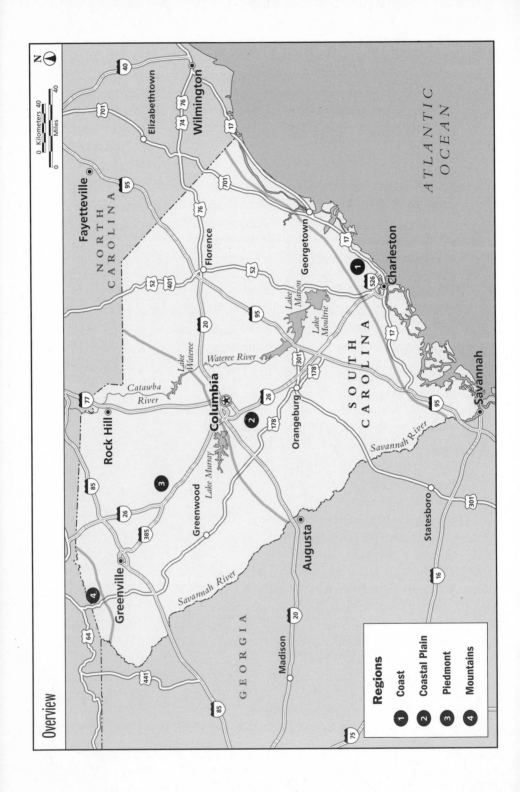

Overview

Acknowledgments

There are so many people and organizations that have helped me during the writing of this guide that it is hard to know where to start. Some people provided places to stay, some offered opinions on favorite birding areas, some helped edit and proofread, and some supported me during the writing process. Without all of these people this guide would not be nearly as informative and would have taken much longer to write.

By far the people who sacrificed the most during the writing of this book were the people I am closest to. So, I would like to begin by thanking my beautiful wife, Meagan, who patiently supported me throughout the writing of this guide, even though I had to give up 90 percent of my free time to complete it. My daughter, Ava Kai, who is the best looking "sea bird" that I have ever seen. My dad and mom, Erik and Kris Mollenhauer, have always believed in me and supported my crazy birding habits. If they had never bought me that first pair of binoculars, who knows what I would be doing right now. My two younger brothers, Ross and Brett, have been my companions on countless adventures and many yet to come. If this book can't sway them to the dark side, then I am at a loss. My aunt/cousin/grandmother, Arly Flaherty, has constantly been an inspiration to me with her strength, spirit, and kindness. It is important to note that she hosted me on my first of many birding trips to south Texas, during which I bought my first FalconGuide. I can't say enough about the generosity of Donn and Sallie James, who provided me with a home away from home, which allowed me to spend countless hours birding the mountains and piedmont. Donn and Sallie showed me the true meaning of "Southern hospitality." Without the love and support of these family members and close friends, this book would never have come to fruition. I can't thank you all enough.

I would also like to thank Frank Holleman for writing the foreword; Will Brown for creating the maps of South Carolina's physiographic regions that I used in presentations about the guide; Robin Carter and Giff Beaton for their help with the status and distribution chart; Kim Counts and Jeff Catlin for providing photos; Charlotte White and Simon and Caroline Harvey for providing me with places to stay during my travels; and Denise Ecker, Irvin Pitts, Laurel Barnhill, Andy Harrison, Jason Giovannone, Paul Koehler, Ross Mollenhauer, Paul Serridge, Dan Tufford, Robin Carter, Anna Martin, Elizabeth Vernon, Mike Walker, Barbara Thomas, Donnie Coody, JB Hines, Jeff Catlin, and Frank Holleman for editing and proofreading. Ann Shahid, Paul Koehler, Steve Tracey, JB Hines, Donnie Coody, Steve Patterson, Jeff Catlin, Lois Stacey, Felicia Sanders, and Mark Spinks were all nice enough to provide me with guided tours of some of the birding areas, and Will Carlisle, Nathan Dias, John Cely, Paul Champlin, Howard Costa, David Chamberlain, Clem Dietze, Lyle Campbell, Richard Moore, Reggie Daves, John Grego, Chip Gilbert, Taylor Drayton Nelson, and

Barry Lowes helped provide valuable information for some of the birding areas. If I have forgotten to mention anyone who contributed to the guide, I am deeply sorry and will grovel for forgiveness the next time we cross paths.

Finally, I would like to thank some of the organizations that helped me out along the way. Were it not for the patience and support of the staff from Audubon South Carolina and the South Carolina Department of Natural Resources, I would never have been able to finish this guide in a timely manner. Special thanks to Norman Brunswig, Linda Renshaw, and Elizabeth Vernon for allowing me to embark on this endeavor. A big thanks to all of the birding organizations in South Carolina that helped me out along the way, including Hilton Head Audubon Society, Charleston Natural History Society, Waccamaw Audubon Society, and the Greenville Bird Club. Thanks to the captain and crew of the *Thunderstar* for allowing me to ride for free while searching for pelagic birds. Last, but not least, thanks to the staff at FalconGuides for offering me this unique opportunity to write a guide about South Carolina's birds.

Foreword

South Carolina is renowned for its natural beauty. Thousands of people visit the state each year and many thousands have moved here because of our beaches, marshes, rolling hills, and beautiful Blue Ridge Mountains. Part and parcel of our natural beauty are South Carolina's birds.

In *Birding South Carolina*, Jeff Mollenhauer has given us longtime South Carolina residents and our welcome visitors an informed and extremely useful guide to seeing and appreciating South Carolina's glorious birdlife. In this convenient volume, Jeff has literally handed us the results of his professional training, years of birding, and extensive research in putting this guide together. Jeff now serves as the Director of Bird Conservation for Audubon South Carolina and is particularly well qualified to tell us not only where to locate South Carolina's birds, but also how to view them responsibly.

By obtaining this one guidebook, we also get the benefit of Jeff's extensive work in putting it together. In one year, he visited birding sites in all corners of the state specifically for the purpose of assembling this guide, running up some 20,000 miles on his car's odometer. As Jeff told me, "That is more driving than I will ever want to do in a year again. But remarkably, the amount of ground that I covered is not even close to the migration of an Arctic Tern, which can fly some 25,000 miles each year from its breeding grounds near the North Pole to its wintering grounds near the South Pole. This year has given me a tremendous amount of respect for a creature that can travel such an amazing distance without the luxury of an automobile." Jeff may not have matched the Arctic Tern in his journey, but through this guide he has given us the benefit of thousands of miles of travel informed by his professional training and experience.

This guide is also a reminder that we cannot take South Carolina's natural beauty or its birdlife for granted. Many of these birding sites—near the coast, the mountains, and our major cities—are in areas that are developing at lightning speed. While South Carolina is one of the nation's smaller states, it ranks near the top of the list of states that are converting open space to subdivisions and shopping centers. It is more urgent than ever that South Carolina residents and visitors who use this guide contribute to the protection of the striking birds and gorgeous places that we South Carolinians and our guests are privileged to enjoy.

Jeff notes in the guide that South Carolina's hunters have contributed a great deal over the years to protecting open spaces in our state. In order to hunt, they must buy licenses, they pay special taxes, and many pay to lease, maintain, and protect wildlife habitat. By contrast, birding is virtually free. We bird-watchers are able to walk through lands protected by federal, state, and local governments and private conservation groups at no charge or for a small fee. Bird-watching doesn't require a license, and we pay no special taxes in South Carolina on the equipment we birders use. It is time that we bird-watchers work to match hunters in our support for protecting South Carolina's birdlife and its natural beauty.

So, as we use Jeff's guide and travel the state looking at some of creation's most memorable creatures, let's also remember that we have a responsibility to help protect South Carolina's birds and natural landscape. Audubon South Carolina works specifically to protect birds and their habitat in our state. The Nature Conservancy, the South Carolina Wildlife Federation, and the Sierra Club statewide; the Coastal Conservation League at the coast and Upstate Forever in the upcountry; and numerous land trusts and river groups in our local communities are working to make sure that South Carolina's natural heritage is preserved. South Carolina's Department of Natural Resources, our State Parks, and our state's Conservation Bank strive every day to preserve areas of particular natural significance. All these organizations and agencies deserve our contributions and our support.

Take this guide, travel South Carolina, and see some of the most beautiful birds in the world. But remember that you can't take them for granted, and that we all have a responsibility to make sure they will be here for our children and grandchildren.

—Frank Holleman
Board Chair, Audubon South Carolina Advisory Board

Introduction

With a wide variety of habitats, South Carolina is an excellent state for bird-watching. The sandy beaches, old rice fields, cypress swamps, blackwater rivers, longleaf pine savannas, and a tiny sliver of the Blue Ridge Mountains provide habitat for the more than 400 bird species that have been observed in South Carolina. Specialty birds of the southeastern United States, such as Black-bellied Whistling-Duck, Anhinga, Reddish Egret, Wood Stork, Swallow-tailed and Mississippi Kites, Purple Gallinule, Common Ground-Dove, Red-cockaded Woodpecker, Swainson's Warbler, Bachman's Sparrow, and Painted Bunting, are all relatively easy to find in South Carolina with a little help from this guide. Pelagic trips from the coast can produce good numbers of shearwaters, petrels, storm-petrels, phalaropes, and even an occasional frigatebird or tropicbird. Tidal mudflats along the coast attract hundreds of thousands of shorebirds during migration and in winter, while the cove hardwood forests of the mountains attract a like number of migrating and breeding songbirds. Barrier islands along the coast serve as important nesting areas for tens of thousands of Brown Pelicans, Royal Terns, Black Skimmers, and other seabirds.

In terms of population, South Carolina is ranked twentieth among the fifty states, with a population density of roughly 116 people per square mile. It is ranked fortieth in state size, with only about 32,000 square miles, so you will rarely be more than a five-hour drive from your next birding site. The summer can be hot and humid, but is a good time to look for many of South Carolina's specialty birds, such as Swainson's Warbler and Swallow-tailed Kite. Temperatures are much milder in the spring, when you can find migrants and breeding birds in their brightly colored breeding plumage. Many of the birds are easier to locate during spring because they are extremely active and vocal as they gear up for the breeding season. Although the birds are less vocal and colorful in the fall, they make up for it in sheer numbers. Millions of migrating shorebirds and songbirds pour through the state from late summer through the fall.

South Carolina's mild winters attract many birds (and birders) from the north. Christmas Bird Count circles along the coast often yield 150 to 180 bird species, numbers that can be rivaled by circles in just a few other states. In fact, of the more than 2,000 Christmas Bird Count circles in the United States, the count circles along the South Carolina coast are consistently among the top fifty counts in the country for total number of bird species. From 2001 to 2007, South Carolina Christmas Bird Count circles had the highest totals in the United States for the twenty-one species listed below. (If a species was the highest in South Carolina during more than one year, the number of years is given in parentheses.)

Common Loon
Little Blue Heron (3)
Wood Duck
American Oystercatcher (4)
Semipalmated Plover (3)
Least Tern
Barred Owl
Red-cockaded Woodpecker (5)
Eastern Kingbird
Blue-headed Vireo
Brown-headed Nuthatch (4)

Eastern Bluebird
Yellow-rumped "Myrtle" Warbler (4)
Yellow-throated Warbler
Eastern Towhee (2)
Chipping Sparrow (2)
Field Sparrow
Henslow's Sparrow
Saltmarsh Sharp-tailed Sparrow (2)
Seaside Sparrow
Rusty Blackbird

No matter your birding skill level, you will find the information contained in this guide to be invaluable to finding birds in South Carolina. The guide provides detailed descriptions of the forty best bird-watching areas in the state, grouped into four regions: coast, coastal plain, piedmont, and mountains. Within each region are descriptions of some of South Carolina's best bird-watching areas. For each area, you will find driving directions, a bird species list, the best season(s) to visit, habitat types, and other useful information. In addition to the detailed descriptions of South Carolina's finest bird-watching sites, the guide also contains many useful tools for finding birds in the state. A status and distribution chart for 349 of South Carolina's bird species, developed specifically for this guide, will help you determine how likely you are to see each species and when to search for it. The birding calendar can help you plan your trips so that you will be in the right place at the right time to witness thousands of migrating Broad-winged Hawks, hundreds of Wood Storks feeding, Reddish Egrets dancing in the surf, and many other dazzling experiences that you won't want to miss. Also included is a list of South Carolina specialty birds, which provides a description of the best habitats and areas to visit for more than 175 of the most sought-after species in the state.

How to Use This Guide

Each of the forty bird-watching areas selected for this guide have been assigned a name and number. An area may contain several birding sites. For example, the Charleston Harbor East birding area contains descriptions of four sites: Patriots Point, Pitt Street Bridge, Fort Moultrie, and Breach Inlet. In order to make this guide as user-friendly as possible, the information for each of the forty birding areas has been divided into the following sections:

Habitats: This section lists all the different types of habitat that can be found in the area. Knowing the habitats found at a site will help give you an idea of what kinds of birds to expect. Refer to this chapter's "Habitats" section for a description of each type and a brief list of the bird species typical of that habitat.

Specialty birds: This section lists some of the bird species that are likely to be encountered in the area. Birds that are considered to be rare or accidental in the area were not included in this section. The specialty birds are divided into four categories: *Resident*—birds that can be found at the site all year long; *Summer*— birds that can be found during June and July; *Winter*—birds that can be found November through March; *Migration*—birds that are seen at the site only during spring (April and May) and/or fall (August through October) migrations. Birds that can be found during summer or winter in South Carolina were omitted from the "Migration" category. See Appendix C, "Specialty Birds of South Carolina," for more information on the best times and locations to find many of the birds listed in this section. In many cases, common birds that have widespread distributions throughout South Carolina have been omitted from the specialty birds section, unless the area contains a particularly high number of the species.

Best times to bird: Certain seasons of the year may be better than others for birding at a particular site. This section suggests the best time(s) of year to visit the area.

Directions: This section includes directions to reach the area. The directions often start from the intersection of two major roads or an interstate highway exit. Directions to specific birding locations within the area are given in the "The Birding" section. For some areas, the driving directions section has been omitted and the directions are given in the "The Birding" section.

The Birding: This section will guide you through the area and help you find the best locations to observe birds. Specific emphasis is given to South Carolina's specialty birds or birds that are difficult to find in the state. Some terms that are used frequently throughout this section are *songbirds, seabirds, pelagic birds, sea ducks, wading birds, raptors,* and *shorebirds. Songbirds* refers to the perching birds such as vireos, warblers, thrushes, tanagers, sparrows, and finches. *Seabirds* are birds that live in the ocean close to shore, like terns, skimmers, gulls, and pelicans. *Pelagic birds* are found in the deep ocean many miles from shore and include petrels, storm-petrels, and shearwaters. *Sea ducks* refers to ducks that are often found only in the ocean, such as scoters, eiders, and the Long-tailed Duck. *Wading birds* are birds in the family Ardeidae, like herons and egrets. *Raptors* refers to birds of prey, such as hawks, eagles, falcons, and kites. *Shorebirds* are birds in the order Charadriiformes and include sandpipers, dowitchers, and phalaropes.

General Information: This section contains information about the logistics of planning your trip, including entrance fees, hours of operation, and facilities. If no information is given about an entrance fee, there was not a fee at the time of this writing. Please keep in mind that entrance fees and hours of operation may have changed since this book was written. If you plan on visiting state parks on a regular basis, it may be worthwhile to buy a $50 annual pass that will give you free admission into all of South Carolina's state parks.

DeLorme atlas: One of the best atlases that you can buy to navigate South Carolina's back roads is the DeLorme *South Carolina Atlas & Gazetteer.* This section provides the DeLorme atlas page number and grid for the area. The DeLorme atlas can be bought at many of the larger bookstores or online at http://shop.delorme.com.

Hazards: This section lists any hazards that may be encountered in the area. These are only *potential* hazards, and in most cases you are unlikely to have any problems with them. This information is not meant to discourage you from visiting the area, but rather to prepare you to avoid potential hazards. For a detailed description of each hazard, see the "Planning Your Trip" section of this chapter.

Nearest food, gas, lodging: Here you will find the nearest town that provides at least a few different options for food, gas, and lodging.

Camping: This section lists the nearest public campground. In cases where there are no public campgrounds within a reasonable distance of the area, this section has been omitted. Contact information for each campground is listed in Appendix E.

For more information: To get more information about the area, look up the organization listed in this section in Appendix E. The appendix contains the addresses and phone numbers for many of the birding areas listed in the guide. With GPS navigation systems in cars becoming more and more prevalent, the addresses listed in Appendix E can be particularly useful in getting directions to a location.

Climate and Topography

For the purposes of this book, I have divided South Carolina into four physiographic regions: coast, coastal plain, piedmont, and mountains. Most South Carolina guides consider the coast to be a part of the coastal plain and often refer to the coast as the "outer coastal plain." However, since there are so many bird species that are found only along the immediate coast, it is necessary to treat the coast as a separate physiographic region. South Carolina has a subtropical climate with hot, humid summers and mild winters.

Coast: The coast extends from beaches along the Atlantic Ocean to roughly 25 miles inland. The elevation in this region ranges from sea level to 150 feet. The average temperatures during the summer are 74 to 87 degrees Fahrenheit. In winter, average temperatures are 43 to 59 degrees. The coast receives an average precipitation of 48 inches per year. This region is typified by its barrier islands, beaches, salt marshes, cypress swamps, and longleaf pine forests. More than 600,000 people live along the coast, and resorts in Myrtle Beach, Charleston, and Hilton Head attract hundreds of thousands of tourists each year. Locals often refer to this region as the "Lowcountry."

Because of the wide variety of habitats in this region, it supports the highest diversity of bird species in the state. Birding on the coast is good to excellent year-round. During the summer the bugs, heat, and humidity at some sites in the region can be unbearable at times. In the winter the coast offers the best birding in South Carolina. Spring and late summer are great times to witness the spectacle of shorebird migration. Some birds that are typical of this region are Wood Stork, Swallow-tailed Kite, Wilson's Plover, Least Tern, Black Skimmer, Red-cockaded Woodpecker, Bachman's Sparrow, and Painted Bunting.

Coastal plain: The coastal plain extends from 25 miles inland to the "Fall Line," an area of elevation change where the flat coastal plain meets the rolling hills of the piedmont. Major rivers on or near the Fall Line often have a series of rapids or waterfalls where the piedmont "falls" into the coastal plain. The Fall Line lies just northwest of the cities of North Augusta and Columbia. The farther inland you travel in the coastal plain, the more hills you will see (the highest are around 300 feet). The average temperatures during the summer are 71 to 93 degrees; in winter, 39 to 59 degrees. The coastal plain receives an average precipitation of 45 inches per year. Over 1.5 million people live in this region.

The coastal plain includes a unique zone at the edge of the piedmont called the "Sandhills," a narrow strip of ancient sand dunes. Millions of years ago the ocean came as far inland as the ancient dunes of the Sandhills, but the dunes have long since been covered by some of the most extensive longleaf pine forest in the state.

The coastal plain is the largest of the physiographic regions and covers roughly half of South Carolina. Some birds that are typical of this region are American Golden-Plover, Buff-breasted Sandpiper, Red-cockaded Woodpecker, Swainson's Warbler, Bachman's Sparrow, Blue Grosbeak, and Painted Bunting.

Piedmont: The piedmont is a series of rolling hills that extends from the Fall Line to the very northwest corner of the state, where it borders with the mountains. It is the most fragmented region in South Carolina because of intense logging, farming, and development. Agriculture is focused in the lower piedmont, while the upper piedmont is the most heavily industrialized region in South Carolina. The elevation range in this region is 300 to 1,200 feet. The average temperatures during the summer are 69 to 87 degrees; in winter, 32 to 52 degrees. The piedmont receives an average precipitation of 45 inches per year. Over 1.75 million people live in the piedmont, mainly in four counties: Anderson, Greenville, Spartanburg, and York. Locals often refer to the piedmont and mountains as the "Upstate."

The best time to visit the piedmont is during spring and fall migrations, when you can expect to find plenty of warblers, vireos, thrushes, tanagers, and grosbeaks. The piedmont has a wider diversity of songbird migrants than any other region of the state. Some birds that are typical of this region are Whip-poor-will; Horned Lark; Yellow Warbler; Dickcissel; and Field, Grasshopper, and White-crowned Sparrows.

Mountains: The mountains are the smallest physiographic region in South Carolina and encompass only the northern portions of three counties—Oconee,

Pickens, and Greenville—in the northwest corner of the state. The elevation ranges from 1,200 to 3,554 feet at Sassafras Mountain. Most of the mountains are below 3,000 feet in elevation and hardly compare to some of the higher peaks just across the North Carolina border. However, the elevations are high enough to support bird species that are not found in any other regions of the state. The average temperatures during the summer are 61 to 84 degrees; in winter, 28 to 51 degrees. The mountains receive more rain than any other portion of the state, with an average precipitation of 70 inches per year.

During spring and fall the mountains provide an excellent spot to observe songbird migration. Migrants such as Blackburnian, Canada, Cerulean, and Cape May Warblers and Rose-breasted Grosbeak are often easier to find here than in the other regions. The mountains are a great place to visit in the summer when heat, humidity, and biting flies drive you away from other areas. Here you can find breeding birds that are difficult to find elsewhere in the state, such as Ruffed Grouse; Common Raven; Red-breasted Nuthatch; Golden-crowned Kinglet; Black-throated Green, Black-throated Blue, Chestnut-sided, and Worm-eating Warblers; and Scarlet Tanager. Some sections of the mountains even have large stands of hemlock/white pine forest, which have produced occasional sightings of Northern Saw-whet Owl, Red Crossbill, Pine Siskin, and Purple Finch.

Habitats

Hardwood forest: Refers to forest that is dominated by deciduous trees. Birds typical of hardwood forests are Red-eyed Vireo, Wood Thrush, and Black-throated Blue Warbler.

Mixed pine-hardwood forest: This is forest that is a mix of coniferous and deciduous trees. Birds typical of pine-hardwood forest are Black-and-white and Yellow-throated Warblers and Summer Tanager. Maritime forests are included within this habitat type, since they typically consist of more than 50 percent live oak with a mixture of pine and palmetto trees. Maritime forest is found only along the coast and is often adjacent to either beach or salt marsh. Birds typically found in maritime forest are Northern Parula, Yellow-throated Warbler, and Painted Bunting.

Pine forest: Refers to forest that is dominated by coniferous trees. Longleaf pine forests, a once-prevalent but now rare type of pine forest found in the southeastern United States, can be found in the coastal plain. Birds typical of pine forest are Red-cockaded Woodpecker, Brown-headed Nuthatch, and Pine Warbler. Some pine forests also contain savannas, where the trees are widely spaced and the understory consists largely of grasses. Birds typical of pine savannas are Northern Bobwhite and Bachman's and Henslow's Sparrows.

Pond: Any small, permanent, enclosed body of water. Birds typical of this habitat include Pied-billed Grebe, Green Heron, Ring-necked and Ruddy Ducks, Green-winged and Blue-winged Teals, Northern Shoveler, and Belted Kingfisher.

Rice fields and waterfowl impoundments are included within this habitat type. Rice fields are a series of canals and dikes along the edges of the rivers in the Lowcountry where rice was cultivated from the late 1600s to 1890. Rice fields have now become important wildlife habitat and support a variety of waterfowl, wading birds, and shorebirds.

Lake: A very large, permanent, enclosed body of water, such as a reservoir. Typical birds found in or near lakes are Common Loon, Horned Grebe, Redhead, Lesser Scaup, Bald Eagle, and Bonaparte's Gull.

Stream: Any permanent, moving watercourse that is less than 20 feet wide. Typical birds found near streams include Louisiana Waterthrush, Eastern Phoebe, and Acadian Flycatcher.

River: Any permanent, moving watercourse that is greater than 20 feet wide. Typical birds found along rivers include Hooded Merganser, Great Blue Heron, Swallow-tailed Kite, and Belted Kingfisher.

Swamp: Refers to flooded or wet forest. In the coast and coastal plain regions, you can find the beautiful bottomland hardwood swamps for which the southeastern United States is so famous. These swamps are often dominated by bald cypress and swamp gum trees that are surrounded by water during the wetter months of the year. Hardwood swamps serve as a buffer along rivers and help prevent flooding of the surrounding area. Birds typically found in swamps are Prothonotary Warbler, Pileated Woodpecker, Barred Owl, and Winter Wren.

Farmland: This habitat type includes crop fields, cattle pastures, and sod farms. Birds typically found in farmland habitat include Sandhill Crane; Buff-breasted, Upland, and Pectoral Sandpipers; American Golden-Plover; Horned Lark; American Pipit; and Bobolink.

Field: A patch of land where the dominant vegetation is grasses and sedges. Typical birds found in fields are Sedge Wren and Field, LeConte's, Henslow's, and Grasshopper Sparrows.

Early successional: This habitat type is dominated by shrubs or young trees. When a grassy field is no longer mowed or managed, it will become an early successional habitat within a couple of years. If left alone, an early successional habitat will eventually develop into a forest. Birds that are typically found in early successional habitat are Yellow-breasted Chat, Blue Grosbeak, Indigo Bunting, Prairie Warbler, and Eastern Towhee.

Beach: This habitat type refers to the sandy beaches and dunes along the coast that are constantly being shaped by wave and wind action. Many shorebirds roost along the beaches during high tide or utilize the dunes for nesting during the summer. Birds typical of the beach include Piping Plover, Red Knot, Sanderling, Ruddy Turnstone, and Willet.

Mudflat: This is an area of muddy, low-lying land that is exposed during low tide but submerged during high tide. Birds typically found on mudflats include

Wilson's and Black-bellied Plovers, American Oystercatcher, Marbled Godwit, and Short-billed Dowitcher.

Salt marsh: This habitat type is only found along the coast where salt or brackish water meets the land. Salt marshes consist mainly of cord grass (*Spartina* spp.) and a soft, pungent mud, which locals refer to as "pluff mud." Salt marshes serve as a nursery for young fish and invertebrates, which are a great food source for many herons, egrets, shorebirds, gulls, and terns. Some other birds that are typically found in the salt marsh are Clapper Rail, Seaside Sparrow, and Saltmarsh and Nelson's Sharp-tailed Sparrows.

Freshwater marsh: This habitat is found along the edges of rivers, ponds, and artificially created wetlands. Along the coast there are numerous old rice fields that have reverted to freshwater marsh. Birds typical of the freshwater marsh are Least and American Bitterns, Virginia and King Rails, Sora, and Common Yellowthroat.

Ocean: Refers to the shallow areas of the Atlantic Ocean near the coast of South Carolina. Birds typically found in this habitat include Red-throated and Common Loons; Horned Grebe; Brown Pelican; Northern Gannet; and Least, Royal, and Sandwich Terns.

Pelagic: Translated literally from its Greek origins, *pelagic* refers to the "open ocean." To see birds in this habitat, you will have to take a boat far out into the ocean. The best pelagic birding is often found where the colder water near the coast meets the warm water of the Gulf Stream. To reach the Gulf Stream in South Carolina, you will have to travel about 50 miles offshore. Birds typical of the pelagic habitat are Cory's Shearwater, Wilson's Storm-Petrel, and Sooty and Bridled Terns.

Planning Your Trip

When to Go Birding

The best time of year for birding in South Carolina is during the spring, when the temperatures aren't too hot, the biting flies and chiggers aren't too vicious, migrating shorebirds and songbirds are passing through in their beautiful breeding plumage, and the forests are alive with the sounds of birds. Summer brings hot and humid weather, biting flies, chiggers, and ticks. As long as you are prepared to deal with these elements, summer is a good time to look for many of South Carolina's breeding specialty birds, such as Black-bellied Whistling-Duck, Wood Stork, Swallow-tailed Kite, Purple Gallinule, and Swainson's Warbler. If you find that the temperatures and bugs along the coast are too much to handle, you may want to try a trip to the mountains, where it is often cool even during the middle of summer.

Late summer brings large flocks of migrating shorebirds and terns to coastal beaches and mudflats. Fall welcomes somewhat cooler temperatures and good numbers of migrating hawks, shorebirds, and songbirds. Fall is often your best chance to find species that are rare in South Carolina, such as Black-billed Cuckoo, Olive-sided Flycatcher, Philadelphia and Warbling Vireos, Golden-winged Warbler, and Clay-colored and Lark Sparrows. Many of the waterfowl, raptors, and sparrows that headed north to breed during the spring will begin returning to their wintering grounds in South Carolina during late fall.

Winter birding in South Carolina can be greatly appreciated for its pleasant temperatures and lack of biting flies. Birds such as Tundra Swan; American Black Duck; Surf, Black, and White-winged Scoter; Common Eider; Long-tailed Duck; Purple Sandpiper; and Lapland Longspur can all be found in South Carolina at the southern edge of their wintering range. Winters are warm enough so that songbirds such as White-eyed Vireo, Blue-gray Gnatcatcher, and Black-and-white and Yellow-throated Warblers are all regular winter residents in the bottomland hardwood swamps.

All this having been said, there is nearly always something interesting to see in any season. Check out Appendix B, "South Carolina Birding Calendar," to see the birding highlights for each month of the year throughout the state.

Hazards

Please keep in mind that this section is not meant to scare you away from birding in South Carolina. The hazards that you will most commonly encounter in the state are those that are rarely life-threatening, such as biting flies, yellow jackets, fire ants, ticks, chiggers, and poison ivy. In all of my birding experience in South Carolina, I have never seen a black bear. Although I have seen many alligators and a few venomous snakes, I have rarely felt threatened by either of them. And I have never been the victim of even the smallest crime while birding in South Carolina.

Again, this section is not meant to frighten you, but rather to prepare you. If you know what the potential hazards are, you can learn to recognize and avoid them.

Alligators: Alligators are quite common in South Carolina, especially in fresh or brackish water near the coast. As long as you have a healthy respect for being in alligator country, they will not be a problem. You may even be lucky enough to see more than a hundred in a single impoundment at Donnelley Wildlife Management Area or Bull Island. Alligators are mainly active during the warmer months, but it is not unusual to see them on a warm, sunny day even in January. Do not swim or stand along the edge of ponds where alligators are known to occur. If you do see an alligator, do not feed it or approach within 60 feet. Alligators that are fed can quickly lose their fear of humans and become very dangerous. There have been only ten alligator attacks in South Carolina since 1948, none of which were fatal. Nearly 20 percent of all attacks are caused by people trying to catch or harass the alligators.

Biting flies: The most common biting flies in South Carolina are mosquitoes, gnats, deerflies, and greenheads. While their bites are not life-threatening, they are capable of running you off from a good birding area if you are not prepared. These flies are at their worst in the marshes along the coast in the summer, but be prepared for them at any time of year. Several areas that are notoriously bad during summer are Bear Island WMA, Donnelley WMA, Cape Romain National Wildlife Refuge, Santee Delta WMA, and Santee Coastal Reserve. The best defense against these flies is wearing long pants and a long-sleeve shirt and dousing yourself with insect repellant. If you plan on birding in the marshes during the summer, you may even want to bring a head net.

Fire ants: This is one of the most common hazards that you will encounter in South Carolina. The tiny fire ants pack a powerful sting, but they are rarely life-threatening. Look for their large dirt mounds in fields, lawns, and pastures, and be careful where you step. If you do step on a mound by accident, move away from that area as quickly as possible. It only takes the ants a few seconds to respond, and before you know it, there will be hundreds on your leg. While one sting by itself is not too painful, getting stung by many at once can be a nasty experience and in extreme cases can lead to anaphylactic shock. If you see the ants on your shoes or pants, brush them off as quickly as possible.

Wasps and bees: These stinging insects can be found along almost any trail during the warmer months, but they rarely pose a hazard unless you should be unfortunate enough to stumble across one of their colonies. The most commonly encountered stinging insect is the yellow jacket. These small wasps build their colonies underground, and if you accidentally step on one, an angry swarm will often emerge. The best way to avoid stepping on a colony is to stay on marked trails.

Ticks: Ticks are often encountered in South Carolina from spring through fall. The problem with ticks is that they can carry Lyme disease and Rocky Mountain spotted fever. Lyme disease can lead to long-term symptoms, such as pain and swelling of joints, chronic muscle pain, and memory loss. In 3 to 5 percent of cases, Rocky Mountain spotted fever is fatal. The best way to avoid getting Lyme disease or Rocky Mountain spotted fever is to take precautions to avoid being bitten by ticks. When in tick country, wear light-colored pants and tuck them into your socks or tape them to your shoes. Every few minutes, stop and check your pants thoroughly for ticks. I also recommend spraying your shoes and pants with insect repellant (high levels of DEET are best). If you do get bitten, remove the tick as soon as possible with a pair of tweezers. An early symptom of Lyme disease is a circular or oval red rash that grows in size daily. Early symptoms of Rocky Mountain spotted fever include a fever and a rash, often on the arms or ankles. Be careful because the tick that is most commonly known to carry Lyme disease, the deer tick (*Ixodes scapularis*), is only about the size of a pinhead. Rocky Mountain spotted fever is often transmitted by the American dog tick (*Dermacentor variabilis*).

Chiggers: These tiny mites, nearly invisible to the naked eye, are commonly found in grassy areas. If you walk through these areas during the summer months, you are bound to get chigger bites. Chiggers usually travel up your shoes and bite your ankles and legs, but if you make the mistake of sitting or lying down in the grass, you can end up with bites all over your body. You can often get bitten by ten to a hundred chiggers per encounter. A couple of days after being bitten, red welts will begin to form around each bite, and they will become incredibly itchy. Use cortisone or anti-itch cream to relieve the itching, which will usually subside after a few days.

Venomous snakes: The majority of snakes that you will encounter in South Carolina are nonvenomous. However, cottonmouths, copperheads, timber and eastern diamondback rattlesnakes, Carolina and dusky pigmy rattlesnakes, and eastern coral snakes can all be found here. There are many myths surrounding venomous snakes, which perpetuate the fear of these amazing creatures. One of the most common myths is that venomous snakes are aggressive, yet studies have shown that this is not the case. If you encounter a snake while birding, whether it is venomous or nonvenomous, the best thing you can do is leave it alone. Snakes will nearly always flee from you if given the opportunity. The best precautions that you can take are to watch where you walk, sit, or place your hands. Never stick your hands into areas that you cannot see. Avoid walking through tall grass, which makes it hard to see snakes. It may seem like common sense, but never try to kill, harass, or catch snakes, which is how many people are bitten. If you are worried about cottonmouths in the swamps or stepping on a snake in grassy areas, you should invest in a pair of snake-proof knee boots. Your chances of being bitten by a snake are very slim, but the boots will provide some protection.

Venomous spiders: South Carolina has only one regularly occurring venomous spider, the southern black widow. Black widows are easily recognized by their jet-black color and red hourglass shape on the underside of their abdomens. They are often found in webs close to the ground, such as at the base of buildings, under porches, in basements, or in the loose bark of trees. Their bite is quite painful, though hardly ever fatal. In rare cases the bite can lead to respiratory failure. If you are bitten by a black widow, you should immediately seek medical attention. People may try to tell you that brown recluse spiders occur in South Carolina, but this is a myth, as their range only extends as far east as northwestern Georgia and Tennessee.

Poison ivy: Contact with the leaves or vines of this plant can leave you with an itchy rash that will last for days. The best way to avoid poison ivy is to learn how to recognize it. Poison ivy grows in two forms: as groundcover (4 to 10 inches high) along forest edges and gaps and as a thick, hairy vine that climbs trees. It can be found in large patches on the ground. The almond-shaped leaves grow in clusters of three and can contain white berries in the fall. Remember the old saying, "Leaves of three, let it be." It is the oil from the plant that causes the itchy rash, and the oil can be transferred from your clothing or shoes to your skin. If you know that you have come in contact with poison ivy, wash the affected area with soap and water as soon as possible, and be sure to wash any clothing that has also come in contact.

Black bears: If you see a bear in South Carolina, consider yourself lucky. There has never been a human fatality or even an attack attributed to a black bear in the state. If you are camping, be sure not to leave any food in your tent. In fact, it is best to put all your food in a bear bag and secure it at least 12 feet off the ground. This will also help protect your food from hungry raccoons, which are much more of a problem than bears in South Carolina.

Hunting: The two hunting seasons during which you should really be careful are deer season (August 15 to January 1) and turkey season (April). On public lands, hunting typically occurs within the wildlife management areas, state forests, national wildlife refuges, and national forests. Hunting season dates vary with each area, so it is always best to call ahead or check the annual South Carolina Department of Natural Resources (SCDNR) *Rules and Regulations* publication at www .dnr.sc.gov/regulations.html. Hunting is not allowed on public lands on Sundays, so that is usually the best day to visit these areas during hunting season. If you do decide to visit an area during hunting season, it is always a good idea to wear a blaze-orange vest or hat. And please be respectful of hunters. Were it not for the conservation efforts of hunters and anglers, we would not have nearly as much public land in the state.

Hurricanes: Hurricane season runs from June 1 through November 30, though you are most likely to encounter hurricanes in South Carolina from early August to mid-October. If you are planning a trip during that time period, keep an eye on the weather. If it looks like a hurricane will strike the coast, your best bet is to head as far inland as you can. If you wait too long to evacuate, you will be stuck in countless hours of traffic. The last major hurricane that struck the South Carolina coast was Hugo in 1989. The effects of this category 4 hurricane can still be seen throughout coastal South Carolina, particularly in Francis Marion National Forest, where the storm made landfall.

Weather: In the summer, when it is hot and humid, be sure to bring plenty of water and avoid direct exposure to the sun for long periods of time. During wet weather, especially in winter, be sure to bring rain gear to avoid hypothermia. Learning to recognize the signs of heat exhaustion, heat stroke, and hypothermia will go a long way toward preventing any weather-related problems.

Crime: This hazard is rarely an issue at the birding areas described in this guide. In all my years of birding in South Carolina, I have never been a victim of any crimes. Use common sense, always lock your car doors, and do not leave valuables exposed to view. If possible, go birding with another person, and/or let someone know your travel itinerary.

Birding Ethics

Everyone who enjoys birds and birding must always respect wildlife, its environment, and the rights of others. In any conflict of interest between birds and birders, the welfare of the birds and their environment comes first.

American Birding Association's Code of Birding Ethics

1. Promote the welfare of birds and their environment.

(a) Support the protection of important bird habitat.

(b) To avoid stressing birds or exposing them to danger, exercise restraint and caution during observation, photography, sound recording, or filming.

Limit the use of recordings and other methods of attracting birds, and never use such methods in heavily birded areas, or for attracting any species that is Threatened, Endangered, of Special Concern, or is rare in your local area.

Keep well back from nests and nesting colonies, roosts, display areas, and important feeding sites. In such sensitive areas, if there is a need for extended observation, photography, filming, or recording, try to use a blind or hide, and take advantage of natural cover.

Use artificial light sparingly for filming or photography, especially for close-ups.

(c) Before advertising the presence of a rare bird, evaluate the potential for disturbance to the bird, its surroundings, and other people in the area, and proceed only if access can be controlled, disturbance minimized, and permission has been obtained from private landowners. The sites of rare nesting birds should be divulged only to the proper conservation authorities.

(d) Stay on roads, trails, and paths where they exist; otherwise keep habitat disturbance to a minimum.

2. Respect the law, and the rights of others.

(a) Do not enter private property without the owner's explicit permission.

(b) Follow all laws, rules, and regulations governing use of roads and public areas, both at home and abroad.

(c) Practice common courtesy in contacts with other people. Your exemplary behavior will generate goodwill with birders and non-birders alike.

3. Ensure that feeders, nest structures, and other artificial bird environments are safe.

(a) Keep dispensers, water, and food clean and free of decay or disease. It is important to feed birds continually during harsh weather.

(b) Maintain and clean nest structures regularly.

(c) If you are attracting birds to an area, ensure the birds are not exposed to predation from cats and other domestic animals, or dangers posed by artificial hazards.

4. Group birding, whether organized or impromptu, requires special care. Each individual in the group, in addition to the obligations spelled out in Items #1 and #2, has responsibilities as a Group Member.

(a) Respect the interests, rights, and skills of fellow birders, as well as people participating in other legitimate outdoor activities. Freely share your knowledge and experience, except where code 1(c) applies. Be especially helpful to beginning birders.

(b) If you witness unethical birding behavior, assess the situation, and intervene if you think it prudent. When interceding, inform the person(s) of the inappropriate action, and attempt, within reason, to have it stopped. If the behavior continues, document it, and notify appropriate individuals or organizations.

Group Leader Responsibilities (amateur and professional trips and tours)

(c) Be an exemplary ethical role model for the group. Teach through word and example.

(d) Keep groups to a size that limits impact on the environment and does not interfere with others using the same area.

(e) Ensure everyone in the group knows of and practices this code.

(f) Learn and inform the group of any special circumstances applicable to the areas being visited (e.g., no tape recorders allowed).

(g) Acknowledge that professional tour companies bear a special responsibility to place the welfare of birds and the benefits of public knowledge ahead of the company's commercial interests. Ideally, leaders should keep track of tour sightings, document unusual occurrences, and submit records to appropriate organizations.

Please follow this code and distribute and teach it to others.

The American Birding Association's code of ethics may be freely reproduced for distribution/dissemination. Please visit the ABA Web site at www.american birding.org.

Coast

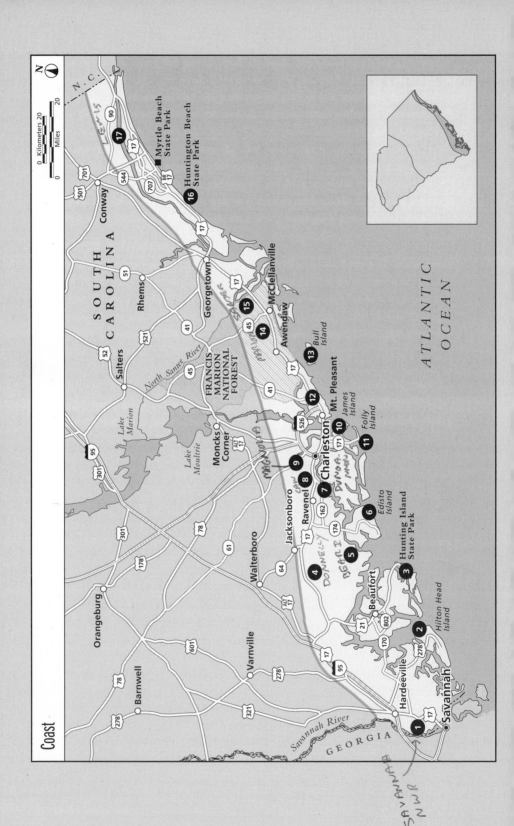

Coast

N

SOUTH CAROLINA

GEORGIA

ATLANTIC OCEAN

N. C.

Myrtle Beach State Park

Huntington Beach State Park

Conway

Rhems

Salters

Georgetown

McClellanville

Awendaw

FRANCIS MARION NATIONAL FOREST

Bull Island

Mt. Pleasant

James Island

Folly Island

Charleston

Ravenel

Jacksonboro

Moncks Corner

Lake Moultrie

Lake Marion

Walterboro

Edisto Island

Hunting Island State Park

Beaufort

Hilton Head Island

Hardeeville

Savannah

Orangeburg

Varnville

Barnwell

North Santee River

Savannah River

SAVANNAH NWR

0 Kilometers 20
0 Miles 20

Savannah National Wildlife Refuge

Habitats: Pond, river, salt marsh, freshwater marsh, mudflats, mixed pine-hardwood forest.

Specialty birds: *Resident*—Anhinga, Little Blue and Tricolored Herons, Glossy and White Ibises, Bald Eagle, Red-shouldered Hawk, Clapper and King Rails, Barn Owl, Yellow-throated Warbler. *Summer*—Yellow-crowned Night-Heron, Least Bittern, Wood Stork, Black-bellied Whistling-Duck, Purple Gallinule, Black-necked Stilt, Least Tern, Common Nighthawk, Summer Tanager, Indigo and Painted Buntings. *Winter*—American Bittern, Canvasback, Sora, Virginia Rail, Sedge Wren, Black-and-white Warbler, Rusty Blackbird. *Migration*—Bobolink.

Best times to bird: Year-round.

Directions: From exit 5 on Interstate 95 in Hardeeville, follow U.S. Highway 17 south toward Savannah, Georgia. After 6.2 miles Highway 170 will split off to the right. Follow Highway 170 for 2.6 miles to the entrance for Savannah NWR on your left.

The Birding

Savannah National Wildlife Refuge is well known as the best place in South Carolina to find breeding Purple Gallinules. In winter the impoundments on the refuge can be loaded with waterfowl. The most commonly seen ducks are Wood Duck, American Black Duck, Blue-winged and Green-winged Teals, Northern Pintail, Northern Shoveler, Gadwall, American Wigeon, Canvasback, Ring-necked Duck, Lesser Scaup, Bufflehead, Hooded Merganser, and Ruddy Duck. Also possible, but not to be expected, are Tundra Swan; Greater White-fronted, Snow, and Ross's Geese; Mottled Duck; Redhead; and Common Goldeneye. The refuge is also full of American Coots in winter and Common Moorhens throughout the year. Numerous wading birds feed in the refuge's many impoundments, including Wood Stork, Glossy and White Ibises, and Tricolored and Little Blue Herons. King Rail can be found in many freshwater impoundments, but beware of misidentification with the more numerous Clapper Rail.

The most accessible part of the refuge is the 5-mile-long **Laurel Hill Wildlife Drive.** There is a kiosk at the entrance with a map and information about bird-watching. Head down the wildlife drive and stop after 0.2 mile at the wooden rice trunk gates, then look into the canal on the right for Clapper Rail year-round and Least Bittern in summer. After another 0.2 mile you will see a small lily pad–covered canal on the left. Stop here in summer and look for Purple Gallinule as well as Least Bittern and Least Tern. The refuge's Purple Gallinules prefer the impoundments and canals that are covered in lily pads. During winter, scan the grassy edges of the canal for American Bittern, Sora, Virginia Rail, and Sedge Wren.

Continue 0.7 mile to the **Cistern Nature Trail.** The short, 0.2-mile trail is a good example of a hammock, which is an island of upland forest surrounded by marsh. This hammock and others along the wildlife drive are good spots to

Lily pad–covered impoundment along Laurel Hill Wildlife Drive

find large flocks of songbirds during migration and in winter. In winter look for White-eyed Vireo, Gray Catbird, Blue-gray Gnatcatcher, and Yellow-throated and Black-and-white Warblers. During summer look for Painted Bunting along the edges of the hammocks. You can often find Northern Waterthrush along the trail during spring and fall. Continue along the wildlife drive, and after 0.4 mile you will start to see flooded agricultural fields on either side of the road. The flooded fields can be good for large rafts of Ring-necked Ducks in the winter, but be sure to search through them carefully for Canvasbacks.

After 0.8 mile you will see a large lily pad–covered impoundment on the left. The impoundment is the best area along the wildlife drive to find Purple Gallinule in summer. If you visit the refuge in June or July, be on the lookout for small black chicks following the adults along the lily pads, begging for food. The large numbers of Common Moorhen that breed on the refuge can make distant identification of the Purple Gallinule difficult at times. The gallinules often appear fast and thin compared to the slow, fat moorhens.

Also be sure to keep an eye out for Least Bittern and Black-bellied Whistling-Duck during summer. In the winter look for rafts of ducks hiding among the lily pads. At dawn and dusk Common Nighthawks are active over many of the impoundments during the summer, and the lucky observer may catch a glimpse of Barn Owls, which are occasionally seen on the refuge throughout the year.

When you reach Highway 170, you will notice a small dirt parking area on the opposite (north) side of road. From the parking lot, you can hike along dikes through the rice fields in the northern portion of Savannah NWR. There are more than 4 miles of dikes that you can hike during the spring and summer. You will find the same types of birds that are found along Laurel Hill Wildlife Drive, but since the north side is closed to vehicles, it often has significantly less people-traffic. Please note, however, that the entire northern section of the refuge is closed from December 1 to February 28. To search for waterfowl, use the pull-outs along Highway 170 that provide good views of the area.

General Information

Laurel Hill Wildlife Drive is open year-round from sunrise to sunset, but the other parts of the refuge are closed from December 1 to February 28 to protect waterfowl.

DeLorme atlas: Page 62, D3.

Elevation: 0 to 10 feet.

Hazards: Alligators, venomous snakes, mosquitoes, ticks.

Nearest food, gas, lodging: Hardeeville.

Camping: Skidaway Island State Park.

For more information: Savannah NWR.

② Hilton Head Island

Habitats: Salt marsh, freshwater marsh, mixed pine-hardwood forest, beach, mudflats, river, pond, swamp, field, early successional.

Specialty birds: *Resident*—Tricolored and Little Blue Herons, Black-crowned Night-Heron, White Ibis, Barred and Great Horned Owls, Eastern Screech-Owl, Pileated Woodpecker, White-eyed Vireo, Brown-headed and White-breasted Nuthatches, Seaside Sparrow. *Summer*—Anhinga; Least Bittern; Reddish Egret; Yellow-crowned Night-Heron; Wood Stork; Gull-billed, Sandwich, and Least Terns; Black Skimmer; Chuck-will's-widow; Painted Bunting. *Winter*—Bald Eagle, Merlin, Peregrine Falcon, Sora, Piping Plover, Marbled Godwit, Red Knot, Sedge Wren, Saltmarsh and Nelson's Sharp-tailed Sparrows. *Migration*—Whimbrel, Black Tern.

Best times to bird: Year-round.

Directions: To reach Pinckney Island NWR from exit 8 on Interstate 95, drive east on U.S. Highway 278 toward Hilton Head. After 17.7 miles turn left into the entrance for the refuge. To reach Fish Haul Creek Park from the intersection of US 278 Express (Cross Island Parkway) and US 278 Business (Fording Island Road), follow US 278 Business. After 2.1 miles turn left at the traffic light on Beach City Road. Follow Beach City Road 2.1 miles and turn right into the parking lot for the park. To reach Sea Pines Forest Preserve from Fish Haul Creek Park, return to US 278 and turn left. After 6.8 miles you will come to a traffic circle. Proceed straight through the traffic circle on Greenwood Drive. After 0.3 mile you will come to a guard station for the Sea Pines Plantation. From the entrance gate, drive 1.0 mile and you will see the parking area for the Sea Pines Forest Preserve on your left.

The Birding

The vast trail network at **Pinckney Island National Wildlife Refuge** is accessible by foot or bike only. It could take you longer than a day to hike the more than 10 miles of trails on the island. The refuge is a popular hiking area for tourists on Hilton Head, so you may want to get started early if you want to beat the crowds. As you drive down the 0.6-mile entrance road to the parking lot, be sure to look for Painted Buntings on the wires during summer. Year-round there are often White Ibis, Little Blue Heron, and other wading birds in the salt marsh along the road.

Before you start hiking the trails, pick up a trail map from the kiosk at the trailhead. The main trail is a gravel road that runs the entire length of the island. The salt marsh along the main trail can be good for Sharp-tailed Sparrow in winter and Seaside Sparrow year-round. In the summer scan the forest edges for Painted Bunting and the salt marsh for Gull-billed Tern. During fall the refuge can be a good area to look for migrating warblers, thrushes, vireos, and other songbirds.

The best birding area on the refuge, **Ibis Pond,** is located 0.6 mile from the trailhead. In the summer there may be a heron rookery in the island of trees at

Salt marsh along the main trail at Pinckney Island National Wildlife Refuge

the center of the pond. During drought years the birds will not nest because of a lack of freshwater. Little Blue and Tricolored Herons, Snowy and Cattle Egrets, and Black-crowned and Yellow-crowned Night-Herons have all been known to breed in the rookery. Although Wood Storks do not breed in the rookery, a few can often be seen roosting with the herons. You should also be able to find Anhinga, Least Bittern, and Painted Bunting around the pond in summer. During winter look for Bufflehead, Sora, White-eyed Vireo, Gray Catbird, Sedge Wren, Common Yellowthroat, and Swamp Sparrow around the pond.

Continue down the main trail from Ibis Pond and you will come to two more ponds, **Osprey** and **Wood Stork Ponds.** These two ponds can contain small numbers of Bufflehead and Hooded Merganser in winter and Wood Duck year-round. During summer you should be able to find more feeding, roosting, and nesting wading birds in the ponds. If you continue farther down the main trail from the ponds, you will come to a longleaf pine forest that can be good for Wild Turkey, Northern Bobwhite, Pileated Woodpecker, and White-breasted Nuthatch year-round.

Fish Haul Creek Park is a great spot to look for shorebirds and terns on the northern end of Hilton Head Island. From the parking area, follow the 0.3-mile trail that leads to the beach, taking you through a live oak forest that can be good for migrating songbirds in spring and fall. The short boardwalk leading out into the salt marsh is a good spot to look for Clapper Rail and Seaside Sparrow year-round. During winter look for Northern Harrier and Saltmarsh and Nelson's

Sharp-tailed Sparrows. In the summer you have a good chance of seeing Wood Stork and Painted Bunting.

Once you reach the beach, start looking for shorebirds, gulls, terns, and skimmers on the **Port Royal Flats,** an extensive stretch of mudflats on the northern end of Hilton Head Island where it borders Port Royal Sound. The Port Royal Flats are more than 5 miles long and can extend up to 0.5 mile from shore during low tide. The best time to see birds is when the tide is about halfway out. At low tide the birds are often too far out to see, while at high tide they find other areas to roost. It is often best to have a spotting scope at all tidal stages. During winter you should be able to find good numbers of Marbled Godwit here, as well as American Oystercatcher; Red Knot; Short-billed Dowitcher; Western Sandpiper; Dunlin; and Black-bellied, Piping, and Semipalmated Plovers. During migration look for Whimbrel and Black Tern. If you are lucky, in the fall or winter you may be able to find a Merlin or Peregrine Falcon hunting along the marsh and beach. During summer the beach and flats are great spots to look for Gull-billed, Royal, Sandwich, and Least Terns and Black Skimmer. Keep an eye out for Reddish Egret on the flats late in the summer.

Sea Pines Forest Preserve, located within Sea Pines Plantation on the southern tip of Hilton Head Island, can be a great spot to look for migrating songbirds in fall. During winter, Christmas Bird Counts can yield more than a hundred species within the preserve. The 605-acre preserve contains a variety of habitats, including mixed pine forest, swamps, grassy fields, and several small freshwater lakes. The preserve is an oasis for birds, surrounded by the ever-increasing development on the southern end of Hilton Head. Be sure to pick up a trail map at the kiosk in the parking lot so that you can navigate the preserve's more than 7 miles of trails.

In the fall look for migrating warblers, thrushes, vireos, and other songbirds throughout Sea Pine Forest Preserve, especially along the forest edges. During winter you should be able to find Ring-necked, Ruddy, and Wood Ducks; Bufflehead; and Hooded Merganser on the lakes. The lakes are so close to the ocean that they even occasionally have scoters and other sea ducks during winter. The island in the middle of Lake Mary once contained a large heron rookery, but the birds abandoned it during a drought several years ago and have not returned. It is hoped that one day the island may once again host a large heron rookery. A night walk through the preserve is a good way to hear and perhaps catch a glimpse of Barred and Great Horned Owls and Eastern Screech-Owl year-round and Chuck-will's-widow during the summer.

General Information

Pinckney Island NWR, Fish Haul Creek Park, and Sea Pines Forest Preserve are all open year-round from dawn to dusk. Admission to Sea Pines Forest Preserve is $5 per car.

DeLorme atlas: Pinckney Island NWR, page 63, C7; Fish Haul Creek Park, page 63, C8; Sea Pines Forest Preserve, page 63, E6.

Elevation: 0 to 10 feet.

Hazards: Ticks, venomous snakes, alligators, mosquitoes.

Nearest food, gas, lodging: Hilton Head.

Camping: Hunting Island State Park.

For more information: Pinckney Island NWR; Sea Pines Forest Preserve Foundation.

3 Hunting Island State Park

Habitats: Salt marsh, freshwater marsh, mixed pine-hardwood forest, beach, mudflats, stream, ocean.

Specialty birds: *Resident*—Tricolored Heron, White Ibis, American Oystercatcher, Marsh Wren, Seaside Sparrow. *Summer*—Yellow-crowned Night-Heron; Wood Stork; Gull-billed, Sandwich, and Least Terns; Black Skimmer; Painted Bunting. *Winter*—Red-throated and Common Loons; Horned Grebe; Northern Gannet; Greater Scaup; White-winged, Black, and Surf Scoters; Bald Eagle; Peregrine Falcon; Saltmarsh and Nelson's Sharp-tailed Sparrows. *Migration*—Red Knot, Marbled Godwit, Black Tern.

Best times to bird: August through May.

Directions: To reach Hunting Island State Park from the intersection of U.S. Highway 21 (Sea Island Parkway) and Highway 802 in Beaufort, drive south on US 21. After 15 miles turn left onto Hunting Island Drive, following signs for the visitor center. Pick up a map and bird checklist from the entrance booth or visitor center. To reach the Port Royal Boardwalk Park from the intersection of US 21 (Ladys Island Road) and Highway 802 (Ribaut Road) in Port Royal, drive south on Highway 802. After 0.8 mile turn left on Paris Avenue, then after 0.7 mile turn left on Seventh Avenue, which turns into Sands Beach Road after 1 block. In 0.5 mile you will reach the parking area for the Port Royal Boardwalk Park.

The Birding

To reach the **Lighthouse Trail** from the visitor center, continue down Hunting Island Drive, following signs for the lighthouse. As you approach the lighthouse, you will begin to see parking lots that are labeled by letter. Park in lot D near the lighthouse. At the end of lot D is the trailhead for 0.3-mile-long Lighthouse Trail, which leads through a swampy maritime forest that can be good for songbirds during migration and in winter. The trail ends at the beach alongside a brackish marsh, where you can continue north along the beach toward the campground. The marsh is a good area to look for rails, but be careful not to walk through the fragile dunes. Scan the ocean and beach for shorebirds, gulls, and terns.

Follow the beach north, and after 0.2 mile you will reach a small creek. At low tide the creek is easy to cross, but at high tide it can be impassable. If you continue north along the beach for 0.8 mile beyond the small creek, you will reach Johnson Creek Inlet, which can be good for American Oystercatcher, migrating shorebirds, and terns. Johnson Creek Inlet is much easier to reach from the campground, but the campground is only accessible to campers. Be sure to visit this area early in the morning, as the large crowds of people and dogs will often scare off most of the shorebirds.

Return to US 21 and turn left. After 0.3 mile turn right into the **Marsh Overlook** area. This small turnout alongside Johnson Creek provides a good view of the salt marsh, where you can scan for waterfowl and raptors in winter and Seaside

Piping Plover and Wilson's Plover resting on the beach

Sparrow year-round. Continue south on US 21 for 1.4 miles and turn right into the parking lot for the **Marsh Boardwalk Trail.** The trail is 0.4 mile long and provides a great opportunity to view the birds of the salt marsh. As you cross the boardwalk at the start of the trail, be sure to look for herons and raptors. The boardwalk leads to a small marsh island, which can be good for songbirds during migration. At the end of the trail is another boardwalk that leads to an observation platform that overlooks Johnson Creek. From the platform, look for Clapper Rail, Marsh Wren, and Seaside Sparrow year-round. In the winter look for Hooded Merganser, Palm Warbler, and Saltmarsh and Nelson's Sharp-tailed Sparrows. During summer look for Wood Stork and Painted Bunting.

Continue south on US 21. After 0.6 mile turn left into the parking lot for the **Nature Center.** During summer you can often find Painted Bunting in the trees around the parking lot or at bird feeders next to the center. A fishing pier at the Nature Center extends 1,120 feet out into Fripp Inlet and provides a good vantage point from which to look for sea ducks, loons, and grebes in winter. During summer look for terns and skimmers. Osprey and Boat-tailed Grackle are common year-round from the pier. The **Island Trail,** which starts at the end of the Nature Center parking lot, runs through maritime forest to a narrow lagoon. During migration the maritime forest can be good for songbirds. After 0.4 mile you will come to a pedestrian bridge that provides a good view of the lagoon. Scan the lagoon and edges for Red-breasted Merganser, Bald Eagle, and American Kestrel in winter. During summer look for Painted Bunting in the trees along the edge of the lagoon.

Port Royal Boardwalk Park is often worth a short stop either on the way to or back from Hunting Island State Park. The park consists of a 0.2-mile-long boardwalk with an enormous, five-story-tall observation platform. The boardwalk runs through the salt marsh and mudflats at the edge of Port Royal Sound. Year-round this is a good place to see Clapper Rail, American Oystercatcher, Marsh Wren, and Seaside Sparrow. In the winter look for waterfowl, Common Loon, Horned Grebe, Bald Eagle, and Saltmarsh and Nelson's Sharp-tailed Sparrows. During spring and fall, check the mudflats at low tide for migrating shorebirds.

General Information

The entrance fee for Hunting Island State Park is $4 per person. The park is open year-round from 6:00 a.m. to 6:00 p.m. during winter and 6:00 a.m. to 9:00 p.m. in the summer. Port Royal Boardwalk Park is open year-round from dawn to dusk.

DeLorme atlas: Hunting Island State Park, page 63, A10; Port Royal Boardwalk Park, page 63, A8.

Elevation: 0 to 15 feet.

Hazards: Ticks, venomous snakes, mosquitoes.

Nearest food, gas, lodging: Beaufort.

Camping: Hunting Island State Park.

For more information: Hunting Island State Park.

④ Donnelley Wildlife Management Area

Habitats: Salt marsh, freshwater marsh, swamp, river, mudflats, mixed pine-hardwood forest, farmland.

Specialty birds: *Resident*—Anhinga, American White Pelican, Black-crowned Night-Heron, Tricolored and Little Blue Herons, Glossy and White Ibises, Wood Stork, Bald Eagle, Red-shouldered Hawk, King Rail, Pileated Woodpecker, Loggerhead Shrike, Brown-headed Nuthatch. *Summer*—Least Bittern, Yellow-crowned Night-Heron, Black-bellied Whistling-Duck, Mississippi Kite, Purple Gallinule, Black-necked Stilt, Common Nighthawk, Red-headed Woodpecker, Eastern Wood-Pewee, Acadian Flycatcher, Yellow-throated Vireo, Prothonotary Warbler, Yellow-breasted Chat, Summer Tanager, Blue Grosbeak, Indigo and Painted Buntings, Orchard Oriole. *Winter*—American Bittern, Northern Pintail, Lesser Scaup, Hooded Merganser, Virginia Rail, Sora, American Pipit, Blue-headed Vireo, Orange-crowned and Palm Warblers, Rusty Blackbird, Fox Sparrow. *Migration*—White-rumped Sandpiper, Long-billed Dowitcher, Black Tern.

Best times to bird: Year-round. From March through October, be prepared for the mosquitoes and gnats, which can sometimes be unbearable.

Directions: From the intersection of U.S. Highway 17 and Highway 64 in Jacksonboro, drive south on US 17. After 10 miles you will see a sign for Donnelley WMA. Turn left on Donnelley Drive, a dirt road that leads into the WMA. If you pass Highway 303, you have gone too far.

The Birding

The wide variety of habitats that are found in Donnelley Wildlife Management Area offer excellent birding in almost any season. You could easily spend a day hiking or biking along the peaceful dirt roads that wind through the 8,048-acre WMA. Donnelley can be quite good in the spring and fall for migrating songbirds and shorebirds. During summer it is the best place in the state to look for Black-bellied Whistling-Duck. Donnelley and the nearby Bear Island WMA are both a part of the ACE Basin, which encompasses more than 700,000 acres of state, federal, and private land. ACE stands for *Ashepoo, Combahee,* and *Edisto,* which are the three rivers that flow into St. Helena Sound to form the basin. If you are planning a trip to Donnelley WMA, be sure to leave enough time to visit Bear Island WMA too. With a visit to both, it is possible to tally more than a hundred species in a day!

From the entrance, drive 0.5 mile until you see the Donnelley WMA office on your left. Park near the kiosk, which usually contains maps with a driving tour of the WMA. In the spring and fall, the forest surrounding the office can often be good for migrating warblers and other songbirds. Year-round you should be able to find Red-headed Woodpecker, Brown-headed Nuthatch, and Pine Warbler. During summer look for Yellow-throated Vireo, Eastern Wood-Pewee, Yellow-throated Warbler, Northern Parula, Summer Tanager, Indigo and Painted Buntings, Blue Grosbeak, and Orchard Oriole. In the winter look for Blue-headed Vireo, Orange-crowned Warbler, and Fox Sparrow.

Rice trunks, like this one at Donnelley Wildlife Management Area, help to regulate the flow of water in and out of the impoundments. KIM COUNTS PHOTO

Continue down the entrance road on foot for 0.1 mile, and you will see a small dirt road on the left that leads to an old rice field. The impoundment is covered in lily pads, making it excellent habitat for Black-bellied Whistling-Duck and

Purple Gallinule in the summer. Wood Storks and egrets nest in a rookery on the far side of the impoundment, and you can watch the birds as they fly to and from their nests. During winter look for American Bittern and Rusty Blackbird. The wet grassy areas of the impoundment can contain King Rail year-round, as well as Sora and Virginia Rail in winter.

Return to your car and continue on the entrance road for 0.6 mile until the road runs alongside a shallow lake. This lake can be a good spot to see Anhinga, Green Heron, Wood Stork, Wood Duck, Common Moorhen, King Rail, and Barred Owl year-round. During summer look for Black-bellied Whistling-Duck, Purple Gallinule, and Prothonotary Warbler. Continue down the road for 0.7 mile and you will see a dirt road on the right that leads to the parking area for the **Boynton Nature Trail.** The trail is 2.2 miles long and leads through old rice fields, loblolly pine forest, and hardwood forest. A publication is available at the kiosk near the Donnelley WMA office that will help guide you along the trail. On the trail you should be able to find a wide variety of wading birds, waterfowl, and songbirds typical of the ACE Basin. The trail is closed from October 15 to February 1 to protect waterfowl.

Once you have finished with the nature trail, return to Donnelley Drive and turn right. After 0.7 mile you will come to a fork in the road. At the fork, bear right, following the sign for the lodge. After 1.1 miles you will see the Donnelley Lodge on your right. During summer the Spanish moss–covered oak trees surrounding the lodge are often full of breeding Yellow-throated Warblers and Northern Parulas.

At the T-intersection 0.1 mile past the lodge, turn right and drive along the dikes of **Fishburn Bank,** an old rice field that is excellent for birding in any season. Beware that the impoundments at Fishburn Bank contain many large alligators, and on some mornings you can easily count more than a hundred. Year-round you can often find good numbers of wading birds in the pond, including Wood Stork, Tricolored and Little Blue Herons, and Black-crowned Night-Heron. In the summer scan the salt marsh of the Old Chehaw River opposite the impoundments for Yellow-crowned Night-Heron. The forest edges and grassy dikes are excellent for Painted Bunting in summer. During winter there may be a few American White Pelicans in the impoundments. In the spring the impoundments can be quite good for shorebirds if the water levels are low enough. If there are large flocks, be sure to keep an eye out for rare birds such as White-rumped Sandpiper.

After you have gone 0.3 mile along the dikes, the road will start to lead away from the impoundments. At this point you should turn around and drive back toward the lodge, but instead of turning left at the lodge, go straight. In 1.1 miles you will reach an agricultural area with some maintenance buildings. This area can be good for American Kestrel, Wilson's Snipe, American Pipit, and sparrows in winter. Year-round look for Wild Turkey, Killdeer, Eastern Bluebird, and Eastern Meadowlark. During summer you can find Mississippi Kite, Eastern Kingbird, and Purple Martin.

Continue down the road for 2.0 miles until you reach Bennetts Point Road. Turning left will take you back to US 17, while turning right leads to Bear Island WMA.

General Information

Donnelley WMA is open Monday through Saturday from 8:00 a.m. to 5:00 p.m., except during special hunts. Call (843) 844-8957 to make sure there are no closures for hunting on the day you intend to visit.

DeLorme atlas: Page 59, D9.

Elevation: 0 to 5 feet.

Hazards: Alligators, venomous snakes, mosquitoes, ticks.

Nearest food, gas, lodging: Jacksonboro for food and gas; Walterboro for lodging.

Camping: Edisto Beach State Park.

For more information: Donnelley WMA.

⑤ Bear Island Wildlife Management Area

Habitats: Pond, river, salt marsh, freshwater marsh, mudflats, mixed pine-hardwood forest, farmland.

Specialty birds: *Resident*—Anhinga, American White Pelican, Black-crowned Night-Heron, Tricolored and Little Blue Herons, Glossy and White Ibises, Wood Stork, Mottled Duck, Bald Eagle, Red-shouldered Hawk, King and Black Rails, Eurasian Collared-Dove, White-winged Dove, Barn Owl, Eastern Screech-Owl, Pileated Woodpecker, Loggerhead Shrike, Brown-headed Nuthatch, Seaside Sparrow. *Summer*—Least Bittern, Yellow-crowned Night-Heron, Roseate Spoonbill, Black-necked Stilt, Least and Gull-billed Terns, Black Skimmer, Common Nighthawk, Chuck-will's-widow, Yellow-breasted Chat, Blue Grosbeak, Indigo and Painted Buntings, Orchard Oriole. *Winter*—Tundra Swan, American Black Duck, Northern Pintail, Lesser Scaup, Hooded Merganser, Merlin, Virginia Rail, Sora, Bonaparte's Gull, American Pipit, Sedge Wren, Orange-crowned and Palm Warblers, Nelson's and Saltmarsh Sharp-tailed Sparrows. *Migration*—White-rumped and Stilt Sandpipers; American Avocet; Black Tern; Bank, Cliff, and Cave Swallows; Bobolink.

Best times to bird: Year-round. Bear Island WMA is closed from October 15 to February 1 to protect waterfowl, but you can still bird along Bennetts Point Road and at Marys House Pond. From March through October, be prepared for the mosquitoes and gnats, which can sometimes be unbearable.

Directions: From Jacksonboro, drive south on U.S. Highway 17. (Be sure to stop for gas in Jacksonboro because there are no gas stations along Bennetts Point Road.) After 7.2 miles on US 17, you will see a sign for Bennetts Point Road and Bear Island WMA. Turn left on Bennetts Point Road.

The Birding

Bear Island Wildlife Management Area offers excellent bird-watching year-round. A combination of old rice fields and marsh, the WMA is the best spot in the state to see Tundra Swan, American White Pelican, and Bald Eagle in the winter. Throughout the year it is good for Wood Stork, Mottled Duck, and King Rail. Several spots along Bennetts Point Road are good for bird-watching, but beware of traffic. There aren't many vehicles on this road, but people drive fast. Don't stop along the road without making sure that you can pull well off it.

After 4.3 miles Bennetts Point Road intersects with Blocker Run Road on the right. Continue on Bennetts Point Road and in 1.5 miles you will see an impoundment on your right that can be good for raptors, waterfowl, and rails. Park on the road shoulder and walk along the gated dike. Year-round look for Bald Eagle and King Rail. During winter you should be able to see waterfowl, Sora, and perhaps a Virginia Rail or American Bittern. In the spring and summer, the dike can be loaded with Least Bitterns.

Continue down Bennetts Point Road for 4.7 miles and you will come to a bridge over the Ashepoo River. Watch for Barn Owls hunting over the marsh

White Ibis taking flight from the rice fields at Bear Island Wildlife Management Area

along the river at dawn and dusk. There is usually an active Osprey nest on the telephone poles near the bridge during the summer. In the spring and fall, the telephone wires near the bridge are often loaded with swallows, including Bank, Cliff, and occasionally Cave Swallows.

Follow Bennetts Point Road for another 1.8 miles to an observation platform on your right. Stop at the platform to scan the marsh for migrating shorebirds, such as Black-necked Stilt and Greater and Lesser Yellowlegs. Mottled Duck and White and Glossy Ibises can often be seen here year-round. In the winter look for Pied-billed Grebe, Tundra Swan, American Black Duck, Bald Eagle, and Sedge Wren. If the birds are distant in the marsh, you can often get a closer look by using the access roads that lead off of Bennetts Point Road to the north and south of the observation platform. At 0.2 mile north of the platform there is an access road that leads to a picnic area, and 0.4 mile to the south there is an access road that leads to a gated dike (look for a sign to Mid Pond).

Continue down Bennetts Point Road from the observation platform for 0.3 mile until you reach **Marys House Pond** and the headquarters of Bear Island WMA. Turn left at the headquarters onto Ti Ti Road and park near the kiosk. Year-round the pond is a good spot to look for American White Pelican, Wood Stork, Tricolored and Little Blue Herons, and Bald Eagle. If water levels are low in the spring and fall, there can be hundreds of shorebirds in the pond. In the summer look for Least Bittern, Roseate Spoonbill, Black Skimmer, Common Nighthawk, Loggerhead Shrike, and Orchard Oriole. During winter look for waterfowl, Tundra Swan, and Bonaparte's Gull. While it may be tempting to scan this area from Bennetts Point Road, there is little room on the shoulder and traffic is often moving quickly.

Continue down Ti Ti Road if conditions permit. (All of the roads in Bear Island WMA are dirt and can get very muddy after a heavy rain.) After 0.4 mile you will see some agricultural fields on your left. Scan the fields for American Pipit (winter), Bobolink (spring), and Eastern Meadowlark (year-round). Eastern Kingbirds (summer) and Loggerhead Shrikes (year-round) will frequently perch on the telephone lines along the road. The forest edges often contain a few Painted Buntings in summer. Numerous side roads run perpendicular to Ti Ti Road. I will only describe a few, but all are worth exploring if you have a full day or two. Most of the side roads end up leading you to impoundments that you can't see from Ti Ti Road.

After you are finished checking the agricultural fields, continue down Ti Ti Road. After 0.4 mile you will see a sign for the observation blind on your right. Park in the small parking area and walk 0.1 mile to a little boardwalk that overlooks a freshwater marsh. In the winter look for waterfowl and Bald Eagle. During spring and late summer, this can be a good spot to look for migrating shorebirds if water levels are low.

After continuing down Ti Ti Road for 0.2 mile, you will see a marshy area on the left that is well known as one of the best places in South Carolina to look for Black Rail. Please do not play back their calls over and over again in this area. The best strategy is to play the calls a couple of times and see if they respond. If not, move on and look for other birds.

Continue down Ti Ti Road another 0.8 mile and you will see a sign for **Hog Island.** Turn left at the road to Hog Island and drive 0.2 mile to the gate. Park at the gate and continue down the road on foot to the impoundments. The Hog Island impoundments are particularly good for waterfowl in winter. In the spring and late summer, you can find migrating shorebirds such as Greater and Lesser Yellowlegs, and perhaps American Avocet or Stilt Sandpiper if you are lucky. During summer look for Least Bittern, Black-necked Stilt, Black Skimmer, Yellow-breasted Chat, Painted Bunting, and Orchard Oriole. Late in the summer, look for large concentrations of egrets, herons, storks, and ibises when the water levels are low. Ti Ti Road continues for 0.8 mile beyond the turn-off for Hog Island, and then it becomes private property. At this point you should turn around and return to Bennetts Point Road.

At Bennetts Point Road, turn left and drive 2.8 miles to the **McKenzie Field Station,** a large green-roofed building on the left. The field station is open to the public and has a variety of publications that may be useful to a visiting bird-watcher. The trees around the field station often contain several Eurasian Collared-Doves, and you might even spot a White-winged Dove if you are lucky. Climb the field station's tower for a fantastic view of the salt marsh along

Birders on the dikes of the Hog Island impoundments. KIM COUNTS PHOTO

Mosquito Creek. For a closer view of the creek, walk out on the metal docks. Clapper Rails can be found stalking the mudflats along the edge of the salt marsh year-round, especially at low tide. During spring and fall thousands of Tree Swallows can be seen roosting in the salt marsh. In the summer, if you are patient, you can often find Marsh Wrens singing from the tops of the salt marsh grass across the creek, or you may see Black Skimmer and Gull-billed, Least, and Royal Terns as they fly past the dock. At dusk Chuck-will's-widows (summer) and Eastern Screech-Owls (year-round) can often be heard calling from the parking lot.

General Information

Bear Island WMA is closed from October 15 to February 1 to protect the large concentrations of wintering waterfowl. It is still possible, however, to visit the Marys House Pond portion of the WMA even when the gates are closed. Throughout the rest of the year, Bear Island WMA is open Monday through Saturday from sunrise to sunset.

DeLorme atlas: Page 59, E10.

Elevation: 0 to 5 feet.

Hazards: Alligators, venomous snakes, mosquitoes, ticks.

Nearest food, gas, lodging: Jacksonboro for food and gas; Walterboro for lodging.

Camping: Edisto Beach State Park.

For more information: Bear Island WMA, SCDNR Marine Resource Division for McKenzie Field Station.

6 Edisto Island

Habitats: Beach, ocean, mudflats, salt marsh, freshwater marsh, swamp, pond, field, mixed pine-hardwood forest, pine forest.

Specialty birds: *Resident*—Anhinga, White Ibis, Wood Stork, King Rail, Barred Owl, Red-headed Woodpecker, Brown-headed Nuthatch, Pine Warbler. *Summer*—Least Bittern; Swallow-tailed and Mississippi Kites; Least Tern; Black Skimmer; Eastern Wood-Pewee; Acadian Flycatcher; Yellow-throated Vireo; Prothonotary, Yellow-throated, and Hooded Warblers; Summer Tanager; Blue Grosbeak; Indigo and Painted Buntings; Orchard Oriole. *Winter*—Common and Red-throated Loons, Horned Grebe, Red-breasted Merganser, Virginia Rail, Sora, Yellow-bellied Sapsucker, Blue-headed Vireo, Sedge Wren, Ruby-crowned Kinglet, Palm and Orange-crowned Warblers, Fox Sparrow. *Migration*—Whimbrel, Black Tern.

Best times to bird: April through June.

Directions: To reach ACE Basin NWR from the intersection of U.S. Highway 17 and Highway 174, drive south on Highway 174 toward Edisto Island. After 3.6 miles you will come to an intersection with Highway 164 (Willtown Road). Turn right on Highway 164 (west) and drive 2.1 miles to the entrance for ACE Basin NWR. To reach Edisto Beach State Park Interpretive Center from the intersection of Highways 164 and 174, drive south on Highway 174 toward Edisto Island. After 16.6 miles turn right on Palmetto Road, following signs for Edisto Beach State Park Interpretive Center. After driving 1.3 miles on Palmetto Road, turn left onto a dirt road. The interpretive center is 0.4 mile down the dirt road on your right. If the center is closed or the parking lot is full, there is additional parking at the boat landing at the end of the dirt road.

The Birding

Along the way to Edisto Island is the **ACE Basin National Wildlife Refuge,** also called the Grove Plantation. Edisto Island and ACE Basin NWR are a part of the ACE Basin, which encompasses over 700,000 acres of state, federal, and private land. ACE stands for *Ashepoo, Combahee,* and *Edisto,* which are the three rivers that flow into St. Helena Sound to make up the ACE Basin. Although the birding and trails around the Grove Plantation are quite good, you will rarely encounter very many visitors.

During summer the open pine forest along the first mile of the entrance road can be good for Bachman's Sparrow, Blue Grosbeak, and Indigo Bunting. Year-round look for Brown-headed Nuthatch and Pine Warbler. After driving 1.4 miles from the start of the entrance road, you will come to a hardwood swamp, which is often a good spot to listen for Acadian Flycatcher, Yellow-throated Vireo, and Prothonotary Warbler during summer. Continue down the entrance road for about 0.5 mile and you come to a kiosk and gate. On weekends and holidays this gate will be closed, but you can park here and walk 0.4 mile to the Grove Plantation House. Surrounding the old plantation house are some beautiful, old live oak trees that are covered in Spanish moss. Year-round the trees contain Barred Owl,

Red-headed Woodpecker, and Eastern Bluebird. During summer look for Ruby-throated Hummingbird, Yellow-throated Warbler, and Summer Tanager.

Behind the house is a network of trails that run through some of the plantation's old rice fields. In the summer the rice fields can be good for Mississippi Kite, Painted Bunting, and the occasional Swallow-tailed Kite. During winter this can be a good area to see Northern Harrier; Belted Kingfisher; Sedge Wren; Palm Warbler; and Chipping, Song, Savannah, and Swamp Sparrows. There is also a freshwater pond behind the plantation house that can contain waterfowl in winter and wading birds throughout the year. Scan the edges of the pond for Virginia Rail and Sora in winter and King Rail year-round.

The maritime forest surrounding the **Edisto Beach State Park Interpretive Center** is one of the best places to find migrating songbirds along the coast in the spring and fall. During spring and summer look for Yellow-billed Cuckoo, Eastern Wood-Pewee, Yellow-throated and Hooded Warblers, Northern Parula, Summer Tanager, and Orchard Oriole. In the winter you can find large flocks of Yellow-rumped Warblers and White-throated Sparrows that also contain smaller numbers of Yellow-bellied Sapsucker, Blue-headed Vireo, Ruby-crowned Kinglet, Orange-crowned Warbler, and Fox Sparrow. Year-round look for Brown-headed Nuthatch and Pine Warbler.

A short trail behind the interpretive center leads to a long boardwalk that extends out over a salt marsh and into the creek. During summer you can usually hear Painted Buntings singing where the forest meets the salt marsh, but they are often difficult to see. In the spring, flocks of Whimbrels feed in the salt marsh on the opposite side of the creek from the boardwalk. In the summer look for Wood Stork, Osprey, and Royal and Least Terns. During winter look for Northern Harrier, Bald Eagle, and Forster's Tern. For a longer walk, try following the Big Bay Trail south from the interpretive center toward the boat landing. After 0.4 mile the trail will dead-end at the Spanish Mount Trail, which leads 1.6 miles east to the state park campground area. The maritime forest along these two trails is often good for songbirds year-round.

The beaches along the western end of Edisto Island where the South Edisto River empties into St. Helena Sound can be a good area to look for shorebirds and resting terns, skimmers, and gulls. The best way to reach this area from the interpretive center is to return to Highway 174 and turn right. After 1.2 miles Highway 174 will bend to the right and become Palmetto Boulevard. Follow Palmetto Boulevard for 3.9 miles, where it splits and Yacht Club Road leads straight ahead. Go straight on Yacht Club Road for 0.3 mile and you will see a small parking area. Park and follow the beach access path through the dunes. Once you reach the beach, turn right and walk 0.2 mile to the northwestern point of Edisto Island. The sandbars and mudflats on the point are the best areas on the island to see shorebirds and resting seabirds. During winter watch for Common and Red-throated Loons, Horned Grebe, and Red-breasted Merganser.

General Information

The ACE Basin NWR visitor center is open Monday through Friday from 7:30 a.m. to 4:00 p.m., but the trails are open year-round from sunrise to sunset. Edisto Beach State Park is open daily from 8:00 a.m. to 6:00 p.m. during winter and 6:00 a.m. to 10:00 p.m. in the summer. The entrance fee is $4 for adults. Edisto Beach State Park Interpretive Center is open Tuesday through Saturday from 9:00 a.m. to 4:00 p.m.

DeLorme atlas: ACE Basin NWR, page 60, D1; Edisto Beach State Park, page 60, G2.

Elevation: 0 to 40 feet.

Hazards: Alligators, venomous snakes, mosquitoes, ticks, chiggers.

Nearest food, gas, lodging: Edisto Island.

Camping: Edisto Beach State Park.

For more information: ACE Basin NWR; Edisto Beach State Park.

⑦ Dungannon Heritage Preserve

Habitats: Swamp, pond, mixed pine-hardwood forest.

Specialty birds: *Resident*—Black-crowned Night-Heron, Red-shouldered Hawk, Barred Owl, Pileated Woodpecker. *Summer*—Anhinga; Yellow-crowned Night-Heron; Wood Stork; Chuck-will's-widow; Eastern Wood-Pewee; Acadian Flycatcher; Yellow-throated Vireo; Wood Thrush; Prothonotary, Yellow-throated, and Kentucky Warblers; Summer Tanager. *Winter*—Yellow-bellied Sapsucker, Blue-headed Vireo, Ruby-crowned Kinglet, Hermit Thrush.

Best times to bird: March through June.

Directions: From the intersection of Highway 162 and U.S. Highway 17 in Rantowles, follow Highway 162 west toward Hollywood. After 3.9 miles turn right into the small dirt parking lot for Dungannon Heritage Preserve.

The Birding

Dungannon Heritage Preserve is perhaps the best place in South Carolina to get a close view of nesting Wood Storks. From April through June more than a hundred Wood Storks nest in a colony deep in the preserve's cypress swamps. Although the 641-acre preserve is within 10 miles of Charleston and the swamp is beautiful in spring, you will rarely encounter other people on the 9-plus miles of trails.

Before you begin your walk, you will need to sign in at the mailbox near the gate. Pick up a trail map from the mailbox because the preserve's many trails can be difficult to navigate without one. You can also get a map online at www .sctrails.net. The mixed pine forest near the entrance gate is a good place to look for Eastern Wood-Pewee and Summer Tanager in summer. At dawn and dusk during the summer, listen for Chuck-will's-widows calling near the parking lot.

Shortly after you walk through the gate, you will come to a dirt road leading right. At the intersection of the two roads, look for a trailhead marked with blue arrows that heads east. The trail drops down into a mixed hardwood forest along the edge of a hardwood swamp. During summer you can see Acadian Flycatcher, Wood Thrush, Yellow-throated Warbler, and occasionally a Kentucky Warbler. In the spring and fall, look for migrating songbirds such as Veery, Ovenbird, and Northern Waterthrush.

After following the blue arrow markers for 1.2 miles, you will come to a small bridge that leads over a dam and spillway to a dike. The 0.2-mile walk on the dike nearly always contains some good birds. Look for Wood Duck, Black-crowned Night-Heron, Red-shouldered Hawk, and Pileated Woodpecker year-round. In the summer you should see Prothonotary Warbler, Northern Parula, and perhaps a Yellow-crowned Night-Heron. The opening in the canopy along the dike provides a good opportunity to scan the sky for Anhinga, Wood Stork, or raptors.

Wood Stork carrying nest material

Cross the dike and take the first road on the left. Following this road 0.2 mile will take you to a boardwalk that ventures out into the center of the Wood Stork nesting colony. From the end of the boardwalk there are fantastic views of the Wood Storks and their nests. As the storks come and go from their nests, they often pass within 25 feet of the boardwalk. Great Egret, Anhinga, and Osprey also nest in the colony, while Black and Turkey Vultures are often seen roosting in the cypress trees. During summer Yellow-throated Vireos and Yellow-throated Warblers can often be heard singing from high in the cypress trees surrounding the boardwalk. Alligators patrol the swamp surrounding the nest trees, keeping the storks safe from land-based predators such as raccoons. However, if water levels drop too low in the swamp during spring due to drought, the storks and other wading birds will abandon their nests.

General Information

The preserve is open year-round from dawn to dusk. There are no facilities for visitors.

DeLorme atlas: Page 60, C3.

Elevation: 0 to 5 feet.

Hazards: Alligators, venomous snakes, biting flies, ticks, chiggers.

Nearest food, gas, lodging: Charleston.

Camping: James Island County Park.

For more information: SCDNR Wildlife and Freshwater Fisheries Division.

8 Caw Caw County Park

Habitats: Swamp, pond, freshwater marsh, salt marsh, mixed pine-hardwood forest.

Specialty birds: *Resident*—Anhinga, Black-crowned Night-Heron, Little Blue and Tri-colored Herons, White Ibis, Wood Stork, Red-shouldered Hawk, King Rail, Barred Owl, Pileated Woodpecker, White-eyed Vireo. *Summer*—Yellow-crowned Night-Heron, Least Bittern, Swallow-tailed and Mississippi Kites, Yellow-throated Vireo, Acadian Flycatcher, Prothonotary Warbler, Blue Grosbeak, Indigo and Painted Buntings. *Winter*—American Bittern; Hooded Merganser; Bald Eagle; Merlin; Virginia Rail; Sora; Sedge Wren; Black-and-white, Yellow-throated, and Orange-crowned Warblers; Fox Sparrow; Rusty Blackbird; Purple Finch. *Migration*—Bobolink.

Best times to bird: Year-round.

Directions: From the intersection of U.S. Highway 17 and Highway 162 in Rantowles, follow US 17 south. After 2.6 miles turn right into the entrance to Caw Caw County Park. Follow the entrance road to the Caw Caw Interpretive Center.

The Birding

Caw Caw County Park contains more than 8 miles of well-maintained hiking trails that lead through rice fields, swamps, and forests. It is an excellent place to look for several specialty birds, including Least Bittern, Wood Stork, Swallow-tailed Kite, King Rail, and Painted Bunting. Start your birding at the **Caw Caw Interpretive Center,** where you can pick up a map and bird checklist for the 654-acre park. Behind the interpretive center is a butterfly garden with bird feeders. There are often many woodpeckers, chickadees, cardinals, titmice, and other common backyard birds around the feeders in winter, but keep an eye out for Purple Finch, which are occasionally seen here. During summer check the feeders for Painted Bunting and Ruby-throated Hummingbird.

Follow the paths behind the interpretive center to the **Rice Field Overlook Boardwalk.** Be sure to keep an eye out for Barred Owls in the trees along the beginning of the path. The short boardwalk will give you your first glimpse of Caw Caw's old rice fields. From the boardwalk, scan the rice fields for Anhinga and Little Blue and Tricolored Herons year-round. During summer look for Wood Stork and Mississippi and Swallow-tailed Kites.

Once you are finished on the boardwalk, follow the trail that leads north out into the rice fields toward the **Waterfowl Trail,** a 1.2-mile loop. An overlook platform on the southern side of the trail provides a good view of the rice fields. The rice field in the center of the trail can have dozens of Mississippi Kites and several Swallow-tailed Kites in late summer. The Waterfowl Trail is also good for King Rail, Least Bittern, Sedge Wren, Blue Grosbeak, and Painted Bunting.

Osprey usually nest on the man-made platforms around the rice fields. In the winter the rice fields can be good for waterfowl, including Blue-winged and Green-winged Teals, Ring-necked Duck, and Hooded Merganser.

You can return to the visitor center via the **Swamp Sanctuary Trail,** which contains a 0.2-mile-long boardwalk through a hardwood swamp. In the summer look for Acadian Flycatcher, Prothonotary Warbler, and Northern Parula. During winter look for Hermit Thrush and Yellow-bellied Sapsucker.

General Information

The park is open Saturday and Sunday from 9:00 a.m. to 5:00 p.m. and Wednesday through Friday from 9:00 a.m. to 3:00 p.m. (closed Monday and Tuesday). The entrance fee is $1 for adults. Guided bird walks are offered on Wednesday and Saturday mornings for $5 per person.

DeLorme atlas: Page 60, B4.

Elevation: 0 to 10 feet.

Hazards: Alligators, venomous snakes, mosquitoes, chiggers.

Nearest food, gas, lodging: Charleston.

Camping: James Island County Park.

For more information: Caw Caw County Park.

⑨ Magnolia Plantation & Gardens

Habitats: Swamp, pond, river, freshwater marsh, mixed pine-hardwood forest.

Specialty birds: *Resident*—Anhinga, Little Blue and Tricolored Herons, Black-crowned Night-Heron, White Ibis, Wood Duck, Red-shouldered Hawk, King Rail, Barred Owl, Pileated Woodpecker. *Summer*—Least Bittern; Wood Stork; Least Tern; Yellow-throated Vireo; Prothonotary, Yellow-throated, Kentucky, and Hooded Warblers; Indigo and Painted Buntings; Orchard Oriole. *Winter*—American Bittern, Hooded Merganser, Bald Eagle, Merlin, Virginia Rail, Sora, Sedge Wren. *Migration*—Bobolink.

Best times to bird: April through July.

Directions: Take Interstate 526 west toward Savannah until you reach the exit for Ashley River Road North (Highway 61). The exit is tricky, so be careful. A few hundred feet beyond the exit ramp is a frontage road on the right that will lead you to Ashley River Road. Follow the frontage road 0.7 mile and turn left on Ashley River Road. After 5.1 miles turn right into the entrance for Magnolia Plantation.

The Birding

Magnolia Plantation is well known as having perhaps the most easily accessible heron rookery in the state. It is largely made up of Anhinga; Green Heron; and Great, Snowy, and Cattle Egrets but also contains smaller numbers of Great Blue, Little Blue, and Tricolored Herons and Black-crowned Night-Herons. The rookery offers a fantastic opportunity to observe bird behavior. In the spring the herons will be busy courting their mates and finding sticks to build their nests. During the summer months the herons will be flying back and forth constantly to feed their young. In addition to the rookery, the plantation also occasionally gets rarities such as Fulvous Whistling-Duck, Limpkin, and Black and Yellow Rails.

Be sure to ask for a trail map of the 500-acre plantation at the entrance booth. The heron rookery is located along the **Audubon Swamp Garden Trail,** a 0.5-mile loop. The trail bears no affiliation with the National Audubon Society, but rather received its name because John J. Audubon wrote about visiting the plantation in his books. It is possible that Audubon obtained his Anhinga specimens from this very swamp. Look for the wading bird nests on the small islands in the middle of the swamp. Great Blue Heron will begin nesting as early as late January, but most of the other species in the rookery will not begin nesting until April and May. This is probably the best place in the state to see Anhinga year-round, especially during the summer, when they are breeding. Other resident birds along the Audubon Swamp Garden Trail include Wood Duck, Red-shouldered Hawk, and Barred Owl. In the summer look for Prothonotary Warbler. During winter you should see large flocks of Green-winged and Blue-winged Teals and smaller numbers of American Wigeon, Gadwall, and Northern Shoveler.

The 2-mile paved **Cattail Wildlife Refuge Trail** winds through 125 acres of old rice fields on the plantation. In the winter the rice fields often contain

Great Egret constructing a nest along the Audubon Swamp Garden Trail

thousands of American Coots. Also look for Ring-necked Duck, Virginia Rail, Sora, Northern Harrier, and Bald Eagle in winter. The observation tower along the trail can be a good spot to scan for waterfowl, raptors, rails, and Anhinga. If you are lucky enough to spot a Fulvous Whistling-Duck or Yellow Rail, the rice fields are where you will find them. The rice fields can be a good spot to find King Rail year-round, but beware because Clapper Rail also occur there. Keep an eye out for other secretive birds hiding in the reeds along the edges of the rice fields, such as American and Least Bitterns and Marsh and Sedge Wren. During spring and fall look for Bobolink, and you may learn how they got the nickname "Rice Birds."

You can rent a canoe and paddle through the rice fields for a close-up view. A nature train, which departs every hour for a forty-five-minute tour of the plantation, can be a great way to see more than 4 miles of trails without all the hard work.

General Information

General admission is $15 for adults, but if you only want to walk through the Audubon Swamp Garden, the cost is $7. The plantation is open year-round from 8:00 a.m. to dusk. Guided bird walks are offered on Sunday mornings.

DeLorme atlas: Page 60, A5.

Elevation: 0 to 5 feet.

Hazards: Alligators, venomous snakes, mosquitoes.

Nearest food, gas, lodging: Charleston.

Camping: James Island County Park.

For more information: Magnolia Plantation & Gardens.

10 James Island

Habitats: Salt marsh, beach, mudflats, ocean, early successional, mixed pine-hardwood forest.

Specialty birds: *Resident*—White Ibis, Clapper Rail, American Oystercatcher, Common Ground-Dove, Loggerhead Shrike, Marsh Wren, Seaside Sparrow. *Summer*—Yellow-crowned Night-Heron; Mississippi Kite; Gull-billed, Sandwich, and Least Terns; Black Skimmer; Painted Bunting. *Winter*—Red-throated Loon, Horned Grebe, Northern Gannet, Bald Eagle, Great Black-backed Gull, Saltmarsh and Nelson's Sharp-tailed Sparrows.

Best times to bird: August through May.

Directions: To reach Fort Johnson from the intersection of U.S. Highway 17 and Highway 171 (Folly Road), drive south on Highway 171 toward Folly Beach. After 1.8 miles turn left on Harbor View Road. In 3.7 miles you will come to a T-intersection with Fort Johnson Road. Turn left and drive 0.8 mile to the entrance gate at Fort Johnson. To reach James Island County Park from the intersection of US 17 and Highway 171 (Folly Road), drive south on Highway 171 toward Folly Beach. After 3.2 miles turn right on Camp Road. In 0.8 mile you will come to a stop sign at Riverland Drive. Turn right and the entrance to James Island County Park is 0.2 mile down the road on the left. Continue 0.6 mile to the parking area for the dog park on the right.

The Birding

Directly across the harbor from Patriots Point is **Fort Johnson.** The site of military operations during both the Revolutionary and Civil Wars, Fort Johnson is now home to the South Carolina Department of Natural Resources Marine Resources Center. Once inside the gates to Fort Johnson, drive 0.3 mile until you see an old, white plantation house on your left called the Marshlands House. Behind the house is a nice view of the harbor and a network of trails that lead through the woods bordering the harbor. In the fall the woods can often contain small flocks of migrating songbirds. Follow the trail closest to the harbor and you will come to a small, wooden viewing platform. If the tide is low, you can walk along the beach and look for Brown Pelican; Bald Eagle; American Oystercatcher; Ruddy Turnstone; Spotted Sandpiper; and Least, Gull-billed, Forster's, and Royal Terns. Common Ground-Doves have occasionally been seen along the beach in front of the convent (look for the rock wall down near the docks).

Another good spot to check out at Fort Johnson is **Fort Johnson Point.** Return to the main road that runs through Fort Johnson, turn left, and follow the road for 0.2 mile until it ends at a boat slip. At the end of the road is a turnaround with a flagpole in the center. The open, grassy area bordering the harbor is Fort Johnson Point, which offers a fantastic view of the harbor and is a great place to watch wading birds, shorebirds, and terns as they fly past the point. It is often worth spending some time sitting in a chair or out on the rocks just to see what will fly past you. In the summer look for Yellow-crowned Night-Heron, Osprey,

Least and Gull-billed Terns, and Black Skimmer. Year-round residents include Brown Pelican, American Oystercatcher, and Royal Tern. During winter look for Red-breasted Merganser, Bald Eagle, Spotted Sandpiper, Great Black-backed Gull, and Forster's Tern. Large flocks of Northern Gannets can occasionally be seen feeding in the harbor during winter, but you often have a better chance of finding them at Folly Beach. In addition to birds, the point is often a great spot to see bottle-nosed dolphins swimming close to shore, and the boat slip can contain Florida manatees in the summer months.

James Island County Park can be a good area to look for migrating warblers, particularly in the fall. From the dog park parking lot, follow the small path that starts in the northeast corner. The short, 0.4-mile trail runs along the shrubby edge of a freshwater lagoon and then loops back around to the northwest corner of the parking lot. On a good day in late September, you may see nearly twenty species of warblers along the trail!

The western edge of the county park is bordered by the salt marsh along the Stono River. To reach the salt marsh, take the paved road called Fisherman's Way, which starts across the street from the dog park parking lot, and follow the signs for the fishing dock. After 0.3 mile you will reach a parking lot for the fishing dock. Follow the paved trail left from the parking lot for 200 feet to the wooden dock. The dock provides a fantastic view of the Stono River and the surrounding salt marsh. Scan the salt marsh grass for Sharp-tailed Sparrow in winter. Year-round look for Clapper Rail, Marsh Wren, and Seaside Sparrow. During summer you should be able to find Painted Bunting in the trees along the marsh. Yellow-crowned Night-Heron and Wood Stork can often be found in the marsh during summer, and many other wading birds are present year-round, including White Ibis and Tricolored and Little Blue Herons. The park is also one of the best areas on James Island to find Mississippi Kite in summer.

General Information

Fort Johnson is open to the public Monday through Friday from 8:30 a.m. to 5:00 p.m. James Island County Park is open 8:00 a.m. to 6:00 p.m. during winter and 8:00 a.m. to 8:00 p.m. in summer. Admission is $1 per person.

DeLorme atlas: Fort Johnson, page 60, C7; James Island County Park, page 60, C6.

Elevation: 0 to 5 feet.

Hazards: Ticks, venomous snakes, mosquitoes, cacti.

Nearest food, gas, lodging: Charleston.

Camping: James Island County Park.

For more information: SCDNR Marine Resources Division; James Island County Park.

11 Folly Island

Habitats: Salt marsh, beach, mudflats, ocean, early successional, mixed pine-hardwood forest.

Specialty birds: *Resident*—White Ibis, American Oystercatcher, Eurasian Collared-Dove, Loggerhead Shrike, Seaside Sparrow. *Summer*—Sandwich and Least Terns, Black Skimmer, Wilson's Plover, Common Nighthawk, Painted Bunting. *Winter*—Red-throated Loon; Horned Grebe; Northern Gannet; Greater Scaup; White-winged, Black, and Surf Scoters; Peregrine Falcon; Piping Plover; Saltmarsh and Nelson's Sharp-tailed Sparrows. *Migration*—Red Knot, Marbled Godwit, Black Tern.

Best times to bird: Year-round.

Directions: See below.

The Birding

Some of the best birding on the west side of Charleston Harbor can be found on Folly Island. With a variety of habitats, good numbers of migrating shorebirds and songbirds, and rare birds possible in any season, Folly Island has something for nearly everyone to enjoy. To reach the island from the intersection of U.S. Highway 17 and Highway 171 (Folly Road), drive south on Highway 171. After 2.5 miles you will come to an area with salt marsh and mudflats on either side of the road. Pull off onto the shoulder or one of the side streets and scan the mudflats for shorebirds. This can be a good spot to see Whimbrel during migration and White Ibis year-round.

After driving another 1.9 miles on Folly Road, you will reach the beach on Folly Island. At the last traffic light, turn right onto Ashley Avenue. As you drive along Ashley Avenue, expect to see Eurasian Collared-Doves on the telephone wires year-round. Rare birds such as White-winged Dove, Gray and Western Kingbirds, and Shiny Cowbird are occasionally found on the telephone wires or in residential yards.

Follow Ashley Avenue 1.5 miles until it ends in **Folly Beach County Park.** In the winter you can expect to see Common and Red-throated Loons, Northern Gannet, Horned Grebe, Greater Scaup, Black Scoter, and Red-breasted Merganser from the beach. The small trees and shrubs around the park's parking lot can occasionally contain small flocks of migrating songbirds. If you walk to the southern tip of the county park, you will come to the Stono River inlet. At the inlet there are some nice sandbars and mudflats where you can find Piping, Semipalmated, and Black-bellied Plovers; Least Sandpiper; Bonaparte's Gull; and Forster's Tern in winter. Brown Pelican, American Oystercatcher, and Black Skimmer can be seen year-round. In the summer look for Least, Sandwich, Gull-billed, and Royal Terns along with numerous Wilson's Plovers. During spring and fall check the mudflats for migrating shorebirds and terns, including Red Knot; Marbled Godwit; and Caspian, Black, and Common Terns.

Morris Island Lighthouse at the north end of Folly Island

Drive back down Ashley Avenue until you reach the traffic light for Folly Road, where you entered the island. Turn right at the light and follow signs for the **Folly Beach Fishing Pier.** The pier extends 1,045 feet out into the ocean and offers a unique opportunity to view seabirds that are hard to see from the beach. In the winter look for loons, gannets, and sea ducks. Long-tailed Duck, White-winged Scoter, and Common Eider are all possible, though not to be expected. Most of the birds are often far out in the ocean, so be sure to bring a scope. During summer look for terns and gulls. Be aware that it can be extremely difficult to find parking near the pier from May through September.

From the pier, work your way back to Ashley Avenue and follow it for 3.4 miles, all the way to the northern tip of Folly Island. Local birders call this area the **Old Coast Guard Station,** though you won't find any signs that refer to it as such. Park in the public parking area on the short road (Sumter Drive) on your right, just before you reach the gate, and follow the narrow paved road beyond the gate at the end of Ashley Avenue. The brush on either side of the road can often be good for migrating songbirds in the fall. During winter this area usually has a few Gray Catbirds mixed in with the large flocks of White-throated Sparrows and Yellow-rumped Warblers.

As you continue down the road, you will come to a speed bump and the foundation of an old building on your left. The open area and dunes beyond the old building are a good area to find Loggerhead Shrike year-round. In the spring and summer it is often easy to find male Painted Buntings singing from the wires and tops of bushes along the paved road. At dusk, look and listen for Common Nighthawks flying over the road. Beware of cacti and sand spurs if you leave the road or trails. At the end of the old parking lot on the left, just past the speed bump, a dirt road heads off into the woods. Several small paths off this road will give you a good view of the salt marsh. Check the marsh for Seaside Sparrows and both Sharp-tailed Sparrows. Follow the dirt road until it ends at the beach, with a good view of the Morris Island Lighthouse and several rock groins extending into the ocean. In the winter scan the railings of the Morris Island Lighthouse for Peregrine Falcon and check the rock groins for loons and sea ducks. From here you can either walk back along the beach or retrace your path through the dunes.

General Information

Folly Beach County Park is open daily from 9:00 a.m. to 7:00 p.m. during summer and 10:00 a.m. to 5:00 p.m. in winter. Admission is $5 per vehicle. Be aware that in the summer Folly Beach can be extremely crowded, which can lead to traffic congestion and difficulty in finding a place to park. Folly Beach Fishing Pier is open daily from 8:00 a.m. to 5:00 p.m. during winter and 6:00 a.m. to 11:00 p.m. in summer.

DeLorme atlas: Page 60, D7.

Elevation: 0 to 5 feet.

Hazards: Ticks, venomous snakes, mosquitoes, cacti.

Nearest food, gas, lodging: Folly Beach.

Camping: James Island County Park.

For more information: Folly Beach County Park; Folly Beach Fishing Pier.

⑫ Charleston Harbor East

Habitats: Salt marsh, beach, mudflats, ocean, hardwood forest, mixed pine-hardwood forest.

Specialty birds: *Resident*—White Ibis, Wood Stork, Black-crowned Night-Heron, Clapper Rail, American Oystercatcher, Eurasian Collared-Dove, Common Ground-Dove, Marsh Wren, Seaside Sparrow, Boat-tailed Grackle. *Summer*—Yellow-crowned Night-Heron; Reddish Egret; Gull-billed, Sandwich, and Least Terns; Black Skimmer; Painted Bunting. *Winter*—Red-throated Loon, Horned Grebe, Hooded and Red-breasted Mergansers, Bald Eagle, Merlin, Peregrine Falcon, Piping Plover, Purple Sandpiper, Saltmarsh and Nelson's Sharp-tailed Sparrows. *Migration*—Red Knot, Marbled Godwit, Whimbrel, Black Tern, Clay-colored Sparrow.

Best times to bird: Year-round.

Directions: To reach Patriots Point, take exit 221 from Interstate 26 and drive north on U.S. Highway 17. As you follow US 17 north across the Arthur Ravenel Jr. Bridge into Mt. Pleasant, move to the farthest right lane on the bridge and follow signs for Coleman Boulevard. After you have exited onto Coleman Boulevard, turn right at the first traffic light on Patriots Point Road. After 0.2 mile turn left into the small parking lot for the nature trail, just before the baseball fields. To reach the Pitt Street Bridge from Patriots Point, return to Coleman Boulevard and turn right. After 1.2 miles you will reach a fork, with Coleman Boulevard going left and Whilden Street continuing straight ahead. Follow Whilden Street for 1.1 miles and turn right on Center Street. After 1 block turn left onto Pitt Street. Follow Pitt Street for 0.4 mile to where it ends at the parking area for the bridge. To reach Fort Moultrie from the intersection of Coleman Boulevard and Ben Sawyer Boulevard (Highway 703), drive south on Ben Sawyer Boulevard toward Sullivan's Island. After 2.1 miles on Ben Sawyer Boulevard, turn right on Middle Street, following signs for Fort Moultrie. After 1.4 miles turn left on Station 12 Street and park in the small dirt lot. If the dirt lot is full, park in the Fort Moultrie lot across the street.

The Birding

During fall migration Patriots Point is well known as one of the best areas in the state to see migrating warblers and other songbirds. As the birds head south in the fall, the small patch of forest at Patriots Point is one of the last refuges for migrants before they cross Charleston Harbor. Birding here during the rest of the year is pretty slow, though you may be able to find a few Painted Buntings during the summer. In the fall scan the area surrounding the parking lot for Clay-colored Sparrow. From the parking lot, follow the nature trail south through the narrow strip of trees between the baseball fields and the golf course. The small patch of deciduous forest that surrounds the nature trail can be excellent for migrating warblers, vireos, thrushes, and other land-bird migrants in the fall. On a good day, you may see over twenty species of warblers!

Walk along the nature trail for 0.6 mile, following signs for the Patriots Point Lookout Deck, and you will come to a paved road near the entrance to the golf

The old causeway at Pitt Street Bridge

course. Cross the road and after 0.2 mile you will reach a small observation platform with a good view of Charleston Harbor. You may find breeding Painted
Buntings in the trees and marsh surrounding the platform in summer. From the
platform you can see **Crab Bank,** one of South Carolina's largest seabird rookeries. Crab Bank is home to thousands of nesting Brown Pelicans, Royal Terns, and
Black Skimmers during the summer, along with lesser numbers of nesting Gull-
billed and Sandwich Terns and American Oystercatchers. To get a good look at
the island from the platform on Patriots Point, you will need a spotting scope. A
great way to get a closer view of Crab Bank and the nesting birds is to arrange a
kayak tour of the island through Coastal Expeditions out of Shem Creek. It is an
experience that you will never forget! *Do not* get off on the island, as it is closed
March through October to protect the nesting birds.

Pitt Street Bridge has a history dating back to before the Revolutionary
War. In 1927 it was rebuilt to allow cars to connect Mt. Pleasant to Sullivan's
Island, but it has long since been closed to vehicles and now serves as a nice area
to observe Charleston Harbor. The 0.2-mile walk leading out to the bridge is one
of the best areas near Charleston to look for salt marsh birds. The salt marsh along
the walkway to the bridge is excellent for Clapper Rail, Marsh Wren, and Seaside
Sparrow year-round, and you may be able to find Saltmarsh and Nelson's Sharp-
tailed Sparrows in winter. Merlins will occasionally perch in snags out in the salt
marsh in late fall and winter, and Wood Storks can be seen soaring above the
marsh year-round.

Fall through spring, the sandbars and mudflats on the harbor side of the walkway are a great place to observe American Oystercatcher, Marbled Godwit, and many other shorebirds. The best time to see the shorebirds is at low tide, when the mudflats are exposed. During the summer look for Reddish Egret; Least, Sandwich, Royal, and Gull-billed Terns; and Black Skimmer. In the winter scan the harbor and waterway for Bufflehead, Red-breasted and Hooded Mergansers, Red-throated and Common Loons, and Horned Grebe. Year-round keep an eye out for Common Ground-Dove, which can occasionally be seen flying by the bridge around dawn or dusk.

Fort Moultrie is a mainland portion of the Fort Sumter National Monument. It provides an excellent location to scan the harbor for seabirds during winter, and is a reliable location to search for Common Ground-Dove year-round. From the dirt lot at the end of Station 12 Street, there is a good view of the harbor and several rock groins. In the winter scan the rock groins along the beach for the occasional Purple Sandpiper and the harbor for loons, grebes, and sea ducks. Year-round look for Common Ground-Dove along the edges of the grassy field and Eurasian Collared-Dove on the telephone wires.

Walk east (toward Isle of Palms) along the forested edge of the field. After 0.3 mile you will come to a beach access at the end of Station 16 Street that leads into the forest. This 90-acre section of forest along Charleston Harbor can be good for migrating warblers, vireos, thrushes, and other birds in the fall. Year-round the scrubby overgrown dunes within the forest are great habitat for Common Ground-Dove.

Return to Middle Street and drive back the way you came. Instead of turning onto Ben Sawyer Boulevard, continue straight on Middle Street. Drive 1.5 miles from the intersection, where Middle Street ends at Highway 703 (Jasper Boulevard). Pull into the parking lot on the right. Here you have a good view of **Breach Inlet,** which divides Sullivans Island from Isle of Palms. Scan the beach for Reddish Egret; Black Skimmer; and Sandwich, Gull-billed, and Least Terns during the summer. Fall through spring, look for flocks of Red Knots and other shorebirds. In the winter, if you are lucky, you may see a Lesser Black-backed Gull or Great Cormorant.

General Information

Patriots Point, Pitt Street Bridge, Fort Moultrie, and Breach Inlet are all open year-round from dawn to dusk.

DeLorme atlas: Patriots Point, page 60, B7; Pitt Street Bridge, page 60, B8; Fort Moultrie, page 60, C8; Breach Inlet, page 60, B8.

Elevation: 0 to 5 feet.

Hazards: Ticks, venomous snakes, mosquitoes, cacti.

Nearest food, gas, lodging: Mt. Pleasant.

Camping: James Island County Park.

For more information: Fort Sumter National Monument; Coastal Expeditions.

13 Cape Romain National Wildlife Refuge

Habitats: Salt marsh, mudflats, ocean, beach, pond, early successional, mixed pine-hardwood forest.

Specialty birds: *Resident*—Black-crowned Night-Heron, Tricolored and Little Blue Herons, White Ibis, Wood Stork, Mottled Duck, American Oystercatcher, Common Ground-Dove, Loggerhead Shrike, Seaside Sparrow. *Summer*—Anhinga, Least Bittern, Reddish Egret, Yellow-crowned Night-Heron, Glossy Ibis, Roseate Spoonbill, Swallow-tailed and Mississippi Kites, Wilson's Plover, Sandwich and Least Terns, Eastern Wood-Pewee, Summer Tanager, Blue Grosbeak, Painted Bunting. *Winter*—Red-throated and Common Loons; Horned Grebe; Northern Gannet; American Bittern; Tundra Swan; American Black Duck; Northern Pintail; Canvasback; Redhead; Greater and Lesser Scaups; Long-tailed Duck; Black, White-winged, and Surf Scoters; Hooded and Red-breasted Mergansers; Bald Eagle; Merlin; Peregrine Falcon; Piping Plover; Whimbrel; Long-billed Curlew; Red Knot; Purple Sandpiper; Bonaparte's and Great Black-backed Gulls; Orange-crowned Warbler; Saltmarsh and Nelson's Sharp-tailed Sparrows. *Migration*—Black-necked Stilt, American Avocet, Marbled Godwit, White-rumped and Stilt Sandpipers, Black Tern, Clay-colored and Lark Sparrows, Bobolink.

Best times to bird: Year-round.

Directions: From the intersection of U.S. Highway 17 and Highway 41 in Mt. Pleasant, drive north on US 17. After 6.9 miles turn right on Seewee Road (following signs for Garris Landing). After 3.4 miles turn right on Bulls Island Road, which leads to Garris Landing after 1.6 miles.

The Birding

Cape Romain National Wildlife Refuge protects a series of barrier islands and salt marsh along a 20-mile stretch of the coast. Cape Romain is truly one of the finest birding areas in the state, especially during winter. It has been estimated that nearly 20 percent of the entire Atlantic population of American Oystercatchers winter within Cape Romain NWR. Many oystercatchers will remain to breed on the washed shell rakes in the Cape Romain tidal creeks. Shell rakes are long mounds of dead, bleached oyster shells, which rise up higher than the surrounding salt marsh.

The refuge is the best spot in South Carolina to see Reddish Egret and Roseate Spoonbill in the summer and Long-billed Curlew during winter. In spring and late summer, the salt marsh and lagoons on Bull Island have some of the highest concentrations of migrating shorebirds in the entire state. It is possible to see thousands of Red Knots and hundreds of Marbled Godwits on the island during late summer as they migrate south. The refuge boasts a large list of rare birds, including Eurasian Wigeon, Golden Eagle, Short-eared Owl, Western Kingbird, Clay-colored and Lark Sparrows, Lapland Longspur, and Snow Bunting.

There are a few things that you will want to keep in mind as you plan your trip to Cape Romain NWR. Access to the refuge is by boat only, but a passenger

Fishing pier at Garris Landing

ferry operated by Coastal Expeditions runs to **Bull Island** several times per week. There is no visitor center on the island and only limited facilities, so be prepared to bring plenty of food and water for your trip. Mosquitoes can be bad here even during winter in some years, so don't forget insect repellant. It may also be worthwhile to bring a mountain bike, since the island is quite large and your time is often limited. You may want to print a map of the island at www .coastalexpeditions.com in order to navigate its many dirt roads.

While you are waiting for the ferry to depart, you can do some birding from the long pier at **Garris Landing.** This small area is the only portion of the refuge that can be accessed without a boat. At low tide the mudflats and oyster beds can be pretty good for migrating shorebirds and wading birds. During summer you should be able to see a few Wood Storks soaring over the salt marsh, and if you are lucky, you may find Swallow-tailed or Mississippi Kites hunting over the marsh or flying along the waterway. Scan the marsh grass year-round for Clapper Rail, Marsh Wren, and Seaside Sparrow. In the winter look for both Nelson's and Saltmarsh Sharp-tailed Sparrows. Although it only lasts about ten minutes, the ferry ride over to Bull Island can often produce a good variety of birds. Scan the shell rakes and oyster beds for American Oystercatcher. During winter look for Horned Grebe, Bufflehead, Bald Eagle, Merlin, and Peregrine Falcon in the creeks and surrounding marsh.

The ferry will drop you off at a dock on Summerhouse Creek, which is located on the north side of the island. From the dock, follow the dirt road south

0.5 mile to the picnic area and restrooms. As you follow the sandy roads on the island, keep an eye out for Common Ground-Dove year-round. The shrubs along the numerous dikes of the refuge can be great areas to look for Painted Bunting during summer and migrating songbirds in the spring and fall. During late fall the shrubs can be literally covered in migrating monarch butterflies. From the picnic area you can proceed in two directions, depending on how much time you have. You can either head south toward the Upper and Lower Summerhouse Ponds, a 2-mile loop, or head northeast toward Jacks Creek, a 5-mile loop. Keep in mind that it is a long walk out to Jacks Creek, and without a bike, it is difficult to make it back in time for the departing ferry.

The **Upper** and **Lower Summerhouse Ponds** are often filled with wading birds, including Tricolored and Little Blue Herons, at any time of year. During spring and late summer, look for shorebirds on the muddy edges of the ponds. In the winter look for good numbers of waterfowl, including American Black Duck, American Wigeon, Northern Pintail, and Green-winged and Blue-winged Teals. If you are on foot, you may want to bird the Summerhouse Ponds by follow-ing the Turkey Walk Trail. The trail starts behind the picnic area and leads to a dike that runs between the two ponds. From the dike, you have a good vantage point to scan for birds on both ponds. Just before you reach the dike, a small trail leading southwest toward Upper Summerhouse will take you to an observation platform with a good view of the pond. For those wanting to take a longer trek, you can follow Summerhouse Road and Mill Road around Upper Summerhouse Pond to create a loop.

The best birding area on the refuge is **Jacks Creek,** especially the section of the road that runs along the eastern end of the island between Jacks Creek and the ocean. During summer Jacks Creek is the most reliable spot in South Carolina to see Reddish Egret and Roseate Spoonbill. In the winter expect to see hundreds, if not thousands, of waterfowl in the marshes, including Tundra Swan, Canvasback, Redhead, Common Goldeneye, and American Black Duck. The marshes are also good hunting areas for Merlin, Peregrine Falcon, and Bald Eagle in winter. Scan the ocean for loons, grebes, gannets, and all three scoter species during winter. In the spring and late summer, the mudflats and beach can be filled with shorebirds, especially Red Knot, Short-billed Dowitcher, Western Sandpiper, and Marbled Godwit. You may also be able to find Piping Plover and White-rumped and Stilt Sandpipers if you are lucky.

Several Long-billed Curlews often spend the winter on **Raccoon Key,** a remote island in the northern portion of the refuge. The only way to access this island is by private boat. Cape Romain Bird Observatory occasionally offers trips out to this area of the refuge to look for the curlews and other rare birds. Dates for upcoming bird-watching trips, along with other valuable information about birding on Bull Island, can be found on the Cape Romain Bird Observatory Web site (see Appendix F).

Reddish Egret chasing fish

If you have never been to the refuge before, you may want to stop by the **Sewee Visitor and Environmental Education Center** on US 17, which serves as the headquarters for the refuge. You can find trail maps for Cape Romain NWR and ferry schedules to Bull Island at the visitor center. In addition to being an outstanding birding area, the refuge serves as an important recovery area for the federally endangered red wolf. Check out the enclosure behind the visitor center for a look at some of these wolves.

General Information

The ferry to Bull Island is $30 per person. A ferry schedule can be viewed at www.coastalexpeditions.com/ferry.htm or call (843) 884–7684.

DeLorme atlas: Page 56, H5.

Elevation: 0 to 10 feet.

Hazards: Alligators, venomous snakes, mosquitoes.

Nearest food, gas, lodging: Awendaw or McClellanville for food and gas; Mt. Pleasant for lodging.

Camping: Francis Marion National Forest.

For more information: Cape Romain National Wildlife Refuge; Coastal Expeditions; Sewee Visitor and Environmental Education Center.

14 Francis Marion National Forest

Habitats: Pine forest, mixed pine-hardwood forest, early successional, field, salt marsh, mudflats, freshwater marsh, pond, stream, swamp.

Specialty birds: *Resident*—Anhinga, White Ibis, Red-shouldered Hawk, King Rail, Red-cockaded and Pileated Woodpeckers, Brown-headed Nuthatch, Bachman's and Seaside Sparrows. *Summer*—Least Bittern; Swallow-tailed and Mississippi Kites; Chuck-will's-widow; Whip-poor-will; Prothonotary, Yellow-throated, Swainson's, Hooded, and Kentucky Warblers; Summer Tanager; Blue Grosbeak; Indigo and Painted Buntings; Orchard Oriole. *Winter*—American Black Duck, Hooded Merganser, Bald Eagle, Sora, Orange-crowned and Black-and-white Warblers, Fox Sparrow, Nelson's and Saltmarsh Sharp-tailed Sparrows, Rusty Blackbird. *Migration*—Broad-winged Hawk, Merlin, Peregrine Falcon.

Best times to bird: March through June. Be aware that the mosquitoes and chiggers at the plantation can be pretty bad during the summer months.

Directions: To reach Ion Swamp from the intersection of Highway 41 and U.S. Highway 17 in Mt. Pleasant, drive north on US 17 for 11 miles. Turn left onto the dirt Ion Swamp Road (FS Road 228). If you pass the Sewee Visitor and Environmental Education Center 0.3 mile north of Ion Swamp Road on US 17, you have gone too far. To reach South Tibwin Plantation from the intersection of Steed Creek Road and US 17 in Awendaw, drive north on US 17 for 6.4 miles and turn right into the entrance for the plantation. To reach Wambaw Bridge from the intersection of US 17 and Highway 45 in McClellanville, drive north on US 17. After 6.4 miles turn left on Rutledge Road, following signs for Hampton Plantation State Historic Site. After 4.3 miles you will reach the Wambaw Bridge.

The Birding

Francis Marion National Forest is a huge area, nearly 250,000 acres, with a diverse selection of habitats. One could almost write an entire book on where to go birding within this national forest, but in order to conserve space, I will only highlight a few key areas. Many birders are drawn to Francis Marion National Forest to look for specialty birds such as Swallow-tailed Kite, Red-cockaded Woodpecker, Swainson's Warbler, and Bachman's Sparrow.

As you drive down **Ion Swamp Road,** keep your eyes on the sky for the Swallow-tailed and Mississippi Kites that occasionally pass over the road during summer. Swainson's and Kentucky Warblers can be heard singing along most of Ion Swamp Road, but the thick brush often prevents you from getting a good look at them. During spring and fall look for migrating warblers along the road, particularly in the swampy areas. In the summer you can often hear numerous Chuck-will's-widows and a few Whip-poor-wills if you drive the dirt roads of the national forest at dawn or dusk.

At 1.2 miles from US 17 you will come to a small bridge where Swainson's and Kentucky Warblers can be found in summer. Also during summer look for

Red-cockaded Woodpecker

Yellow-billed Cuckoo, Acadian Flycatcher, Yellow-throated and Red-eyed Vireos, Northern Parula, and Prothonotary Warbler. Year-round you can find Red-shouldered Hawk, Barred Owl, and White-eyed Vireo.

Continue another 1.3 miles along Ion Swamp Road and you will see a small parking area on the left and the trailhead for the **Ion Swamp Interpretive Trail,** a 2-mile loop. The trail takes you through what remains of an old rice field that has reverted to a hardwood swamp. The trail follows the old levees that used to surround the patchwork of rice fields. Along the trail you should be able to find Wood Duck and Barred Owl year-round, and Yellow-crowned Night-Heron, Yellow-billed Cuckoo, Acadian Flycatcher, Northern Parula, and Prothonotary Warbler in the summer. You may also be able to find a couple Swainson's and Kentucky Warblers at the beginning of the trail during summer. In the spring and fall, you can often see Northern Waterthrush and other migrant warblers along the old levees.

Continue another 1.3 miles on Ion Swamp Road, until it dead-ends on Willow Hall Road (FS Road 202). At the junction of these two roads, you will see several Red-cockaded Woodpecker nest trees marked with white paint rings at the base. The best time to look for the woodpeckers is at dawn and dusk, when they are entering and exiting their nest holes. During summer you should also be able to find Eastern Wood-Pewee, Yellow-throated and Prairie Warblers, and Bachman's Sparrow. Look for Brown-headed Nuthatch, Pine Warbler, and Eastern Towhee year-round.

Turn left on Willow Hall Road and drive 2.0 miles to a small pond on the left, just before you reach FS Road 202A. This 2-mile stretch of Willow Hall Road is an excellent area to find foraging Red-cockaded Woodpeckers. Park near the pond and search the area around the pond and along Willow Hall Road for these woodpeckers in any season. In the summer look for Bachman's Sparrow, Indigo Bunting, and Blue Grosbeak. During winter, search the pine savannas and early successional habitat for sparrows. The small pond can contain Anhinga, Bald Eagle, Osprey, Belted Kingfisher, and even a few alligators.

South Tibwin Plantation contains over 5 miles of primitive roads that are accessible only by foot or bicycle. Park at the entrance gate and pick up a trail map from the kiosk, then walk or bike the main road through the gate. From the fall through spring, the woods along this road can be good for flocks of migrating and wintering songbirds. In the winter look for Blue-headed Vireo, Orange-crowned and Black-and-white Warblers, and Fox Sparrow. Continue straight on the road, past the USDA Forest Service house, and after 0.4 mile the road will cross a small creek. During summer this creek can be filled with Wood Storks, White and Glossy Ibises, and numerous egrets and herons.

Continue straight along the road for another 0.5 mile and you will come to an impoundment, which can occasionally have Roseate Spoonbill mixed in with other common wading birds in late summer. During winter the impoundment can be good for waterfowl, but it is closed to the public from November 1 to February 15. There are often good numbers of waterfowl still present in late February and early March. In the summer keep an eye out for Mississippi and Swallow-tailed Kites soaring over the forests and impoundments. Painted Buntings are fairly common breeders along the edges of the salt marsh and impoundments. During fall watch for migrating raptors such as Bald Eagle, Broad-winged Hawk, Peregrine Falcon, and Merlin flying southwest along the coast. The impoundments and salt marsh that border the eastern edge of the plantation offer a wide view to scan for the raptors.

In the summer the **Wambaw Bridge** is a good spot to watch for Swallow-tailed Kites, particularly in the early afternoon as they fly along Wambaw Creek. The woods on either side of the bridge can sometimes contain breeding Swainson's and Kentucky Warblers, as well as numerous Acadian and Great Crested Flycatchers, Yellow-throated and Red-eyed Vireos, Northern Parulas, and Prothonotary Warblers.

Continue north on Rutledge Road and after 0.9 mile you will come to a Red-cockaded Woodpecker colony. During summer the longleaf pine forest surrounding the colony is an excellent spot to look for Bachman's Sparrow, as well as Common Yellowthroat, Kentucky Warbler, Summer Tanager, Indigo Bunting, and Blue Grosbeak. Year-round you should be able to find Brown-headed Nuthatch and Pine Warbler. Another Red-cockaded Woodpecker colony with similar habitat lies 1.0 mile farther north on Rutledge Road.

General Information

The dirt roads in Francis Marion National Forest are open year-round twenty-four hours a day.

DeLorme atlas: Ion Swamp, page 56, G4; South Tibwin Plantation, page 57, E6; Wambaw Bridge, page 57, C6.

Elevation: 0 to 20 feet.

Hazards: Alligators, venomous snakes, mosquitoes, ticks, chiggers, logging trucks.

Nearest food, gas, lodging: Awendaw or McClellanville for food and gas; Mt. Pleasant for lodging.

Camping: Francis Marion National Forest.

For more information: Sewee Visitor and Environmental Education Center; Francis Marion National Forest.

15 Santee River Delta

Habitats: Pine forest, mixed pine-hardwood forest, early successional, salt marsh, mud-flats, freshwater marsh, pond, river, stream, swamp.

Specialty birds: *Resident*—American White Pelican, Anhinga, White and Glossy Ibises, Wood Stork, Mottled Duck, Red-shouldered Hawk, Black and King Rails, Barn Owl, Red-cockaded Woodpecker, Brown-headed Nuthatch, Bachman's and Seaside Sparrows. *Summer*—Least Bittern, Swallow-tailed and Mississippi Kites, Yellow-throated Vireo, Prothonotary and Hooded Warblers, Summer Tanager, Blue Grosbeak, Indigo and Painted Buntings, Orchard Oriole. *Winter*—American Black Duck, Gadwall, American Wigeon, Canvasback, Redhead, Hooded Merganser, Bald Eagle, Merlin, Peregrine Falcon, Sora, Nelson's and Saltmarsh Sharp-tailed Sparrows, Rusty Blackbird. *Migration*—White-rumped and Stilt Sandpipers, Bobolink.

Best times to bird: March to May. The mosquitoes and deerflies are awful from late May through October and make it virtually impossible to do any birding here, even with a head net and insect repellant.

Directions: To reach the Santee Coastal Reserve from the intersection of U.S. Highway 17 and Highway 45 in McClellanville, follow US 17 north toward Georgetown. After 3.0 miles turn right on South Santee Road, then in 2.6 miles turn right onto the dirt entrance road to the Santee Coastal Reserve. To reach the Santee Delta WMA, from the intersection of South Santee Road and US 17 in South Santee, drive north on US 17. After 2.7 miles turn right into the entrance for Santee Delta WMA, just before the bridge over the North Santee River.

The Birding

The **Santee Coastal Reserve** offers good birding year-round, but during the warmer months the mosquito and deerfly swarms along the Marshland Loop Trail and Bike/Hike Loop Trail become large enough to carry you away. The entrance road is a great area to look for Red-cockaded Woodpecker and Brown-headed Nuthatch year-round. To locate the Red-cockaded nest trees, look for the pines with white paint rings at the base. Nesting colonies of Red-cockaded Woodpeckers are located along the entrance road at 1.3 and 1.7 miles from South Santee Road. In the spring and summer, look and listen for numerous Bachman's Sparrows.

After driving 2.7 miles from the entrance at South Santee Road, you will come to a gate and kiosk. Park in the designated area near the gate and follow the signs for the 1.9-mile **Marshland Loop Trail** that starts in the woods behind the kiosk. Within 0.2 mile you will come to the boardwalk for the Washo Reserve. This boardwalk leads 0.2 mile into a beautiful cypress swamp. In the winter the swamp is often filled with waterfowl such as Wood Duck, Gadwall, and American Wigeon. The Washo Reserve contains a large nesting colony of Wood Storks during spring and summer. The nests are not visible from the end of the boardwalk, but you can often see Wood Storks dropping down just behind the tree line. Return to the Marshland Loop Trail and follow it for 0.3 mile until you

Swallow-tailed Kite

come to an impoundment. In the winter look for waterfowl, Sora, and Rusty Blackbird. Permanent residents include Anhinga, Wood Stork, Red-shouldered Hawk, Black and King Rails, White-eyed Vireo, and Common Yellowthroat.

Continue following the Marshland Loop Trail for another 0.6 mile and you will come to an intersection with the **Bike/Hike Loop Trail,** a 6.5-mile trek should you choose to attempt the whole loop. The Bike/Hike Loop Trail winds through several thousand acres of brackish water impoundments. If you aren't up to the whole loop, you can reach the beginning of the impoundments within 0.5 mile of the intersection of the two trails. In the winter the impoundments are excellent for waterfowl, and you can expect to see Green-winged and Blue-winged Teals, Northern Shoveler, Northern Pintail, American Wigeon, Gadwall, Ring-necked Duck, Lesser Scaup, and Bufflehead. If you are lucky, you may even be able to find Canvasback or Redhead. Please note that the reserve is closed from November through January, but a trip here in February or March can still turn up thousands of waterfowl. Also in winter expect to see many Bald Eagles and Northern Harriers and perhaps a small flock of American White Pelicans.

During spring the impoundments often contain thousands of migrating shorebirds. With enough patience, you can often find White-rumped and Stilt Sandpipers and Long-billed Dowitcher among the thousands of Western and Semipalmated Sandpipers, Dunlins, Semipalmated Plovers, and Short-billed Dowitchers. Rarities such as Ruff, Wilson's Phalarope, and American Avocet have been seen here as well. In the spring you may also find Swallow-tailed and

Mississippi Kites and the occasional Roseate Spoonbill. Scan the marsh grasses for shy birds such as Black and King Rails, Least Bittern, Seaside Sparrow, and Sharp-tailed Sparrows. Barn Owl, Merlin, and Peregrine Falcon are occasionally seen near the fire tower at the northeast corner of the loop.

Return to the Marshland Loop Trail and continue for 0.3 mile, and you will come to a set of buildings. During winter you can usually find American Kestrel in this area. The last 0.5 mile is through an open habitat that has Eastern Bluebird year-round. The live oak trees near the houses across the field often have a few Red-headed Woodpeckers in the spring and summer.

Santee Delta Wildlife Management Area is well known as one of the most reliable areas in the state to find Swallow-tailed Kites during summer. From the parking area, follow the gated road that parallels the North Santee River. Barn Owl nest towers have been set up in the reserve, so there is potential for seeing this rare species here, but you will still need a lot of luck. During spring scan the trees along the edges of the marsh for Blue Grosbeak, Indigo and Painted Buntings, and Orchard Oriole. Breaks in the trees will allow you to look out over the Santee Delta. In the summer you can often find numerous Mississippi Kites as well as a few Swallow-tailed Kites soaring over the delta. From mid-July to early August, the numbers of kites will rise as they gear up for migration, and this is your best bet for a sure sighting. The only downside to birding the delta is that you may have to brave hordes of biting flies and mosquitoes to get good looks at the kites. If you are lucky, you will find the kites within minutes of the parking lot. Santee Delta WMA can be good for waterfowl during the winter, but it is closed November through January.

General Information

The Santee Coastal Reserve is closed from November 1 to January 31 to protect wintering waterfowl. During February the reserve is open daily from 1:00 to 5:00 p.m. March through October, the reserve is open Monday through Saturday from 8:00 a.m. to 5:00 p.m. and Sunday from 1:00 to 5:00 p.m. Santee Delta WMA is open February through October from dawn to dusk.

DeLorme atlas: Santee Coastal Reserve, page 57, D8; Santee Delta WMA, page 57, C7.
Elevation: 0 to 20 feet.
Hazards: Alligators, venomous snakes, mosquitoes, ticks, chiggers.
Nearest food, gas, lodging: McClellanville for food and gas; Georgetown for lodging.

Camping: Francis Marion National Forest.
For more information: Santee Coastal Reserve; Sewee Visitor and Environmental Education Center.

16 Huntington Beach State Park

Habitats: Salt marsh, mudflats, ocean, beach, rock jetty, pond, freshwater marsh, mixed pine-hardwood forest.

Specialty birds: *Resident*—Brown Pelican, Black-crowned Night-Heron, Little Blue and Tricolored Herons, White Ibis, Bald Eagle, Common Ground-Dove, Seaside Sparrow. *Summer*—Anhinga, Reddish Egret, Yellow-crowned Night-Heron, Glossy Ibis, Wood Stork, Wilson's Plover, Sandwich and Least Terns, Painted Bunting. *Winter*—Red-throated and Common Loons; Horned Grebe; Northern Gannet; Great Cormorant; American Bittern; American Black Duck; Northern Pintail; Canvasback; Redhead; Greater and Lesser Scaups; Common Eider; Black, White-winged, and Surf Scoters; Long-tailed Duck; Hooded and Red-breasted Mergansers; Merlin; Peregrine Falcon; Sora; Virginia Rail; Piping Plover; American Oystercatcher; Red Knot; Purple Sandpiper; Bonaparte's Gull; Great and Lesser Black-backed Gulls; Razorbill; Cave Swallow; Sedge Wren; Orange-crowned Warbler; Salt-marsh and Nelson's Sharp-tailed Sparrows. *Migration*—Black-necked Stilt, American Avocet, Marbled Godwit, White-rumped and Stilt Sandpipers, Black Tern, Whimbrel.

Best times to bird: Year-round.

Directions: To reach Huntington Beach State Park from the intersection of Highway 707 and U.S. Highway 17 in Murrells Inlet, drive 4.3 miles south on US 17. Turn left into the park entrance and stop at the booth to pay the entrance fee and pick up a map of the park. To reach Myrtle Beach State Park from the intersection of US 17 and Highway 544 near Surfside Beach, follow Highway 544 east toward the beach. After 1.8 miles turn left on US 17 Business (Kings Highway). Follow US 17 Business for 1.9 miles and turn right into the entrance for Myrtle Beach State Park.

The Birding

Huntington Beach State Park is considered by many South Carolina birders to be the best bird-watching spot in the state. The park contains 3 miles of beach and nearly 2,500 acres of land. It boasts an impressive checklist, with more than 300 species having been observed in the park, including many rare birds for the state such as Dovekie, Thick-billed Murre, Smith's Longspur, and Snow Bunting. During winter it is the best spot in the state to see difficult-to-find species such as Great Cormorant, Razorbill, Common Eider, Long-tailed Duck, Purple Sandpiper, Piping Plover, and Cave Swallow. Huntington Beach is also an excellent spot for observing shorebird migration in the spring and fall.

After you pay the entrance fee, continue into the park until you reach a causeway with water on either side. A salt marsh is on the north side of the causeway, and a freshwater lagoon is on the south side. Drive to the far end of the causeway and park in one of the parking lots. From the parking lot, you can walk back to the observation platforms on either side of the causeway. Look for Bald Eagle, Northern Pintail, Gadwall, Ruddy Duck, Lesser and Greater Scaups, Hooded Merganser, Cave Swallow, and Sharp-tailed sparrows in winter. In the spring and

Observation platform overlooking the freshwater lagoon along the causeway at Huntington Beach State Park

fall, look for large numbers of migrating shorebirds. Most commonly seen are Semipalmated Plover; Greater and Lesser Yellowlegs; Western, Semipalmated, and Least Sandpipers; Dunlin; Short-billed Dowitcher; and Black-necked Stilt, along with lesser numbers of Solitary, White-rumped, Pectoral, Stilt, and Buff-breasted Sandpipers and American Avocet.

The park has a history of turning up rare shorebirds every once in a while, such as Spotted Redshank; Long-billed Curlew; Hudsonian Godwit; and Red-necked, Red, and Wilson's Phalarope, so be prepared for anything! Numerous wading birds often search for fish along the causeway, including Tricolored and Little Blue Herons year-round, while Wood Stork and Yellow-crowned Night-Heron are found only during summer. The birds along the causeway are often quite used to the presence of people, which makes for great photo opportunities.

Two short boardwalks lead out into the freshwater lagoon, and if there are any interesting birds in the lagoon near the causeway, they are often easier to see from the boardwalks. The first boardwalk is at the end of the causeway road. To reach the second boardwalk at the south end of the freshwater lagoon, turn right at the T-intersection at the end of the causeway and drive toward the campground. After 0.3 mile stop at the parking area for Atalaya, a castle that served as Anna Huntington's art studio. From the west end of parking lot follow the 0.3-mile Kerrigan Nature Trail until it ends at the second boardwalk. During winter scan the freshwater marsh at the south end of the lagoon for American Bittern, Sora,

Virginia Rail, and Sedge Wren. An old causeway road that leads west from Atalaya offers additional views of the south end of the freshwater lagoon and marsh. The old causeway road and brushy woods surrounding Atalaya can often be good for songbirds year-round, including Painted Bunting in the summer.

Return to the T-intersection at the end of the new causeway and drive straight (north) for 0.2 mile, where you will see the visitor center on your left. Check the bird feeders at the visitor center for Common Ground-Dove and Painted Bunting year-round, but be sure to go inside the building to see the educational displays. Just outside the visitor center is a boardwalk that leads 0.2 mile out into the salt marsh. This boardwalk provides one of the best opportunities in the state to get a good look at the elusive Clapper Rail and Seaside Sparrows year-round. During winter look for Nelson's and Saltmarsh Sharp-tailed Sparrows, and in the summer look for numerous singing Marsh Wrens perched in the salt marsh grass.

After exiting the visitor center, continue driving north until you reach the parking lot at the end of the road. Park and follow the boardwalk down to **North Beach.** During winter scan the wax myrtle bushes along the edge of the trail and parking lot for Orange-crowned Warbler and Gray Catbird mixed in with the large flocks of Yellow-rumped Warblers. Once you reach the beach, look to your left (north) and you will see a rock jetty 1.2 miles down the beach. If you have the time, walk down to the jetty, which is an outstanding birding area, especially in winter. It is often well worth hauling a spotting scope, if you have one, down to the jetty. Along the beach between the parking lot and jetty you may find Piping Plover, Red Knot, and Great Black-backed Gull in winter. Also in winter be sure to scan the dunes periodically for rare birds such as Lapland Longspur and Snow Bunting. During summer look for Wilson's Plover.

About halfway from the parking lot to the jetty, if you look over the sand dunes, you will begin to see a tidal pond. This pond can be good for waterfowl in winter, and even sea ducks such as Surf Scoter will occasionally appear here. When the mudflats of the pond are exposed, there can be large flocks of foraging shorebirds. Continue down the beach until you reach the jetty. From the jetty, you are likely to see Red-throated and Common Loons, Horned Grebe, Northern Gannet, Greater Scaup, Black and Surf Scoters, and Purple Sandpiper in winter. Also be on the lookout for rare birds such as Great Cormorant, Common Eider, Long-tailed and Harlequin Ducks, White-winged Scoter, and Razorbill.

At the base of the jetty is a paved trail alongside a salt marsh. This marsh is an excellent place to look for Savannah, Seaside, and both Sharp-tailed Sparrows in winter. The best time to look for the sparrows is at high tide; at other times they can be difficult to find. You may even see the sparrows hopping along the rocks at the edge of the jetty if you are lucky. Mink can often be seen hunting along the rocks of the jetty. If you follow the paved trail until it ends, you will see a fenced-in Least Tern management area, which is closed in the summer. Turn right (north) at the end of the paved trail and walk counterclockwise around the

Whimbrel

Least Tern area. The mudflats and beach surrounding the inlet are often good for shorebirds, gulls, and terns. Look for Piping Plover in winter and American Oystercatcher year-round. Reddish Egrets can be found stalking the edges of the marsh around the inlet during late summer. In the spring and late summer, look for large numbers of shorebirds roosting in the Least Tern area at high tide. A few pairs of Wilson's Plovers will often nest in the Least Tern area during summer.

Return to the parking lot and you will see a trailhead for the **Sandpiper Pond Nature Trail** on the south side. The trail is 2 miles long and ends across from the visitor center. Less than 0.1 mile down the trail from the parking lot is an observation platform that provides a nice view of the north end of Sandpiper Pond. From the platform, look for Green Heron, swallows, Common Yellowthroat, and Painted Bunting in spring and summer. If you don't find Painted Bunting from the platform, try walking along the trail. Also keep an eye out for animals such as river otters, American alligators, and water snakes in the pond.

There are a few other small platforms along the trail, but none of them offer the unobstructed view that first one does. To view the south end of Sandpiper Pond, try walking south along the beach from the parking lot. After 0.6 mile you will see a small kiosk and a man-made inlet that leads through the dunes to the pond. This can be a good spot to look for herons, egrets, Glossy Ibis, Black-necked Stilt, and other shorebirds.

For those in the Myrtle Beach area, another spot to look for seabirds in winter and migrating songbirds during fall is **Myrtle Beach State Park.** Though the park is much smaller than Huntington Beach State Park and has less variety of habitats and species, it offers a convenient location within Myrtle Beach. A fishing pier, which extends over 500 feet into the Atlantic Ocean, provides close-up views of sea ducks, loons, grebes, and gannets during winter. Also look for flocks of Bonaparte's Gulls flying around the pier. In the fall the small maritime forest in the park can be quite good for migrating songbirds, since there is little suitable habitat in the surrounding Myrtle Beach area. Look for the migrating warblers, thrushes, and vireos along the Sculptured Oak (0.5 mile) and Yaupon (0.4 mile) Trails, which start near the park office. The entrance road is another good area to search for migrants, particularly the stretch alongside the small pond 0.4 mile from the park entrance. With all of the development surrounding the park, it is no wonder so many migrants stop there in the fall.

General Information

Huntington Beach State Park is open daily from 6:00 a.m. to 6:00 p.m. during winter and 6:00 a.m. to 10:00 p.m. in the summer. The park offers guided bird walks on Wednesdays and Fridays at 10:00 a.m. from March to October. The entrance fee is $5 for adults. Myrtle Beach State Park is open daily from 6:00 a.m. to 8:00 p.m. during the winter and 6:00 a.m. to 10:00 p.m. in the summer. The entrance fee is $4 for adults.

DeLorme atlas: Huntington Beach State Park, page 50, F1; Myrtle Beach State Park, page 50, D3.

Elevation: 0 to 10 feet.

Hazards: Alligators, venomous snakes, mosquitoes.

Nearest food, gas, lodging: Murrells Inlet.

Camping: Huntington Beach State Park.

For more information: Huntington Beach State Park; Myrtle Beach State Park.

Lewis Ocean Bay Heritage Preserve

Habitats: Pine forest, mixed pine-hardwood forest, stream, field.

Specialty birds: *Resident*—Northern Bob-white, Red-cockaded Woodpecker, Brown-headed Nuthatch. *Summer*—Prairie Warbler, Yellow-breasted Chat, Summer Tanager, Bachman's Sparrow, Blue Grosbeak, Indigo Bunting. *Winter*—Grasshopper, Henslow's, and LeConte's Sparrows.

Best times to bird: December through May.

Directions: From the intersection of U.S. Highway 501 and Highway 90 in Conway, follow Highway 90 east toward Nixonville. After 6.8 miles turn right on International Boulevard. From here all of the roads are dirt and can be difficult to drive on if it has recently rained. Follow International Boulevard for 1.5 miles and turn left onto an unmarked dirt road that leads into Lewis Ocean Bay Heritage Preserve.

The Birding

Lewis Ocean Bay Heritage Preserve can be good for sparrows during the winter and pine-forest species year-round. The preserve gets its name from the twenty-three Carolina bays found within the 9,383 acres of pine forest. Carolina bays are elliptical or oval depressions, which can be easily seen in aerial photos, and are a type of isolated freshwater wetland. The bays often fill with water during the winter months and dry out in the summer. When the bays are dry during the summer months, they can be more difficult to locate on the ground, but look for the sandy rims that mark the edges of the bays. Interestingly, scientists have yet to determine how these unique bays formed in the Carolinas and a few other states along the Atlantic Coast.

To access the preserve from International Boulevard, follow the unmarked dirt road 0.8 mile until you come to a power line right-of-way. The grassy, shrubby areas below the power lines can be great areas to look for sparrows during the winter months. If you are lucky, you may be able to find Henslow's, Grasshopper, or LeConte's Sparrows. During summer look for Indigo Bunting and Blue Grosbeak along the right-of-way. Continue 0.1 mile down the road and you will see a Red-cockaded Woodpecker colony on your left—just look for the trees with white paint rings around the base. Listen for singing Bachman's Sparrows around the woodpecker colony during summer.

Continue another 0.3 mile and you will come to a T-intersection. Surrounding the intersection is a beautiful grassy meadow and pine savanna. The grassy pine savanna is great for Bachman's Sparrow during summer and Henslow's, Grasshopper, and LeConte's Sparrows in winter. Driving 0.5 mile to the left at the intersection will take you to a stream crossing. This small stream corridor can be a good spot to look for songbirds during migration. A right turn at the T-intersection

Longleaf pine savanna at Lewis Ocean Bay Heritage Preserve

will lead you through more beautiful pine savannas. Northern Bobwhite, Brown-headed Nuthatch, and Pine Warbler are common year-round in the pine savannas. During summer look for Prairie Warbler and Yellow-breasted Chat. After 1.1 miles you will come to another power line right-of-way that can be good for sparrows in winter, and in another 1.6 miles you will arrive at yet another power line right-of-way to scan for winter sparrows.

General Information

Lewis Ocean Bay Heritage Preserve is open year-round from dawn to dusk.

DeLorme atlas: Page 50, A4.

Elevation: 5 to 15 feet.

Hazards: Venomous snakes, mosquitoes.

Nearest food, gas, lodging: Conway.

Camping: Myrtle Beach State Park.

For more information: SCDNR Wildlife and Freshwater Fisheries Division.

Coastal Plain

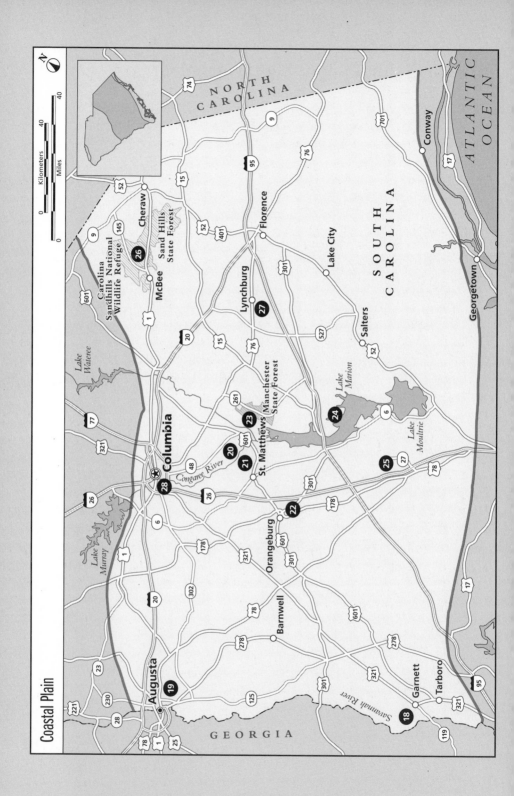

Coastal Plain

18 · Webb Wildlife Management Area

Habitats: Pine forest, mixed pine-hardwood forest, early successional, field, freshwater marsh, lake, swamp.

Specialty birds: *Resident*—Anhinga, Red-shouldered Hawk, Northern Bobwhite, Red-cockaded and Hairy Woodpeckers, Brown-headed Nuthatch, Bachman's Sparrow. *Summer*—Wood Stork; Swallow-tailed and Mississippi Kites; Purple Gallinule; Chuck-will's-widow; Red-headed Woodpecker; Yellow-throated Vireo; Prothonotary, Swainson's, Kentucky, and Hooded Warblers; Yellow-breasted Chat; Summer Tanager; Blue Grosbeak; Indigo and Painted Buntings; Orchard Oriole. *Winter*—American Black Duck, Hooded Merganser.

Best times to bird: April through June.

Directions: From the intersection of U.S. Highway 321 and U.S. Highway 601 in the small town of Tarboro, follow US 321 north. After 5.8 miles you will come to an intersection with Highway 119 in Garnett. At the intersection turn left onto Augusta Stage Coach Road (S-25-20), the road that crosses the railroad tracks within 500 feet of the intersection. Be careful not to make the mistake of taking the hard left onto Highway 119, which leads south to Clio, Georgia. After 2.6 miles on Augusta Stage Coach Road, turn left onto the dirt entrance road for Webb WMA.

The Birding

Webb Wildlife Management Area is made up largely of pine forest, but also contains cypress swamp, farm fields, and a couple of ponds. Red-cockaded Woodpecker can be found along the entrance road. Look for nest holes in the trees marked with orange or white paint rings. The pine forest around the colony is also good for Red-headed Woodpecker, Yellow-breasted Chat, Bachman's Sparrow, and Orchard Oriole in summer. Year-round look for Northern Bobwhite, Brown-headed Nuthatch, and Pine Warbler.

After 1.5 miles you will come to a group of buildings that serves as the headquarters for Webb WMA. Stop here and get a map, as there are numerous roads that run through the management area. Continue past the headquarters on Bluff Lake Road, following TRAIL and LAKES AND PONDS signs. After 0.6 mile you will come to another Red-cockaded Woodpecker colony. Drive another 0.2 mile and you will see a FISHING PONDS sign that points to a side road on the right. The side road will lead you to the Upper and Lower Ponds, which are the best place in the WMA to find Purple Gallinule in summer. The Lower Pond can also be good for Wood Stork and other wading birds in summer.

Return to Bluff Lake Road and turn right. After 0.6 mile you will see an agricultural field on your left. The edges of the field are often good for Painted and Indigo Buntings and Blue Grosbeak in summer. Continue down the road 1.3 miles to the Bluff Lake Picnic Area and observation deck on the right. The observation deck and nearby field are often good spots to scan for Swallow-tailed and

Mississippi Kites in summer. You may be able to hear Kentucky Warbler in the woods across the road from the observation platform.

Continue another 0.2 mile to the end of Bluff Lake Road and you will come to a gate that marks the start of the Savannah River Swamp Trail, a 2-mile-long trail that leads through a cypress swamp to the Savannah River. After heavy rains, much of this trail is underwater. If you are able to hike the trail, it can be good for Anhinga; Swallow-tailed Kite; Yellow-throated Vireo; and Prothonotary, Hooded, and Swainson's Warblers during summer. Look for Yellow-bellied Sapsucker, Hermit Thrush, and Winter Wren in the winter, and for Wood Duck, Hairy Woodpecker, and Yellow-throated Warbler year-round.

As you depart Webb WMA, if you are headed back to Interstate 95, there are a couple of boat landings on the Savannah River that are worth a stop if you are still looking for a Swallow-tailed Kite or Swainson's Warbler. From the intersection of Highway 119 and US 321 in Garnett, follow US 321 south. After 13.1 miles turn right on Sand Hills Road in Tillman and follow the signs to the B & C Landing. When you are done exploring the B & C Landing, return to US 321 and turn right (south). After 9.0 miles turn right on Becks Ferry Road, which will lead you to the Becks Ferry Landing.

General Information

Webb WMA is open daily year-round, except for scheduled hunt days during spring and fall. Call ahead at (803) 625-3569 to find out if there is a scheduled hunt.

DeLorme atlas: Page 61, G10.
Elevation: 30 to 70 feet.
Hazards: Alligators, venomous snakes, mosquitoes, ticks.

Nearest food, gas, lodging: Ridgeland.
For more information: Webb WMA.

19 Central Savannah River Area

Habitats: Lake, pond, stream, field, farmland, pine forest, hardwood forest.

Specialty birds: *Resident*—Red-shouldered Hawk; Wild Turkey; Northern Bobwhite; Red-headed, Hairy, and Pileated Woodpeckers; White-breasted and Brown-headed Nut-hatches. *Summer*—Wood Stork; Mississippi Kite; Chuck-will's-widow; Whip-poor-will; Yellow-throated Vireo; Northern Parula; Prairie, Yellow-throated, Swainson's, and Kentucky Warblers; Louisiana Waterthrush; Yellow-breasted Chat; Bachman's Sparrow; Blue Grosbeak; Indigo Bunting. *Winter*—Hooded Merganser, Bald Eagle, American Woodcock, Wilson's Snipe, Winter Wren, American Pipit, Orange-crowned and Palm Warblers, Fox Sparrow. *Migration*—Solitary and Pectoral Sandpipers, Black Tern, Rose-breasted Grosbeak, Bobolink.

Best times to bird: April through October.

Directions: To reach Silver Bluff Audubon Sanctuary from the intersection of Highway 125 and U.S. Highway 278 in Beech Island, drive south on Highway 125 (Atomic Road). After 4.5 miles turn right on Silver Bluff Road (SR 32). Follow Silver Bluff Road for 4.4 miles to the Silver Bluff visitor center on the right. To reach Aiken State Natural Area from the intersection of Highway 302 and U.S. Highway 78 near Aiken, drive east on US 78. After 10.4 miles turn left onto State Park Road. Follow State Park Road 5.0 miles and turn left onto Tory Trail Road. Take an immediate right into the entrance for the natural area. To reach J. Strom Thurmond Dam from exit 1 on Interstate 20, drive north on Highway 230 for 5.6 miles and turn left on Highway 53 (Woodlawn Road). After 7.1 miles turn right on Highway 28, then in 5.4 miles turn left on U.S. Highway 221. After 1.3 miles turn right into the small parking lot above the dam.

The Birding

The Central Savannah River Area, which locals refer to as simply "the CSRA," is a metropolitan area encompassing five counties in Georgia and South Carolina. The best birding area on the South Carolina side of the CSRA can be found at **Silver Bluff Audubon Sanctuary.** The main attraction at Silver Bluff is the hundreds of Wood Storks that visit the sanctuary from mid-July through mid-September. A series of three impoundments, named the Kathwood Ponds, are stocked each year with fish to feed the Wood Storks. During late summer the ponds are slowly drawn down one by one in order to provide the storks easy access to the fish.

Many other wading birds are also found here at this time, including Green, Great Blue, and Little Blue Herons; Cattle, Great, and Snowy Egrets; White Ibis; and occasionally even a Roseate Spoonbill! The muddy edges of the ponds attract a good variety of shorebirds, such as Greater and Lesser Yellowlegs and Solitary, Pectoral, Spotted, and Least Sandpipers. Rare shorebirds such as American Avocet; Black-necked Stilt; and White-rumped, Baird's, and Stilt Sandpipers have occasionally been seen as well. During winter you may be able to find a few ducks in the ponds, usually Mallard, Wood Duck, and Hooded Merganser. Also look for Bald Eagle, Wilson's Snipe, American Pipit, and Palm Warbler in winter.

Wood Storks feeding in the Kathwood Ponds

Visitors planning to go to the stork ponds from July through September should call ahead to arrange a tour with the sanctuary manager, as access to the ponds is often restricted during this time to protect the Wood Storks. To reach the stork ponds from the visitor center, drive 1.0 mile back toward Highway 125 and you will see a parking area along the fence on the right.

Silver Bluff also has two hiking trails: a 0.7-mile loop and a 2-mile loop, both of which start at the visitor center. The trails are actively managed for birds and provide quite a variety of forest successional stages, from fields to eighty-year-old trees. The sanctuary serves as a model to the timber industry for balancing forest management with bird conservation. The most common habitat found along these trails is pine forest, but there is a small section of hardwood forest and swamp about halfway along the 2-mile loop. In the pine forests look for Northern Bobwhite, Wild Turkey, Hairy Woodpecker, Brown-headed and White-breasted Nuthatches, and Pine Warbler year-round. In the summer look for Red-headed Woodpecker, Prairie Warbler, Yellow-breasted Chat, Summer Tanager, Indigo Bunting, and Blue Grosbeak.

The hardwood forests and swamps often contain Northern Parula, Prothonotary and Hooded Warblers, and Louisiana Waterthrush in the summer. Keep an ear out for breeding Kentucky Warblers in the forest near the visitor center. The trails can also be quite good during spring and fall migration, particularly in the sections that contain hardwood forest. The Silver Bluff bird list contains an impressive twenty-nine species of warblers that have been recorded in the sanctuary. During winter keep a sharp eye out for American Woodcock. Before you leave, be sure to check the bird feeders near the visitor center for Ruby-throated Hummingbird, Rose-breasted Grosbeak (migration), and American Goldfinch.

Another good area to check out during migration is the agricultural fields just outside the Silver Bluff sanctuary. The fields can be good for Mississippi Kite, Bobolink, and Eastern Meadowlark. To reach the fields, drive 2.0 miles from the visitor center back toward Highway 125. The fields are private property, so bird from the road only.

Silver Bluff Audubon Sanctuary is only open from 9:00 a.m. to 5:00 p.m., but you can still bird by car along Silver Bluff Road after dark. The dirt section of Silver Bluff Road is often good for finding both Chuck-will's-widows and Whip-poor-wills in summer. They will often be sitting in the dirt roads around dusk, so drive slowly and look for the tiny orange reflection of their eyes. The Chuck-will's-widows outnumber the Whip-poor-wills by about ten to one.

The swampy thickets of **Aiken State Natural Area** provide excellent habitat for songbirds year-round. The 3-mile Jungle Trail can be good for Blue-headed Vireo, Winter Wren, Hermit Thrush, Gray Catbird, Orange-crowned Warbler, and Fox Sparrow in winter. In the summer you can find Ovenbird; Hooded, Kentucky, Prothonotary, and Black-and-white Warblers; and perhaps even Swainson's Warbler if you are lucky. During migration the swampy thickets can be loaded with migrating warblers and thrushes. Year-round look for Wild Turkey, Red-shouldered Hawk, Red-headed Woodpecker, White-eyed Vireo, White-breasted and Brown-headed Nuthatches, and Pine Warbler. Walk the edges of Fishing Lake and Cabin Lake to look for flocks of migrant and wintering songbirds. The primitive campground can be a good area to listen for Eastern Screech-Owl and Great Horned Owl year-round.

About 15 miles northwest of North Augusta is **J. Strom Thurmond Dam** on the Savannah River. In the winter the parking lot above the dam offers a good vantage point to scan Lake Thurmond for Redhead, Common Loon, Horned Grebe, and Bonaparte's Gull. During late summer you may even be able to find a few Black Terns cruising the lake. Once you have finished looking for these species, exit the parking lot and turn left. In 0.3 mile you will see a road on the right that leads down to the spillway below the dam. In the winter this can be a good place to scan for gulls and Bald Eagles, especially when the floodgates are open. During spring and fall migration, a brief walk along roads and the short fitness trail can produce a good number of warblers, thrushes, and other songbirds.

General Information

Silver Bluff Audubon Sanctuary is open Monday through Saturday from 9:00 a.m. to 5:00 p.m. Be sure to call ahead at (803) 471-0291 during late summer if you want to schedule a time to see the Wood Storks. Aiken State Natural Area is open daily from 9:00 a.m. to 6:00 p.m. J. Strom Thurmond Dam is open year-round from 8:00 a.m. to 8:30 p.m.

DeLorme atlas: Silver Bluff Audubon Sanctuary, page 51, A8; Aiken State Natural Area, page 44, E2; J. Strom Thurmond Dam, page 42, D4.
Elevation: 100 to 450 feet.
Hazards: Venomous snakes, mosquitoes, ticks.

Nearest food, gas, lodging: North Augusta.
Camping: Aiken State Natural Area.
For more information: Silver Bluff Audubon Sanctuary; Aiken State Natural Area; J. Strom Thurmond Dam and Lake.

⓴ Congaree National Park

Habitats: Hardwood forest, mixed pine-hardwood forest, pine forest, river, swamp.

Specialty birds: *Resident*—Anhinga; Barred and Great Horned Owls; Eastern Screech-Owl; Hairy, Red-headed, and Pileated Woodpeckers; White-eyed Vireo; White-breasted Nuthatch; Yellow-throated Warbler. *Summer*—Yellow-crowned Night-Heron; Mississippi Kite; Chuck-will's-widow; Yellow-billed Cuckoo; Ruby-throated Hummingbird; Acadian Flycatcher; Red-eyed and Yellow-throated Vireos; Northern Parula; Prothonotary, Swainson's, Kentucky, and Hooded Warblers; Summer Tanager; Blue Grosbeak; Indigo Bunting. *Winter*—Yellow-bellied Sapsucker, Blue-headed Vireo, Brown Creeper, Winter Wren, Ruby-crowned Kinglet, Hermit Thrush, Orange-crowned and Black-and-white Warblers, Fox Sparrow, Rusty Blackbird.

Best times to bird: Year-round.

Directions: From exit 5 on Interstate 77, take Highway 48 East (Bluff Road), following the brown signs for Congaree National Park. Travel southeast on Highway 48 for 11.9 miles and turn right onto Mt. View Road. Follow Mt. View Road for 0.8 mile, then turn right onto Old Bluff Road and travel 0.6 mile. At the large park entrance sign, turn left and follow the park entrance road to the Harry Hampton Visitor Center. If you arrive before 8:30 a.m. and the gate is closed, park in the after-hours parking lot and walk down the main road 0.5 mile to the visitor center. At the visitor center, be sure to pick up a trail map and bird checklist for the park.

The Birding

For an unforgettable trip into a bottomland hardwood swamp, visit Congaree National Park, which contains a vast network of trails and boardwalks through large bald cypress and sweet gum trees. The park has more than 15 miles of trails, with more than 2 miles of boardwalks. In March, Congaree National Park is usually one of the first places to get early migrating songbirds, such as Prothonotary Warbler and Northern Parula. During winter the park is probably the best place in South Carolina to see Yellow-bellied Sapsucker, Winter Wren, Ruby-crowned Kinglet, and Hermit Thrush. In the summer you should be able to find plenty of Acadian and Great Crested Flycatchers, Yellow-throated and Red-eyed Vireos, Northern Parula, and Prothonotary and Hooded Warblers on the trails in the park, along with lesser numbers of Louisiana Waterthrush and Swainson's and Kentucky Warblers. During spring and fall you can expect to see good numbers of warblers and thrushes, though perhaps not quite the diversity that you might find at nearby Saluda Shoals Park. Listen for nocturnal species, such as Great Horned Owl, Eastern Screech-Owl, and Chuck-will's-widow, at the primitive campground near the after-hours parking lot.

The park gets a tremendous number of visitors year-round, most of whom hike the boardwalk loop on the **Elevated** and **Low Boardwalk Trails.** If you are planning on birding from the boardwalks, be sure to arrive early to beat the

Low boardwalk near visitor center at Congaree National Park

crowds or you may not see very many birds. The weekends are often much more crowded than weekdays. Luckily there are plenty of other good trails for birding in the park that don't receive nearly the amount of people-traffic that the boardwalks get. As you head down the bluff behind the visitor center on the boardwalk, listen for Kentucky Warbler in summer. These birds are most easily found along the edge of the bluff, so if you don't find them here, your best bet is hiking the Bluff Trail. Swainson's Warbler can be found throughout the swamp during summer, particularly in areas where the understory is thick.

To get a good feel for the park, try hiking the **Oakridge Loop** (7.5 miles) or the shorter **Weston Loop** (4.6 miles). Take the Low Boardwalk Trail 0.7 mile to the intersection with Weston Loop and follow the trail counterclockwise. Just before the intersection with the Oakridge Loop, you will come to a small clearing with bamboo around the edges and an old pump house. For several weeks in March 2006, this area had a Yellow-bellied Flycatcher. During winter Yellow-bellied Sapsucker, Blue-headed Vireo, Winter Wren, Golden- and Ruby-crowned Kinglets, Hermit Thrush, and American Robin are all numerous along the Oakridge and Weston Loops. Also keep an eye out for smaller numbers of White-eyed Vireo; Brown Creeper; Black-and-white, Yellow-throated, and Orange-crowned Warblers; and Fox Sparrows in winter. Year-round the swamp is often alive with the sounds of drumming woodpeckers, and you should be able to find at least five species at any time of year, including Pileated, Downy, Hairy, Red-headed, and Red-bellied Woodpeckers and Northern Flicker. Other common resident birds are Wood Duck, Red-shouldered Hawk, Barred Owl, and Pine Warbler.

If you are trying to avoid bumping into a lot of people, you may want to consider the **Kingsnake Trail.** This trail is 3.6 miles long and contains many of the same birds found along the Oakridge and Weston Loops. The first mile of the trail from the Cedar Creek Road trailhead contains some thick understory, where you may be able to find Swainson's Warbler. You can reach the Kingsnake Trail from the eastern side of the Oakridge Loop or from the trailhead at the end of Cedar Creek Road. To reach the Cedar Creek Road trailhead, return to Old Bluff Road and turn right. After 2.6 miles turn right at Cedar Creek Road. In 1.8 miles you will see a dirt road on the right that leads to the small parking lot for the Cedar Creek canoe access and the trailhead for the Kingsnake Trail.

General Information

The Congaree National Park visitor center is open daily from 8:30 a.m. to 5:00 p.m. The trails in the park are open year-round twenty-four hours a day. Back-country camping is allowed with a permit from the visitor center.

DeLorme atlas: Page 46, A1.

Elevation: 100 to 120 feet.

Hazards: Alligators, venomous snakes, mosquitoes.

Nearest food, gas, lodging: Columbia.

Camping: Available on-site, with very limited facilities.

For more information: Congaree National Park.

㉑ Congaree Bluffs Heritage Preserve

Habitats: Hardwood forest, mixed pine-hardwood forest, pine forest, early successional, stream, river.

Specialty birds: *Resident*—Anhinga, Barred and Great Horned Owls, Eastern Screech-Owl, Hairy and Pileated Woodpeckers, White-eyed Vireo, Brown-headed Nuthatch. *Summer*—Mississippi Kite; Chuck-will's-widow; Yellow-billed Cuckoo; Ruby-throated Hummingbird; Eastern Wood-Pewee; Acadian Flycatcher; Red-eyed and Yellow-throated Vireos; Northern Parula; Prairie, Yellow-throated, Prothonotary, Swainson's, Kentucky, and Hooded Warblers; Yellow-breasted Chat; Summer Tanager; Blue Grosbeak; Indigo Bunting. *Winter*—Brown Creeper, Winter Wren, Fox Sparrow.

Best times to bird: April through October.

Directions: To reach the heritage preserve from the intersection of Highway 419 and U.S. Highway 601 near St. Matthews, drive west on Highway 419. After 3.4 miles turn right on Turkey Track Lane.

The Birding

Congaree Bluffs Heritage Preserve offers a unique bird's-eye view of the Congaree Swamp. The bluffs rise about 90 feet above the swamp! As you enter the heritage preserve, Turkey Track Lane passes through a mix of pine and early successional habitat that is excellent for species such as Eastern Wood-Pewee, Brown Thrasher, Prairie Warbler, Yellow-breasted Chat, Summer Tanager, Eastern Towhee, Indigo Bunting, and Blue Grosbeak during summer.

After 0.6 mile you will reach the first parking lot on the left. This is a good spot to look for some of the pine and early successional breeding species. To reach the second parking lot, continue down Turkey Track Lane and bear left at the fork in 0.3 mile. Drive 0.1 mile past the fork and you will see the second parking lot on the left. Continue on foot through the gate at the end of Turkey Track Lane. At the end of the road in 0.3 mile, you will see a couple buildings on the right side of the road. An observation deck just past the last building provides a fantastic view of the Congaree Swamp. From August to November a hawk watch is occasionally conducted from this deck. In August you can often see good numbers of Mississippi Kites as they migrate over the swamp, but the peak of the hawk migration is from mid-September to mid-October. On a good day, observers might expect to see twenty or thirty migrating raptors. Commonly observed species include Osprey and Sharp-shinned, Cooper's, and Broad-winged Hawks, with lesser numbers of Bald Eagle, Peregrine Falcon, and American Kestrel. During summer look for Mississippi Kites and Red-shouldered Hawks as they soar over the swamp.

Continue down the road that you followed to reach the buildings and observation deck. A couple hundred feet past the buildings, the road narrows to a small footpath, which bends left and heads downhill to a small stream surrounded by deciduous forest. In the summer you should be able to find Acadian Flycatcher, Northern Parula, and Hooded Warbler near the stream. You can hike a loop on the trails by the stream or choose a route that will lead you back to the parking lot, but be aware that there are numerous trail intersections and you will probably want to have a map with you. For a map of the area, check out www.sctrails.net.

After you are done exploring the small stream, head back to the parking lot. Across the road from the parking lot is a gated trail that leads downhill through deciduous forest to the Congaree River. Follow the trail 0.3 mile to the banks of the river, at which point the trail will fork and you can hike a 0.6-mile loop. This is a good area to look for migrant warblers in the spring and fall. In the summer you should be able to find Northern Parula; Yellow-throated, Prothonotary, Kentucky, and Hooded Warblers; and Indigo Bunting. During winter look for Winter Wren, Brown Creeper, and Fox Sparrow.

General Information

Congaree Bluffs Heritage Preserve is open year-round from dawn to dusk.

DeLorme atlas: Page 46, B2.

Elevation: 100 to 260 feet.

Hazards: Alligators, venomous snakes, mosquitoes.

Nearest food, gas, lodging: St. Matthews for food and gas; Columbia for lodging.

Camping: Available on-site, with very limited facilities.

For more information: SCDNR Wildlife and Freshwater Fisheries Division.

22 Orangeburg Super Sod Farm

Habitats: Farmland, mixed pine-hardwood forest.

Specialty birds: *Resident*—Eurasian Collared-Dove, Common Ground-Dove, Loggerhead Shrike, Horned Lark. *Summer*—Cattle Egret, Mississippi Kite, Eastern Kingbird. *Winter*—Northern Harrier, American Kestrel, American Pipit, Palm Warbler, Vesper and Savannah Sparrows, Lapland Longspur. *Migration*—American Golden-Plover; Upland, Pectoral, Solitary, and Buff-breasted Sandpipers; Bank and Cliff Swallows.

Best times to bird: August through October.

Directions: From exit 154 on Interstate 26, follow U.S. Highway 301 north toward Orangeburg. After 0.7 mile turn left on Super Sod Boulevard. The building on the right immediately after you turn left is the Super Sod office.

The Birding

The Orangeburg Super Sod farm is well known as the best place in South Carolina to find American Golden-Plover and Upland, Pectoral, and Buff-breasted Sandpipers during late summer and fall. Loggerhead Shrike and Horned Lark are easy to find at the farm throughout the year, and you may be able to spot a few Common Ground-Doves and Eurasian Collared-Doves. Rarities such as Sandhill Crane, Sprague's Pipit, and Yellow-headed Blackbird are possible during fall and winter.

From the office, follow Super Sod Boulevard as it turns into a dirt road and leads through a gate. The Super Sod farm is private, and you can only enter the property during business hours. Be sure to stop at the office to get permission before you drive into the farm. Once you enter the farm, stay on the roads and stay out of the way of farm operations. If the office and gate are closed, do not try to enter the farm; instead, turn around and follow the alternate route provided at the end of this section.

The best time to look for the shorebirds is after a heavy rain, when the fields are wet and muddy. Peak diversity occurs early in September, when you may be able to find ten or more species of shorebirds. Keep an eye out for rare birds such as Sharp-tailed Sandpiper or Wilson's Phalarope, which have both been known to occur here. The best strategy to look for the shorebirds is to drive along Super Sod Boulevard, stopping frequently and scanning the fields along both sides of the road. A spotting scope is often very useful here, as the shorebirds can be distant from the main road. You may be able to use some of the side roads to get better looks at the shorebirds, but be careful not to get stuck if they are muddy.

Summer is often pretty slow for birding at the sod farm, but you should be able to find a few Mississippi Kites hunting over the fields. During late summer and

The open, grassy fields at the Super Sod farm provide a perfect habitat for migrating shorebirds after a good rain.

early fall, the large flocks of swallows hunting over the fields often contain Bank and Cliff Swallows. In the winter the fields are one of the best spots in South Carolina to look for American Pipit, Vesper Sparrow, and Lapland Longspur.

Follow this alternate route if the Super Sod farm is closed: Return to US 301 and turn right. After 0.4 mile turn right on Millennium Drive and scan the fields on your right for migrating shorebirds, Horned Lark, and sparrows in winter. After 1.3 miles turn right on Big Buck Boulevard (Road 196) and scan the fields on both sides of the road for grassland birds. After 1.1 miles turn right on Dynasty Drive, which runs along a large sod field on the west side of the Super Sod farm. After 1.9 miles you will reach US 301. Turn right to return to I-26.

General Information

Super Sod is open Monday through Friday from 8:00 a.m. to 5:00 p.m. and occasionally from 8:00 a.m. to noon on Saturday. If the farm is closed, you can always take the alternate route provided above.

DeLorme atlas: Page 46, G1.
Elevation: 180 feet.
Hazards: Biting flies.

Nearest food, gas, lodging: Orangeburg.
Camping: Santee State Park.
For more information: Super Sod.

Purple Gallinule on lily pads at Savannah National Wildlife Refuge

Sora at Pinckney Island National Wildlife Refuge

Forster's Tern catching a small fish at Hunting Island State Park

Eastern Bluebird at ACE Basin National Wildlife Refuge

Black Skimmer at Bear Island Wildlife Management Area

Eastern Screech-Owl at Bear Island Wildlife Management Area

Juvenile Seaside Sparrow at Bear Island Wildlife Management Area

Flock of Tundra Swans at Bear Island Wildlife Management Area

Wood Stork at Bear Island Wildlife Management Area

Magnolia Warbler at James Island County Park

American Oystercatcher at Folly Beach County Park

Flock of Dunlin at Folly Beach County Park

Loggerhead Shrike at Old Coast Guard Station on Folly Beach

Flock of Red Knots near Old Coast Guard Station on Folly Beach

Ruddy Turnstone at Folly Beach County Park

Ruby-throated Hummingbird at Patriots Point

Sandwich Tern at Cape Romain National Wildlife Refuge

Purple Sandpiper on the jetty at Huntington Beach State Park

Semipalmated Sandpiper at Huntington Beach State Park

White-rumped Sandpiper at Huntington Beach State Park

Orchard Oriole at Webb Wildlife Management Area

Indigo Bunting at Silver Bluff Audubon Sanctuary

Yellow-throated Warbler at Silver Bluff Audubon Sanctuary

Northern Parula at Saluda Shoals Park

Painted Bunting at Santee National Wildlife Refuge

Pileated Woodpecker at Francis Beidler Forest Audubon Sanctuary

Prothonotary Warbler at Francis Beidler Forest Audubon Sanctuary

American Woodcock blending with the leaf litter at Francis Beidler Forest Audubon Sanctuary

Yellow-bellied Sapsucker at Carolina Sandhills National Wildlife Refuge

Scarlet Tanager at Croft State Natural Area

American Redstart at Walhalla State Fish Hatchery

Ovenbird at Burrell's Ford

23 Poinsett State Park

Habitats: Mixed pine-hardwood forest, hardwood forest, pond, stream, swamp.

Specialty birds: *Resident*—Barred and Great Horned Owls, Pileated Woodpecker, White-breasted and Brown-headed Nuthatches. *Summer*—Mississippi Kite; Broad-winged Hawk; Yellow-billed Cuckoo; Chuck-will's-widow; Whip-poor-will; Acadian Flycatcher; Yellow-throated Vireo; Wood Thrush; Northern Parula; Prothonotary, Yellow-throated, Swainson's, Kentucky, and Hooded Warblers; Summer Tanager. *Winter*—Yellow-bellied Sapsucker, Blue-headed Vireo, Hermit Thrush, Orange-crowned Warbler.

Best times to bird: April through October.

Directions: From exit 119 on Interstate 95, follow Highway 261 west toward Paxville. After 19.2 miles turn left on Poinsett Park Road (SR 63). In 1.7 miles you will reach the entrance to the state park. Follow the road through the park for another 1.1 miles, where you will come to the park office.

The Birding

Poinsett State Park contains a unique combination of habitats that incorporate features of both the coastal plain and piedmont. This is one of the few places in the state where you can find mountain laurel covered in Spanish moss. The park also has a surprising amount of topography for the coastal plain region.

The best route for birding in the park is to hike around Old Levi Mill Lake. The trailhead for the **Coquina Nature Trail,** a 1.5-mile loop, is located behind the park office. Follow the trail clockwise around the lake. The Spanish moss hanging from the trees and mountain laurel provides great habitat for nesting Northern Parula and Yellow-throated Warbler in summer. Also look for Prothonotary Warbler along the edge of the lake during summer. When you reach the east end of the lake, you will come to an intersection with the **Hilltop Trail,** a 0.5-mile loop. The Hilltop Trail leads through the swampy areas along Shanks Creek, which can be good for Yellow-billed Cuckoo; Acadian Flycatcher; Louisiana Waterthrush; and Prothonotary, Kentucky, and perhaps Swainson's Warblers in summer. During spring and fall migration, look for flocks of migrating warblers, thrushes, and vireos in the vegetation along Shanks Creek. In the winter check the swamp for Yellow-bellied Sapsucker, Blue-headed Vireo, Hermit Thrush, and Orange-crowned Warbler.

At the east end of the Hilltop Trail you will come to an intersection with the **Laurel Group Trail.** This trail continues along Shanks Creek for another 0.5 mile, at which point you will reach the paved entrance road. Return to the intersection of the Laurel Group and Hilltop Trails. Turn left on the Hilltop Trail and you will discover that it is aptly named. The trail climbs uphill until you are more than 100 feet above the swamp. During summer look for Yellow-throated Vireo,

Wood Thrush, Hooded Warbler, and Summer Tanager in the hardwood forests in the hilly areas, and keep an eye out for Mississippi Kites and Broad-winged Hawks soaring overhead as well.

When you reach the intersection with the Coquina Nature Trail, turn left and follow the trail as it winds through more hills covered in hardwood forest along the southern end of the Old Levi Mill Lake. After 0.7 mile you will reach the park office. At dusk listen for Chuck-will's-widows and Whip-poor-wills calling around the office during summer. Year-round you may hear Great Horned Owls.

General Information

Poinsett State Park is open daily 9:00 a.m. to 6:00 p.m. during winter and 9:00 a.m. to 9:00 p.m. in the summer.

DeLorme atlas: Page 46, A3.

Elevation: 80 to 220 feet.

Hazards: Alligators, venomous snakes, biting flies.

Nearest food, gas, lodging: Sumter.

Camping: Poinsett State Park.

For more information: Poinsett State Park.

24 Santee National Wildlife Refuge

Habitats: Lake, pond, swamp, hardwood forest, mixed pine-hardwood forest, pine forest, farmland, field, early successional.

Specialty birds: *Resident*—Anhinga, Red-shouldered Hawk, Northern Bobwhite, Brown-headed Nuthatch, Marsh Wren. *Summer*—Least Bittern, Little Blue and Tricolored Herons, Purple Gallinule, Yellow-billed Cuckoo, Yellow-throated Vireo, Wood Thrush, Prothonotary and Yellow-throated Warblers, Blue Grosbeak, Indigo and Painted Buntings, Orchard Oriole. *Winter*—Common Loon, Tundra Swan, Redhead, Canvasback, Lesser Scaup, Northern Harrier, American Kestrel, Sandhill Crane, American Woodcock, Wilson's Snipe, Bonaparte's Gull, Forster's Tern, Blue-headed Vireo, Sedge and Winter Wrens, Palm Warbler, Rusty Blackbird. *Migration*—Caspian Tern, Bobolink.

Best times to bird: Year-round.

Directions: From exit 102 on Interstate 95, follow signs for U.S. Highways 15 and 301 north. Follow US 15/301 north for 0.4 mile, then turn left onto the entrance road to the refuge's visitor center and the Bluff Unit.

The Birding

Santee National Wildlife Refuge lies along the eastern shore of Lake Marion, a vast artificially created lake. The 15,095-acre refuge is divided into four units: Bluff Unit, Cuddo Unit, Dingle Pond Unit, and Pine Island Unit. Pick up maps and a bird checklist at the refuge's visitor center on the **Bluff Unit.** While at the visitor center, scan the area around it for Golden- and Ruby-crowned Kinglets in winter.

Before leaving the Bluff Unit, drive down to the **Wrights Bluff Nature Trail,** a 1-mile loop. This trail is the best spot to look for waterfowl and geese in the coastal plain in the winter. Rarities such as Cackling, Ross's, and Greater White-fronted Geese and Sandhill Crane are often found in the farm fields on the back side of the loop. In order to get good views of the geese and waterfowl, you will need to have a scope. Start by heading clockwise around the loop. During winter the woods can be loaded with Hermit Thrush and White-throated Sparrow. After 0.3 mile you will come to a long boardwalk leading through cypress trees. The boardwalk is a good area to look for Winter Wren and Rusty Blackbird in winter and Prothonotary Warbler in summer.

At the end of the boardwalk you will reach an agricultural field and the trail will take a 90-degree turn to the right. During winter the field is closed to protect waterfowl, but in the summer you can walk the edges of the field to look for Painted and Indigo Buntings, Blue Grosbeak, and Orchard Oriole. In fact, one of the best places to see Painted Buntings in South Carolina is along the grassy road on the east side of the field that runs parallel to a small ditch. Continue along the Wrights Bluff Nature Trail from the 90-degree turn and in 0.1 mile you will

Bald Eagle

come to an observation tower that provides good views of the fields. During winter the fields often contain hundreds of Canada Geese, but be sure to check for any Ross's, Snow, or Greater White-fronted Geese that may be mixed in with the flock. In addition to the geese, look for Northern Harrier, American Kestrel, Sandhill Crane, Wilson's Snipe, American Pipit, Palm Warbler, Savannah and Field Sparrows, and Eastern Meadowlark. Vesper Sparrow and Brewer's Blackbird are possible in the fields, but they are not to be expected.

The pond beyond the fields often contains hundreds of Ring-necked Ducks and American Coots, but you may also find smaller numbers of Tundra Swan, American Black Duck, Mallard, American Wigeon, Canvasback, Redhead, Lesser Scaup, Ruddy Duck, Bufflehead, and Wood Duck. Bald Eagles can often be seen perched in the trees near the pond or flying overhead, which usually spooks the geese and waterfowl. Look for Anhinga and Red-shouldered Hawk year-round near the pond.

Continue down the Wrights Bluff Nature Trail and you will come to an opening that looks out over Cantey Bay, which often contains a wide variety of ducks and geese, Bonaparte's Gull, and Forster's Tern in winter. During late summer and spring, scan the mudflats along the edge of Cantey Bay for shorebirds; most commonly seen are Semipalmated Plover; Greater and Lesser Yellowlegs; and Pectoral, Solitary, Least, and Spotted Sandpipers.

The **Cuddo Unit** contains a 7.5-mile wildlife drive and several hiking trails. To reach the Cuddo Unit from the visitor center, return to US 15/301 and turn left (north). After 3.7 miles turn right on Liberty Hill Road (Road 373), then in 2.0 miles turn left on Bill Davis Road. After 4.0 miles turn right on William Brunson Road. In 3.4 miles you will come to an intersection with Rogers Road. Turn right and after 0.4 mile you will come to an intersection with Log Jam Road. Turn left and the entrance to the Cuddo Unit will be a few hundred feet down the road on your left. In the winter check the grassy and shrubby fields for Sedge Wren, Common Yellowthroat, and large flocks of sparrows, including Song, Swamp, and Savannah. If you search the fields long enough, you may even turn up a hard-to-find species, such as Henslow's, Grasshopper, LeConte's, or Vesper Sparrows. During summer the fields are loaded with Yellow-breasted Chat, Indigo Bunting, and Blue Grosbeak. Be sure to check the forest edges for breeding Painted Buntings.

After 2.9 miles on the wildlife drive, you will come to the trailhead of two nature trails: the North Loop (1.9 miles) and the South Loop (1.4 miles). Continue down the drive for 0.5 mile and you will arrive at a swamp that often has Wood Duck, Blue-headed Vireo, Swamp Sparrow, and Rusty Blackbird in winter. During summer the swamp can be good for Little Blue Heron, Yellow-throated Vireo, Wood Thrush, and Yellow-throated Warbler.

The **Dingle Pond Unit** has a 0.8-mile hiking trail that provides views of a unique Carolina bay habitat. Though levels in the pond fluctuate, it has water most of the year, unlike many other Carolina bays in South Carolina. (Carolina bays are elliptical or oval-shaped isolated freshwater wetlands of uncertain origin.) To reach the Dingle Pond Unit from the visitor center, retrace your steps back to exit 102 on I-95, but instead of getting on I-95, follow the service road underneath the interstate. A few hundred feet past the interstate, turn left on Road 400 (Dingle Pond Road). After 0.1 mile you will come to a stop sign. Turn left and continue to follow Road 400. In 1.7 miles look for a small gated road on the right that marks the trailhead for the Dingle Pond hiking trail.

Be warned that there is barely enough room to park two cars at the trailhead and the trail can be poorly maintained and overgrown. However, those who are daring enough to embark on this adventure can often find dabbling ducks such as American Wigeon and Green-winged Teal on the pond during winter. The edges of Dingle Pond can be good for sparrows in the winter, especially Song and Swamp Sparrows. American Bittern, Sora, Virginia Rail, and American Woodcock are occasionally found around the pond in the winter, while Least Bittern and Purple Gallinule are occasionally seen during summer.

The **Pine Island Unit** has 3.8 miles of trails through a variety of habitats. To reach the Pine Island Unit from Dingle Pond, continue down Dingle Pond Road for 0.5 mile to a stop sign at Road 400. Turn right on Road 400 and drive 2.0 miles, at which point the paved road becomes dirt. Follow the dirt road 1.3 miles and park on the left before the closed gate, then head out on foot through the gate. During winter the pine forest along the road can be good for Golden-crowned Kinglet, Brown Creeper, and Dark-eyed Junco.

After 0.2 mile you will come to a road that heads left through the fields and marsh. The fields are an excellent place to look for Wilson's Snipe, Sedge Wren, Palm Warbler, and a variety of sparrows in winter. The most common sparrows are Swamp, Song, and Savannah, but with a little luck, you may turn up a Grasshopper, LeConte's, or Henslow's. Look for raptors over the fields in winter, including Northern Harrier, Red-shouldered and Red-tailed Hawks, and Bald Eagle. During summer you can find breeding Marsh Wrens in the marshes and perhaps a Purple Gallinule or Least Bittern if you are lucky. The edges of the grassy fields often have good numbers of breeding Painted Buntings.

General Information

Be sure to check for closures from November 1 to March 1, as there are some areas that are closed to public access to protect waterfowl. The wildlife drive on the Cuddo Unit is closed on Saturdays, but the other three units of Santee NWR are open all week. The refuge is open to the public from 7:00 a.m. to 7:00 p.m. during summer and 8:00 a.m. to 5:00 p.m. in the winter.

DeLorme atlas: Page 46, F5.

Elevation: 70 to 85 feet.

Hazards: Alligators, venomous snakes, mosquitoes, ticks, chiggers.

Nearest food, gas, lodging: Santee.

Camping: Santee State Park.

For more information: Santee NWR.

25 Francis Beidler Forest Audubon Sanctuary

Habitats: Swamp, hardwood forest, mixed pine-hardwood forest, farmland.

Specialty birds: *Resident*—Anhinga, Wild Turkey, Barred Owl, Pileated Woodpecker, White-breasted and Brown-headed Nuthatches, Yellow-throated Warbler. *Summer*—Yellow-crowned Night-Heron; White Ibis; Swallow-tailed and Mississippi Kites; Eastern Wood-Pewee; Acadian Flycatcher; Yellow-throated Vireo; Northern Parula; Prothonotary, Swainson's, Kentucky, and Hooded Warblers; Louisiana Waterthrush; Summer Tanager; Indigo and Painted Buntings. *Winter*—American Woodcock, Brown Creeper, Winter Wren, Black-and-white Warbler, Fox Sparrow.

Best times to bird: April through June.

Directions: Take Interstate 26 to exit 187 (Highway 27 south). At the end of the exit ramp, turn left on Highway 27. After 1.2 miles turn right on U.S. Highway 78, and in 2.7 miles bear right on U.S. Highway 178. After 0.7 mile turn right on Beidler Forest Road. In 4.1 miles, when Beidler Forest Road makes a 90-degree turn to the left, continue straight on Mims Road. After 1.1 miles turn right onto the dirt entrance road to Francis Beidler Forest.

The Birding

Francis Beidler Forest is home to the Audubon South Carolina state office and a 1.7-mile-long boardwalk that leads into the heart of Four Holes Swamp. Before starting the walk, you may want to ask one of the Audubon staff in the visitor center about any recent wildlife sightings. The boardwalk starts off in a mixed hardwood forest, but quickly works its way into an old-growth hardwood swamp. The swamp contains the largest remaining stand of virgin bald cypress and black gum trees in the world. Some of the bald cypress trees are over 1,000 years old. On one area of the boardwalk you can actually step inside one of the old, hollow cypress trees and imagine what it would be like if you were a Barred Owl.

The mixed hardwood forest at the beginning of the boardwalk can be good for Red-shouldered Hawk, Wild Turkey, and Brown-headed Nuthatch year-round. Barred Owls can often be heard and seen along the wetter areas of the boardwalk, particularly near Goodsen Lake. Six species of woodpecker are commonly found in the swamp: Downy, Hairy, Red-bellied, and Pileated Woodpeckers; Northern Flicker; and Yellow-bellied Sapsucker (winter). In the winter the numerous fallen logs in the swamp often provide good foraging habitat for Winter Wren and Hermit Thrush. Be sure to scan the leaf litter along the edges of the swamp for the highly camouflaged American Woodcock during winter. In the spring and summer, the swamp is probably the best location in South Carolina to see and photograph Prothonotary Warbler. These birds are truly fearless at Beidler Forest and it is an amazing experience to be within an arm's reach of a singing male. During May and June you can often find these brilliantly colored warblers nesting in hollow cypress knees within feet of the boardwalk.

Winter Wren

During summer look for Yellow-crowned Night-Herons patrolling the swamp in search of crayfish, and you may spot Swallow-tailed and Mississippi Kites gliding over the observation tower at Goodsen Lake. You may hear singing Kentucky and Swainson's Warblers near the visitor center and along the first 0.4 mile of the boardwalk in the summer, but they are often difficult to see. Yellow-throated Warbler and Northern Parula nest in the large clumps of Spanish moss hanging from the trees, and it is possible to find Yellow-throated Warbler even in the winter months.

In addition to the birds, the fallen logs and cypress stumps are favorite hangouts for snakes, turtles, and frogs during the summer months. The boardwalk is a great spot to see cottonmouths from a safe distance, as they sun themselves on cypress knees and logs. Also watch for American alligator, white-tailed deer, bobcat, beaver, and river otter.

As you leave the sanctuary, be sure to scan the grassy and weedy fields along Mims Road just outside the entrance to the sanctuary, which often contain Blue Grosbeak and Painted and Indigo Buntings during summer. Year-round look for Red-shouldered Hawk, Red-headed Woodpecker, and Loggerhead Strike. Swainson's Warblers can occasionally be heard singing in the thick brush at the intersection of Mims Road and Beidler Forest Road during summer. These areas are private property, so please do not leave the road.

General Information

The Francis Beidler Forest Audubon Sanctuary is open Tuesday through Sunday from 9:00 a.m. to 5:00 p.m. General admission is $7 for adults.

DeLorme atlas: Page 55, C6.

Elevation: 55 to 80 feet.

Hazards: Alligators, venomous snakes, mosquitoes.

Nearest food, gas, lodging: Harleyville for food and gas; Summerville for lodging.

Camping: Givhans Ferry State Park.

For more information: Francis Beidler Forest Audubon Sanctuary.

26 Carolina Sandhills National Wildlife Refuge

Habitats: Pine forest, early successional, lake, stream, field.

Specialty birds: *Resident*—Wood Duck; Red-shouldered Hawk; Northern Bobwhite; Red-cockaded, Hairy, and Red-headed Woodpeckers; Brown-headed Nuthatch; Field Sparrow; Eastern Meadowlark. *Summer*—Common Nighthawk, Chuck-will's-widow, Whip-poor-will, Eastern Wood-Pewee, Prairie and Hooded Warblers, Yellow-breasted Chat, Summer Tanager, Bachman's Sparrow, Blue Grosbeak, Indigo Bunting. *Winter*—American Black, Ring-necked, and Ruddy Ducks; Hooded Merganser; Bald Eagle.

Best times to bird: April through October.

Directions: From the intersection of U.S. Highway 1 and Highway 145 just west of McBee, follow US 1 north toward Patrick. After 1.2 miles turn left on the entrance road to Carolina Sandhills NWR.

The Birding

With more than a hundred nest clusters of Red-cockaded Woodpeckers, Carolina Sandhills National Wildlife Refuge is one of the best places in South Carolina, if not the entire Southeast, to see this federally endangered species. The ponds and lakes that are scattered throughout the refuge can be good places to look for Pied-billed Grebe; Hooded Merganser; American Wigeon; and American Black, Ring-necked, and Ruddy Ducks in winter. At dusk during the summer, the refuge is full of nightjars, especially Common Nighthawk and Chuck-will's-widow, but you may be able to find a couple Whip-poor-wills too. The refuge is full of roads and trails that are good for birding, but this book will only cover a few key areas.

To get started, follow the road from the visitor center for 0.7 mile until you come to an intersection with Wildlife Drive. Turn left on Wildlife Drive and after 0.7 mile you will see a parking area for the **Woodland Pond Trail** on the left. The short, 1-mile loop trail can be good year-round for pine forest specialists such as Brown-headed Nuthatch and Pine Warbler. During summer look for Hooded Warbler in the bay thickets along the trail. In the fall the thickets can be good for migrating warblers and thrushes, and during winter they are full of Gray Catbird, Hermit Thrush, American Robin, Eastern Towhee, and White-throated Sparrow.

Continue down Wildlife Drive for 0.4 mile and you will come to an intersection with Wire Road. There is a nesting colony of Red-cockaded Woodpeckers on the right side of the road at the intersection. The best way to find the woodpeckers is to look for them near their nest trees in the early morning or late evening. The nest trees are easily identified by the white paint rings around the base. The woodpeckers are often easiest to find during May and June, when they are busy creating nest cavities and feeding their young. There are numerous nesting

Northern Bobwhite

colonies throughout the refuge; all you have to do is look for the white rings on the trees.

Continuing on Wildlife Drive, after 2.6 miles you will see a road on the right leading down to **Martin Lake,** one of the best birding areas on the refuge. Along the dirt road that leads to Martin Lake from Highway 145 there are several clusters of Red-cockaded Woodpecker nest trees. From the Martin Lake parking lot, follow Tate's Trail 0.2 mile to an observation tower that overlooks the lake. During winter this is a good spot to scan for Pied-billed Grebe and American Black, Ring-necked, and Ruddy Ducks, while Canada Geese and Wood Ducks are permanent residents. The thickets along the lakeshore are often full of songbirds during winter, including Gray Catbird, Hermit Thrush, American Robin, and White-throated Sparrow. Year-round look for Brown-headed Nuthatch, Pine Warbler, and Eastern Towhee. If you hike 0.4 mile north along Tate's Trail from the observation platform, you will see an old wooden photography blind along the shore of the lake. The blind often provides good views of waterfowl on the lake that can't be seen from the tower.

Continue on Wildlife Drive and after 0.9 mile you will reach a T-intersection. Turn left and drive 1.1 miles to the **Lake Bee Recreation Area.** Look for Red-cockaded Woodpecker in the many nest trees surrounding the picnic area, and scan the picnic area year-round for Brown-headed Nuthatch, Eastern Bluebird, and Pine Warbler. In the winter look for Yellow-bellied Sapsucker, Blue-headed

Vireo, and Dark-eyed Junco. During summer look for Eastern Wood-Pewee, Prairie Warbler, and Bachman's Sparrow.

Continuing down Wildlife Drive, after 2.1 miles you will reach a road on the right that leads to the **Oxpen Farm Unit.** Follow the dirt road 0.6 mile to the observation tower. The road can be severely eroded, so if you don't have a high-clearance vehicle, you may want to park at the start of the dirt road and walk. The fields that surround the observation tower are good for grassland species. Search the fields year-round for Loggerhead Shrike, Eastern Bluebird, Field Sparrow, and Eastern Meadowlark. During winter look for raptors such as American Kestrel and Northern Harrier. A walk through the fields in winter should produce a variety of sparrows, including Dark-eyed Junco; Savannah, Song, White-throated, and Chipping Sparrows; and the occasional White-crowned or Vesper Sparrow. During summer look for Eastern Kingbird, White-eyed Vireo, and Yellow-breasted Chat.

General Information

The refuge is open year-round from one hour before sunrise to one hour after sunset.

DeLorme atlas: Page 29, E7.
Elevation: 300 to 550 feet.
Hazards: Venomous snakes, mosquitoes.
Nearest food, gas, lodging: Hartsville.

Camping: Cheraw State Park.
For more information: Carolina Sandhills NWR.

27 Longleaf Pine and Lynchburg Savanna Heritage Preserves

Habitats: Pine forest, early successional, field.

Specialty birds: *Resident*—Wild Turkey; Northern Bobwhite; Red-cockaded, Hairy, and Red-headed Woodpeckers; Brown-headed Nuthatch; Chipping and Field Sparrows. *Summer*—Prairie Warbler, Yellow-breasted Chat, Bachman's Sparrow, Indigo Bunting, Blue Grosbeak, Orchard Oriole. *Winter*—Yellow-bellied Sapsucker; House Wren; Grasshopper, LeConte's, Henslow's, Fox, and Lincoln's Sparrows.

Best times to bird: November through June.

Directions: To reach Longleaf Pine Heritage Preserve from the intersection of U.S. Highway 76 and Highway 527 (Elliot Highway) near Lynchburg, drive east on US 76. After 4.0 miles turn right on Atkins Avenue, then in 1.4 miles turn right on McKnight Road. After 2.0 miles turn left into the entrance to Longleaf Pine Heritage Preserve and park in the dirt lot near the gate. See directions below to Lynchburg Savanna Heritage Preserve.

The Birding

Two heritage preserves near Lynchburg offer great opportunities to view birds that specialize on longleaf pine forest ecosystems. The 843-acre **Longleaf Pine Heritage Preserve** consists largely of mature longleaf pine forest that is interspersed with pond cypress depressions. The area around the preserve's parking lot is often good for Yellow-breasted Chat, Indigo Bunting, Blue Grosbeak, and Orchard Oriole. Year-round look for Chipping and Field Sparrows.

From the parking lot, follow the road through the gate on foot. After 0.7 mile you will come to a power line right-of-way. Look for a nesting colony of Red-cockaded Woodpeckers on the far (east) side of the right-of-way. During winter walk the grassy right-of-way and look for House Wren and sparrows. If you are lucky, you may find a Henslow's Sparrow. In the summer the longleaf pine forest on either side of the right-of-way often contains Eastern Wood-Pewee, Summer Tanager, and Bachman's Sparrow. Year-round look for Wild Turkey, Northern Bobwhite, Red-headed and Hairy Woodpeckers, Brown-headed Nuthatch, and Eastern Towhee. If you missed the Red-cockaded Woodpeckers at the right-of-way, try driving 0.5 mile south from the parking lot on McKnight Road to find another colony on the left side of the road.

Not far from Longleaf Pine Heritage Preserve is **Lynchburg Savanna Heritage Preserve,** which is largely made up of early successional longleaf pine habitat. To get to Lynchburg Savanna from Longleaf Pine, return to Atkins Avenue. When you reach US 76, continue straight on Atkins Avenue for 0.9 mile, then turn left on CC Road. After 1.0 mile turn right into the entrance for Lynchburg Savanna Heritage Preserve. Park in the lot and follow the dirt road through the

Bachman's Sparrow

gate. The dirt road will go 0.5 mile through the preserve before it ends, but there are several shorter roads that branch off from the main road that you can also explore. During summer the preserve is an excellent place to look for Prairie Warbler, Yellow-breasted Chat, Indigo Bunting, and Blue Grosbeak, and you may find a few Bachman's Sparrows. Year-round look for Northern Bobwhite, Brown-headed Nuthatch, Pine Warbler, Eastern Towhee, and Chipping and Field Sparrows. In the winter the preserve is an excellent area to look for sparrows. The most commonly observed are Song, Swamp, White-throated, and Fox Sparrows, but you may get lucky and find a Lincoln's, Grasshopper, LeConte's, or Henslow's Sparrow.

General Information

Both heritage preserves are open year-round from dawn to dusk.

DeLorme atlas: Longleaf Pine Heritage Preserve, page 38, E4; Lynchburg Savanna Heritage Preserve, page 38, E3.

Elevation: 150 feet.

Hazards: Venomous snakes, mosquitoes.

Nearest food, gas, lodging: Bishopville.

Camping: Lee State Natural Area.

For more information: SCDNR Wildlife and Freshwater Fisheries Division.

28 Columbia Area

Habitats: Mixed pine-hardwood forest, hardwood forest, early successional, field, swamp, river, stream, pond.

Specialty birds: *Resident*—Red-shouldered Hawk, Barred Owl, Hairy Woodpecker, Brown-headed Nuthatch, House Wren. *Summer*—Mississippi Kite; Acadian Flycatcher; Red-eyed Vireo; Wood Thrush; Northern Parula; Yellow-throated, Prothonotary, Swainson's, and Kentucky Warblers; Summer Tanager; Blue Grosbeak; Indigo and Painted Buntings;

Orchard Oriole. *Winter*—Common Loon, Horned Grebe, Bald Eagle, Bonaparte's Gull, Brown Creeper, Winter Wren, White-crowned and Fox Sparrows. *Migration*—Solitary and Pectoral Sandpipers, Caspian Tern.

Best times to bird: Saluda Shoals Park is best in April and May and again in September and October. Lake Murray Dam Park is best from December through March. Congaree Creek Heritage Preserve is good year-round.

Directions: To reach Saluda Shoals Park from exit 104 on Interstate 26, drive west on Piney Grove Road toward Whitehall. After 1.5 miles turn right on St. Andrews Road, then in 0.2 mile take a left on Bush River Road. Drive 1.5 miles and turn left into the entrance for Saluda Shoals Park. To reach Lake Murray Dam Park from exit 102 on I-26, drive west on Highway 60 (Murray Boulevard). After 3.6 miles you will come to an intersection with Highway 6 (Lake Drive). Continue straight for 0.1 mile and the entrance to the park will be on your left. To reach Congaree Creek Heritage Preserve from exit 2 on Interstate 77, drive north on Highway 35 (12th Street) towards Cayce. After 2.0 miles turn right on Godley Road, then in 0.2 mile turn right on New State Road. At the fork in 0.5 mile, bear right on Old State Road. Drive 1.3 miles and turn right into the parking lot for Congaree Creek Heritage Preserve.

The Birding

Saluda Shoals Park is a small section of woods and fields that runs along the eastern bank of the Lower Saluda River. It is probably the best location in the Columbia area to see migrating songbirds in the spring. After you pay the entrance fee at the booth, follow the road downhill and park in the lot on your right. Walk across the street and follow the trail that leads past the enclosed dog park. The trail winds through a wide, brushy right-of-way, which can be loaded with Song, Swamp, and White-throated Sparrows in winter. Other birds to look for in winter are House and Winter Wrens, Common Yellowthroat, Eastern Towhee, and Fox Sparrow.

Brown-headed Nuthatch and Pine Warbler are common residents of the small sections of pine forest along the edges of the rights-of-way. During summer look for Mississippi Kite soaring over the open areas, as well as House Wren, Indigo Bunting, Blue Grosbeak, and Orchard Oriole in the brushy areas. Painted Buntings have occasionally been spotted here during the summer.

The main attraction of the park is the paved trail that follows the bank of the Lower Saluda River for 1.5 miles. This trail can get a little crowded at times, so you may want to arrive early during weekends or visit on a weekday. In the spring and fall, this trail is the best place in the park to look for migrating warblers and thrushes. During winter you should be able to find numerous Hermit Thrushes along the trail. Scan the river at various points along the trail for Wood Duck, Bald Eagle, and Spotted Sandpiper. Check the area by the boat landing for Red-headed Woodpecker year-round.

Not far from Saluda Shoals Park is **Lake Murray Dam Park,** which is owned and operated by South Carolina Electric & Gas (SCE&G). The park is quite small and consists mainly of a parking lot, picnic area, and boat ramp on the north side of the Lake Murray Dam. The park's main attraction to bird-watchers is the commanding view that it offers of Lake Murray. In the winter it is worth a stop to scan the lake for Common Loon, Horned Grebe, Red-breasted Merganser, Redhead, Lesser Scaup, Bald Eagle, and Bonaparte's Gull. Rare waterfowl such as Common Goldeneye and Common Merganser are possible, and don't forget to scan the thousands of Ring-billed Gulls for rare gulls. During spring and fall watch for Caspian and Forster's Terns.

Located in the southwest corner of Columbia is the beautiful **Congaree Creek Heritage Preserve.** Its 627 acres of hardwood swamp and upland forest are often pretty good for songbird migrants in the spring and fall. From the parking lot you should be able to hear Eastern Wood-Pewee, Kentucky Warbler, and Indigo Bunting during summer. Follow the Guignard Brickworks Trail at the south end of the parking lot for 0.2 mile to reach a large group of clay pits that were used in the early 1900s to create bricks. The pits have now become ponds that attract a wide variety of wildlife. Watch your step along the trail because there is plenty of poison ivy in this area, but it shouldn't be a problem unless you leave the trail.

At the clay pits, the trail splits and forms a 2.5-mile loop that works its way around and occasionally even through the pits. One of the big attractions of the preserve are the alligators that can occasionally be seen in the ponds, as they are not very common this far inland in South Carolina. During winter look for Yellow-bellied Sapsucker, Winter Wren, Hermit Thrush, and Rusty Blackbird. In the summer you should be able to find Acadian Flycatcher, Northern Parula, Prothonotary Warbler, and Summer Tanager. The trail can also be quite good in the summer for both Kentucky and Swainson's Warblers.

Head clockwise around the loop and after 0.4 mile you will reach the banks of Congaree Creek. In another 1.0 mile you will pass through a couple brushy power line rights-of-way. Look for Yellow-breasted Chat, Indigo Bunting, and Blue Grosbeak in the brushy areas during summer.

After you are finished birding at Congaree Creek Heritage Preserve, there are a couple of nearby areas that you may also want to check out. As you exit the parking lot, turn right on Old State Road and head south. Old State Road becomes a dirt road shortly past the preserve. Follow this road as it goes through pine forest and mixed pine-hardwood forest. During spring and fall the road offers good opportunities to find migrating songbirds, since it parallels the Congaree River. The entire length of Old State Road is private property, so please do not leave the road. After 2.5 miles you will see agricultural fields on your left and a sludge farm on your right. During summer you can usually find a few Mississippi Kites and Painted Buntings around the farms. In the winter look for good numbers of sparrows, and you may even be able to find a couple White-crowned Sparrows.

Another spot that you may want to check out is Newman Boat Landing, which lies just north of the heritage preserve along the Congaree River. To reach the boat landing, drive north on Old State Road from the heritage preserve. After 0.4 mile turn right on Granby Landing Road and drive 0.1 mile to the boat landing. Look for wading birds year-round, including Black-crowned Night-Heron. If the river is low during spring and fall, scan the sandbars for migrating shorebirds such as Spotted, Solitary, Least, and Pectoral Sandpipers.

General Information

Saluda Shoals Park is open daily from 7:00 a.m. to sunset. Admission is $4 for Lexington County residents and $5 for nonresidents. Lake Murray Dam Park is open twenty-four hours a day year-round. Admission is $3 per vehicle. Congaree Creek Heritage Preserve is open year-round from sunrise to sunset.

DeLorme atlas: Saluda Shoals Park, page 36, E1; Lake Murray Dam Park, page 35, E10; Congaree Creek Heritage Preserve, page 36, G2.

Elevation: 130 to 300 feet.

Hazards: Alligators, venomous snakes, mosquitoes, poison ivy.

Nearest food, gas, lodging: Columbia.

Camping: Sesquicentennial State Park; Congaree National Park (primitive sites only).

For more information: Saluda Shoals Park; SCDNR Wildlife and Freshwater Fisheries Division.

Piedmont

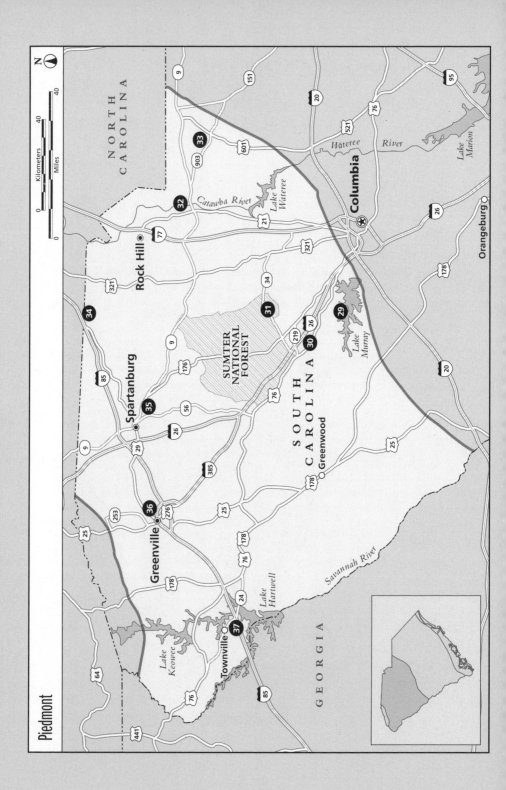

Piedmont

29 Dreher Island State Park

Habitats: Lake, mixed pine-hardwood forest.

Specialty birds: *Resident*—Great Horned Owl, Hairy and Pileated Woodpeckers, Brown-headed Nuthatch. *Summer*—Yellow-billed Cuckoo, Cliff Swallow, Prothonotary Warbler, Summer Tanager. *Winter*—Common Loon, Horned Grebe, American Black and Ring-necked Ducks, Lesser Scaup, Bufflehead, Common Merganser, Bald Eagle, Bonaparte's Gull, Brown Creeper, Winter Wren, Hermit Thrush, American Pipit.

Best times to bird: December through March.

Directions: From exit 85 on Interstate 26, follow Highway 202 (Pomaria Avenue) south toward Little Mountain. After 1.9 miles turn right on U.S. Highway 76 (Chapin Road), then in 0.5 mile turn left on Wheeland Road. Travel 5.9 miles and turn left on Macedonia Church Road. After 1.3 miles turn left on Dreher Island Road, then in 0.6 mile turn right on State Park Road. In 2.6 miles you will reach the entrance booth for the state park.

The Birding

Dreher Island State Park is made up of a series of small islands that extend out into Lake Murray, a 50,000-acre artificially-created reservoir. In winter it is one of the best areas in the piedmont to look for Common Loon and Horned Grebe. Waterfowl that are rare away from the coast, such as Common and Red-breasted Mergansers and Surf Scoter, can occasionally be found on Lake Murray.

One of the best places to scan the lake is from the causeway just past the entrance booth. Park in the lot to the right of the booth and walk out to the causeway. The pines at the beginning of the causeway often have Brown-headed Nuthatch and Pine Warbler year-round. In the winter scan the lake for waterfowl, Common Loon, Bonaparte's Gull, and perhaps a few Horned Grebes. The summer months are pretty slow for birding in the park, but you can find Cliff Swallows nesting underneath the bridge in the center of the causeway.

Walk back to your car and drive farther into the park, following signs for the visitor center. Along the way, you will see numerous spots to get out and scan the lake for waterfowl, loons, grebes, and gulls. Once you reach the visitor center, pick up a map of the park. There are three trails that you can hike to look for songbirds: Billy Dreher Nature Trail (0.25 mile), Bike Trail (0.3 mile), and Little Gap Trail (2.1 miles). During summer look for Yellow-billed Cuckoo, Prothonotary Warbler, and Summer Tanager. Year-round the pine forests in the park are good for Brown-headed Nuthatch and Pine Warbler. In the spring and fall, the park can be good for migrating warblers and other songbirds. More than twenty species of warblers have been observed here during migration, including Golden-winged, Blue-winged, Blackburnian, and Cape May.

Lake Murray

General Information

Dreher Island State Park is open daily from 6:00 a.m. to 6:00 p.m. during winter and 6:00 a.m. to 9:00 p.m. in the summer. The entrance fee is $2 per person.

DeLorme atlas: Page 35, E8.

Elevation: 370 to 420 feet.

Hazards: Poison ivy.

Nearest food, gas, lodging: Columbia.

Camping: Dreher Island State Park.

For more information: Dreher Island State Park.

30 Lynch's Woods Park

Habitats: Field, mixed pine-hardwood forest, stream.

Specialty birds: *Resident*—Northern Bob-white, Hairy Woodpecker. *Summer*—Common Nighthawk, Acadian Flycatcher, Eastern Wood-Pewee, Red-eyed and Yellow-throated Vireos, Wood Thrush, Northern Parula, Yellow-throated Warbler, Summer Tanager, Orchard Oriole. *Winter*—American Woodcock, Winter Wren.

Best times to bird: April and May and again in September and October.

Directions: From exit 76 on Interstate 26, follow Highway 219 west toward Newberry. After 3.2 miles turn left on U.S. Highway 76. Follow US 76 for 0.7 mile, then turn left at the entrance to Lynch's Woods Park.

The Birding

Lynch's Woods Park is excellent for migrating songbirds in the spring and fall. On a good day during migration, you may see close to twenty species of warblers. Lynch's Woods has been a public park for more than seventy years. As you travel along the 4-mile dirt road that loops through the 286 acres of nearly pristine upland forest, you will drive over several stone bridges that were built by the Civilian Conservation Corps back in the 1930s. The road is open to vehicles, but the best way to look for the migrating songbirds is to walk the loop or the maze of hiking, biking, and equestrian trails on the inside of the loop. If you aren't up to walking the whole loop, you can drive and stop at various points.

To get started on the dirt road, follow the one-way signs and go clockwise around the loop. After 0.2 mile you will come to a power line right-of-way. In the winter the brushy areas in the right-of-way can be good for Field, Chipping, White-throated, and Song Sparrows. The road gradually works its way down through mixed hardwood forest to a stream. At about 0.8 mile from the right-of-way, find a good place to park along the side of the road to do some walking. For the next 0.7 mile the road is relatively flat while it follows the stream, until it eventually works its way back uphill to the start of the loop. During winter this section of road is good for Hermit Thrush and Winter Wren. In the spring and fall, look for migrating warblers, thrushes, and Baltimore Oriole. During summer look for Acadian Flycatcher, Yellow-throated Vireo, Northern Parula, and Yellow-throated Warbler. The edge of the cow pasture is a good spot to listen for Common Nighthawk and look for Orchard Oriole in the summer. During late winter listen for American Woodcock around dusk.

As it heads uphill, the last 2.3 miles of the road can be good for Red-eyed Vireo, Wood Thrush, and Summer Tanager in the summer. During migration scan the sides of the road for migrating thrushes such as Veery, Gray-cheeked Thrush, and Swainson's Thrush.

Gray-cheeked Thrush

General Information

The park is open year-round twenty-four hours a day.

DeLorme atlas: Page 35, A6.

Elevation: 420 to 550 feet.

Hazards: Venomous snakes, mosquitoes, ticks.

Nearest food, gas, lodging: Newberry.

Camping: Lynch's Woods Park (primitive sites only); Dreher Island State Park.

For more information: Newberry Soil & Water Conservation District.

31 Sumter National Forest—Enoree District

Habitats: Pond, river, swamp, pine forest, mixed pine-hardwood forest, hardwood forest, early successional.

Specialty birds: *Resident*—Red-shouldered Hawk, Wild Turkey, Northern Bobwhite, American Woodcock, Barred Owl, Hairy and Pileated Woodpeckers, Loggerhead Shrike, Brown-headed Nuthatch, Eastern Bluebird, Pine Warbler, Field Sparrow, Eastern Meadowlark, American Goldfinch. *Summer*—Red-headed Woodpecker; Yellow-throated Vireo; Prairie, Black-and-white, Prothonotary, Yellow-throated, and Kentucky Warblers; Ovenbird; Yellow-breasted Chat; Blue Grosbeak; Indigo Bunting. *Winter*—Northern Pintail, Green-winged Teal, Gadwall, American Wigeon, American Black and Ring-necked Ducks, Lesser Scaup, Bald Eagle, American Kestrel, Brown Creeper, Winter Wren, Hermit Thrush, Orange-crowned Warbler, Fox Sparrow.

Best times to bird: February through May and again in September and October.

Directions: To reach the Broad River Waterfowl Management Area from exit 74 on Interstate 26, drive 12 miles east on Highway 34. Turn right on Strothers Road, the first street after the bridge over the Broad River, and drive 1.2 miles on Strothers Road to the gated road on the right (look for signs to the waterfowl area).

The Birding

One of the best areas to look for waterfowl in the piedmont during winter is the **Broad River Waterfowl Management Area.** From the gate, head down the road for about a mile and you will see a storage equipment area on the right. Just past the equipment area, the road will bend to the left and run parallel to the railroad tracks. Follow the road out onto the dike and begin looking through the flooded agricultural fields for waterfowl. During winter you should be able to find Mallard, American Black Duck, Northern Pintail, Green-winged Teal, Gadwall, and American Wigeon. You may see a few Lesser Scaup or Ring-necked Ducks, but they are not as common. Year-round you should be able to find good numbers of Wood Duck. Also in winter look for Winter and House Wrens and sparrows in the grasses along the edges of the dikes.

Nearby Shelton Ferry Road and Enoree River Waterfowl Management Area are not as good for waterfowl in winter, but they can be good for migrating and breeding songbirds. To reach **Shelton Ferry Road,** return to Highway 34 and turn left. After 1.2 miles turn right on Mt. Pleasant Road (Road 28), then in 3.6 miles turn right on Maybinton Road (Road 45). Travel 4.4 miles and turn right on Tyger River Road (Road 54). After 1.1 miles turn right on Dogwalla Road (Road 702), then in 0.9 mile bear left on Shelton Ferry Road. As you drive through the mixed pine forest along Shelton Ferry Road, listen for Wood Thrush, Black-and-white Warbler, and Ovenbird during spring and summer. After 1.7 miles you will reach a clear-cut with regenerating pine forest. The clear-cut

Gadwall

provides excellent nesting habitat for Red-headed Woodpecker, Prairie Warbler, Yellow-breasted Chat, Indigo Bunting, and Blue Grosbeak. Scan the clear-cut year-round for Northern Bobwhite, Field Sparrow, and American Goldfinch.

Continue for 1.0 mile and you will come to a small patch of bottomland hardwood forest along the Broad River. Walk the road leading to the boat ramp to look for Red-shouldered Hawk, Barred Owl, and American Woodcock year-round. During summer you can find Yellow-throated Vireo and Prothonotary, Yellow-throated, and Kentucky Warblers. In the spring and fall, the hardwood forest can be a good area to look for migrating warblers and other songbirds. The hardwood forest surrounding the boat ramp is private property, so don't stray from the road.

To reach the **Enoree River Waterfowl Management Area,** return to Dogwalla Road and turn left. After 0.5 mile bear right at the yield sign and continue to follow Dogwalla Road. Travel another 1.8 miles and then turn left on FS Road 401E. After 0.8 mile park on the left just before the gate. Walk down the road through a pine forest, and after about 0.3 mile you will reach a series of farm fields that are flooded during winter to provide waterfowl habitat. In the spring and fall, look for migrating songbirds in the forest around the edges of the fields. The mixed pine forest can be good for Brown-headed Nuthatch and Pine Warbler year-round.

When you finish birding the waterfowl management area, return to Dog-walla Road and turn left. Dogwalla Road runs through a mixture of pine forest and clear-cuts for 3.6 miles to Maybinton Road. Turn left on Maybinton Road and retrace your steps to I-26. As you follow the roads through numerous farms and fields, be sure to keep an eye on the telephone wires for typical farmland species such as American Kestrel, Loggerhead Shrike, Eastern Bluebird, and Eastern Meadowlark.

General Information

Broad River and Enoree River Waterfowl Management Areas are closed from mid-October to early February to protect waterfowl. During the rest of the year, both waterfowl management areas are open twenty-four hours a day. There are no visitor facilities at either waterfowl management area.

DeLorme atlas: Broad River Waterfowl Management Area, page 26, H3; Enoree River Waterfowl Management Area, page 26, G3.

Elevation: 200 to 400 feet.

Hazards: Venomous snakes, poison ivy.

Nearest food, gas, lodging: Newberry.

Camping: Rocky Branch Campground.

For more information: Sumter National Forest—Enoree District.

32 Landsford Canal State Park

Habitats: Hardwood forest, pine forest, river.

Specialty birds: *Resident*—Bald Eagle, Red-shouldered Hawk, Northern Bobwhite, Brown-headed Nuthatch. *Summer*—Ruby-throated Hummingbird; Acadian and Great Crested Fly-catchers; Yellow-throated Vireo; Wood Thrush; Northern Parula; Prairie, Prothonotary, Yellow-throated, Kentucky, and Hooded Warblers; American Redstart; Summer and Scarlet Tanagers; Grasshopper Sparrow; Blue Grosbeak; Indigo Bunting. *Winter*—Hooded Merganser, Bonaparte's Gull, Winter Wren, Hermit Thrush. *Migration*—Cliff Swallow.

Best times to bird: April and May and again in September and October.

Directions: From exit 65 on Interstate 77, follow Highway 9 east toward Fort Lawn. After 1.4 miles turn left on Highway 223, then in 6.6 miles turn left on U.S. Highway 21. Travel 1.6 miles and turn right on Landsford Road. In 1.7 miles turn left into the main entrance of Landsford Canal State Park.

The Birding

Landsford Canal State Park lies on the western bank of the Catawba River. This park is one of the best areas in the state to observe songbird migration in the spring and fall. On a good day in spring, you should easily find more than fifteen species of warblers in their beautiful breeding plumage. The park contains three trails: Canal Trail (1.5 miles), Nature Trail (0.5 mile), and Eagle Point Trail (0.2 mile).

From the parking area, follow the Canal Trail south along the river. The trail runs parallel to the old, abandoned canal that was built in the early 1800s. After 0.1 mile the Nature Trail will split off to the left. Either of these trails is excellent during migration, and you may find such migrants as Blackpoll, Chestnut-sided, Cape May, Yellow, and Black-throated Blue Warblers; Northern Waterthrush; and Baltimore Oriole in spring. During summer look for Red-eyed and Yellow-throated Vireos; Wood Thrush; Northern Parula; Prothonotary, Yellow-throated, and Kentucky Warblers; American Redstart; and Ovenbird.

After 0.5 mile the Canal Trail and Nature Trail will rejoin to form a loop. Continue another 0.4 mile after the trails rejoin and you will see a viewing platform at the edge of the river. This platform was designed for viewing the Rocky Shoals spider lilies, which bloom from early May to mid-June. The Catawba River contains the Southeast's largest population of these beautiful lilies, and they literally cover the river in white. The platform is also a good spot to look for migrating swallows, Canada Goose, Bald Eagle, and Spotted Sandpiper. The park is usually pretty slow for birding in the winter, but you may be able to find Hooded Merganser, Bald Eagle, and Bonaparte's Gull along the river. As you hike along the river during winter, scan the hardwood forest for Yellow-bellied Sapsucker, Winter Wren, Cedar Waxwing, Hermit Thrush, and Golden- and

Ruby-crowned Kinglets. Even if the birding is slow, the beautiful scenery and fascinating history of the canal make the trip well worth it.

A parking lot at the south end of the Landsford Canal provides access to the southern portion of the Canal Trail. To reach the parking lot, return to Landsford Road and turn left. The early successional pine forest along this road can be good for Northern Bobwhite, Brown-headed Nuthatch, Pine Warbler, and Field Sparrow year-round. During summer look for Prairie Warbler, Indigo Bunting, and Blue Grosbeak. After 1.2 miles turn left at the stop sign on Canal Road and drive 0.5 mile to the parking lot. From the south parking lot, follow the Canal Trail north through the lifting locks of the nearly 200-year-old canal. Seeing Blackburnian, Chestnut-sided, Canada, and Cape May Warblers; Scarlet Tanager; Baltimore Oriole; and many other beautiful migrants while surrounded by the history of the old canal is an amazing experience!

When you are finished birding in the park, be sure to look for American Kestrel, Eastern Bluebird, and Eastern Meadowlark in the fields along Landsford Road. Keep an ear out for singing Grasshopper Sparrows, which have been known to breed in some of the fields during summer.

General Information

The park is open daily from 9:00 a.m. to 6:00 p.m. The entrance fee is $2 for adults.

DeLorme atlas: Page 27, A9.

Elevation: 430 to 550 feet.

Hazards: Venomous snakes, mosquitoes.

Nearest food, gas, lodging: Lancaster.

Camping: Andrew Jackson State Park.

For more information: Landsford Canal State Park.

33 Forty Acre Rock Heritage Preserve

Habitats: Hardwood forest, pine forest, early successional, pond, stream.

Specialty birds: *Resident*—Wood Duck, Red-shouldered Hawk, American Woodcock, Brown-headed Nuthatch, Pine Warbler. *Summer*—Yellow-billed Cuckoo; Northern Parula; Prothonotary, Prairie, Kentucky, and Hooded Warblers; Louisiana Waterthrush; American Redstart; Scarlet and Summer Tanagers. *Winter*—American Black and Ring-necked Ducks, Winter Wren.

Best times to bird: April and May and again in September and October.

Directions: From the intersection of Highway 903 and U.S. Highway 601, follow US 601 north toward Pageland. After 1.6 miles turn left on Nature Reserve Road. Follow Nature Reserve Road for 2.0 miles and turn left on Conservancy Road. Follow the road until it ends at the upper parking lot after 0.8 mile.

The Birding

The main attraction for birders at Forty Acre Rock Heritage Preserve is songbird migration in the spring. **Forty Acre Rock** (which is actually only about 14 acres) is a huge unbroken rock that provides great views of the surrounding area. Seeing the rock is well worth the 0.5-mile hike from the upper parking lot, but the birding around the rock is not very good. The pine forest that surrounds Forty Acre Rock can be good for Brown-headed Nuthatch and Pine Warbler year-round, and you may be able to find a few Prairie Warblers in the summer.

The best area for birding in the park is the trail around the beaver pond near the lower parking lot. During spring and fall the hardwood forest around the pond can be good for migrating songbirds. To reach the lower parking lot, return to Nature Reserve Road and turn right. After 1.6 miles turn right into the lower parking lot. To reach the beaver pond, follow the trail from the parking lot for 0.2 mile. Just before you reach the lake, a small path will lead off to the left. This path will take you up along the hillside and around the beaver pond. A large oval-shaped rock on the south end of the pond provides a great lookout platform to scan the water. In the winter you may be able to find a few Ring-necked or American Black Ducks on the pond, and keep an eye out for the occasional American Bittern. Permanent residents near the pond include Wood Duck, Red-shouldered Hawk, and American Woodcock.

Continue along the trail as it heads over a short boardwalk and runs between Flat Creek and a swampy area along the edge of the pond. During spring the swamp is great for migrating songbirds such as Northern Waterthrush; Black-throated Blue, Black-throated Green, and Yellow Warblers; and many others. In the summer look for Northern Parula; American Redstart; Prothonotary, Hooded, and Kentucky Warblers; Summer Tanager; and perhaps even a few Scarlet

Prothonotary Warbler

Tanagers at the edge of their breeding range. Keep an eye out for breeding Louisiana Waterthrush along Flat Creek.

After 0.6 mile you will come to an intersection with the main trail that runs along the northern shore of the beaver pond. Turning left at the intersection will take you through a power line right-of-way and uphill to Forty Acre Rock. Turning right at the intersection will lead you 0.4 mile back to the lower parking lot.

General Information

The heritage preserve is open year-round from sunrise to sunset. There are no facilities at the preserve.

DeLorme atlas: Page 28, C4.
Elevation: 360 to 630 feet.
Hazards: Venomous snakes, mosquitoes.
Nearest food, gas, lodging: Lancaster.

Camping: Andrew Jackson State Park.
For more information: SCDNR Wildlife and Freshwater Fisheries Division.

34 Kings Mountain

Habitats: Hardwood forest, mixed pine-hardwood forest, stream, lake.

Specialty birds: *Resident*—Barred Owl, Red-headed and Pileated Woodpeckers, White-breasted Nuthatch, Chipping Sparrow. *Summer*—Great Crested Flycatcher; Eastern Wood-Pewee; Red-eyed Vireo; Wood Thrush; Kentucky, Hooded, and Black-and-white Warblers; Ovenbird; Summer and Scarlet Tanagers. *Winter*—Brown Creeper, Fox Sparrow, Purple Finch. *Migration*—Spotted Sandpiper.

Best times to bird: April and May and again in September and October.

Directions: Follow Interstate 85 north into North Carolina. Get off at exit 2 and follow Highway 216 south back into South Carolina. At 2.4 miles from the interstate, you will reach the entrance to Kings Mountain National Military Park. Continue on Highway 216 into the park, and after 1.7 miles turn left into the visitor center parking lot.

The Birding

Kings Mountain is made up of two parks, Kings Mountain National Military Park and Kings Mountain State Park. Combined, the two parks contain nearly 11,000 acres of protected land and more than 30 miles of trails. The elevation rises to just over 1,000 feet in the park, though there are no great views of the surrounding area. Kings Mountain contains many breeding songbirds typical of the piedmont and can be good for warblers, thrushes, and other migratory songbirds in spring and fall. Birding is pretty slow during winter, but you may find Brown Creeper or Purple Finch if you are lucky.

Behind the Kings Mountain National Military Park visitor center is the **Battlefield Trail,** a paved 1.5-mile loop trail. The trail is best during fall migration, when you should be able to find many different types of warblers and other songbirds. During summer you will likely find Red-eyed Vireo, Eastern Wood-Pewee, and Summer Tanager along the trail. Year-round the area is pretty good for Red-headed and Pileated Woodpeckers and White-breasted Nuthatch. If the birding is slow or you are with a non-birding spouse or friend, the trail has numerous interpretive signs and monuments to help you learn all about the Revolutionary War battle that took place here in 1780.

From the visitor center parking lot, turn left and head into the state park. After 2.9 miles turn left on Lake Crawford Road. In 0.9 mile you will come to a large parking lot. From here, follow the Living History Farm trail down to Lake Crawford. During spring and fall check the dam and lake edges for Spotted Sandpiper. Uphill from the parking lot is a picnic area with a trailhead for the **Kings Mountain Hiking Trail,** a 16-mile trail that loops around the outer edges of the two parks. The trail winds through hardwood forest and ravines and runs along several small streams. It can be good for Wood Thrush; Black-and-white, Hooded, and

Battlefield Trail in Kings Mountain National Military Park

Kentucky Warblers; Ovenbird; and Scarlet Tanager in summer. During spring and fall the trail can be good for migrating warblers and other songbirds. Hiking the loop counterclockwise from the state park picnic area will lead you to the Kings Mountain National Military Park visitor center, while hiking the loop clockwise will take you to the lesser-visited southern end of the park.

General Information

Kings Mountain National Military Park is open daily from 9:00 a.m. to 5:00 p.m. Kings Mountain State Park is open daily from 8:00 a.m. to 6:00 p.m. during winter and 8:00 a.m. to 9:00 p.m. in the summer. Admission to the state park is $2 for adults.

DeLorme atlas: Page 20, C3.

Elevation: 600 to 1,000 feet.

Hazards: Venomous snakes, mosquitoes, ticks.

Nearest food, gas, lodging: Blacksburg.

Camping: Kings Mountain State Park.

For more information: Kings Mountain National Military Park; Kings Mountain State Park.

35 Spartanburg Area

Habitats: Hardwood forest, mixed pine-hardwood forest, stream, lake, pond.

Specialty birds: *Resident*—Red-shouldered Hawk, Barred Owl, Hairy Woodpecker, Eastern Phoebe, White-breasted and Brown-headed Nuthatches, Pine Warbler. *Winter*—Winter Wren, Rusty Blackbird. *Summer*—Acadian Flycatcher,

Red-eyed and Yellow-throated Vireos, Wood Thrush, Northern Parula, Yellow-throated and Hooded Warblers, Summer and Scarlet Tanagers, Indigo Bunting, Orchard Oriole. *Migration*—Spotted and Solitary Sandpipers.

Best times to bird: April and May and again in September and October.

Directions: To reach the Edwin M. Griffin Nature Preserve from exit 21 on Interstate 26, drive east on U.S. Highway 29. After 6.3 miles turn right on Fernwood Drive, then in 0.9 mile turn left onto Beechwood Drive (don't turn at the Beechwood Drive that you reach in 0.4 mile). In 0.1 mile you will see the parking lot for the Edwin M. Griffin Nature Preserve. To reach Croft State Natural Area from exit 22 on I-26, drive east on Highway 296 (Reidville Road) toward Spartanburg. After 1.0 mile turn right onto Highway 295 (Southport Road), then in 6.0 miles turn right onto Highway 56 (Cedar Springs Road). Travel 2.2 miles and turn left on Dairy Ridge Road. In 0.3 mile turn right into the entrance for Croft State Natural Area. Follow the entrance road 3.1 miles to a four-way intersection and the park office. Continue straight on the entrance road to the parking area near the corral just behind the office.

The Birding

Right in the heart of Spartanburg lies the **Edwin M. Griffin Nature Preserve,** also known as the Cottonwood Nature Trail Preserve. The preserve has more than 5 miles of trails and is particularly good for songbirds during spring and fall migration. Follow the trail from the parking lot down to Lawsons Fork Creek. At the creek turn left on the Cottonwood Nature Trail, which runs along the creek bank. The forest along the creek often harbors a couple of Barred Owls and Red-shouldered Hawks year-round. During winter look for Winter Wren and Rusty Blackbird.

After 0.4 mile you will come to a bridge that crosses the creek and takes you to an open field. Scan the shrubs and forest edges for Yellow-breasted Chat and Indigo Bunting during summer. Cross back over the bridge and continue down the Cottonwood Nature Trail, and in 100 feet you will see a trail on the left with a sign that points to wetlands. The trail leads to a 550-foot-long boardwalk that crosses a beaver pond filled with dead snags. During migration the pond can be good for Solitary Sandpiper, and you may be able to find a few waterfowl. In the summer look for swifts, swallows, and martins flying low over the wetlands to catch insects. The dead snags provide nesting habitat for several woodpecker species, including Red-headed and Red-bellied Woodpeckers and Northern Flicker. At the end of the boardwalk is the start of the Highlands Trail, a 0.4-mile loop.

Cottonwood Nature Trail in Edwin M. Griffin Nature Preserve

This trail is another good spot to look for migrating warblers and thrushes in spring and fall.

Just south of Spartanburg is **Croft State Natural Area,** another outstanding area to look for songbirds during migration. The pine trees surrounding the parking area near the corral can be good year-round for Brown-headed Nuthatch and Pine Warbler. From the parking area, continue down the dirt entrance road on foot toward the horse stables. After 0.2 mile you will come to the trailhead for the Nature Trail on your right (it is the second trailhead). This trail is not only a beautiful hike, but also an excellent area to look for migrating warblers and thrushes during spring and fall.

Follow the Nature Trail downhill toward Fairforest Creek. After 0.3 mile the trail will fork and form a 1.2-mile loop. Take the left side of the fork and walk clockwise around the loop. During summer look for Yellow-billed Cuckoo, Yellow-throated and Red-eyed Vireos, Northern Parula, Hooded Warbler, and Summer Tanager. Eventually the trail will loop around and you will see Fairforest Creek. The trail runs parallel to the creek until you return to the start of the loop.

For a longer trail that runs through similar habitat in the park, try the Fosters Mill Trail, a 6.5-mile loop. This trail starts near the horse stables 0.1 mile farther up the road from the Nature Trail trailhead.

To check out a different habitat in the park, head back to the four-way intersection near the park office and turn right. The road leads down to a boat ramp on the edge of Lake Craig. Follow the small trail at the end of the parking lot that runs along the edge of the lake. The woods here can be good for migrating thrushes in spring and fall. After 0.3 mile the trail ends at a gravel road. During summer the woods can be good for Wood Thrush, Yellow-throated Warbler, and Ovenbird. Following the road left will take you to the Lake Craig Dam, where you have a great vantage point to view the lake. During winter look for Ring-necked and Ruddy Ducks and Red-breasted Merganser. Look for Spotted Sand-piper in spring and late summer, especially along the edge of the dam. During summer the forest edge along the dam is a good spot to look for Eastern Phoebe, Indigo Bunting, and Blue Grosbeak.

General Information

Edwin M. Griffin Nature Preserve is open from dawn to dusk year-round. Croft State Natural Area is open daily from 7:00 a.m. to 6:00 p.m. during winter and 7:00 a.m. to 9:00 p.m. in the summer. The entrance fee is $2 per person.

DeLorme atlas: Edwin M. Griffin Preserve, page 19, F7; Croft State Natural Area, page 19, G8.

Elevation: 550 to 700 feet.

Hazards: Venomous snakes, mosquitoes, ticks.

Nearest food, gas, lodging: Spartanburg.

Camping: Croft State Natural Area.

For more information: Edwin M. Griffin Nature Preserve; Croft State Natural Area.

36 Greenville Area

Habitats: Field, early successional, mixed pine-hardwood forest, river, pond, lake.

Specialty birds: *Resident*—Red-shouldered Hawk, Northern Bobwhite, Red-headed and Hairy Woodpeckers, Brown-headed and White-breasted Nuthatches, Field and Song Sparrows. *Summer*—Whip-poor-will; Acadian Flycatcher; Red-eyed Vireo; Wood Thrush; Black-and-white, Hooded, and Kentucky Warblers; Ovenbird; Yellow-breasted Chat; Scarlet Tanager; Blue Grosbeak; Indigo Bunting; Orchard Oriole. *Winter*—American Bittern; Wilson's Snipe; American Woodcock; Red-breasted Nuthatch; Winter Wren; Fox, White-crowned, and Lincoln's Sparrows; Rusty Blackbird. *Migration*—Spotted and Solitary Sandpipers.

Best times to bird: April and May and again in September and October.

Directions: To reach Bunched Arrowhead Heritage Preserve, follow U.S. Highway 25/276 north toward Traveler's Rest, where US 25 and US 276 split. Bear right and follow US 25 north. After 3.3 miles turn right on Tigerville Road, then in 0.9 mile turn left on Shelton Road. Travel 0.8 mile and turn right on McCauley Road. After 0.5 mile turn right into the parking lot for Bunched Arrowhead Heritage Preserve. To reach Paris Mountain State Park from the intersection of Highway 253 and Highway 291 in Greenville, drive north on Highway 253. After 2.5 miles bear left on State Park Road, then in 0.8 mile turn left at the entrance to Paris Mountain State Park. To reach Lake Conestee Nature Park, take exit 46B from Interstate 85 and follow Pleasantburg Road south. After 0.7 mile turn left on Old Augusta Road, then in 0.5 mile turn left on Fork Shoals Road. Travel 0.2 mile and turn left on Henderson Avenue. In 0.6 mile turn right into the gravel parking lot for Lake Conestee Nature Park.

The Birding

Bunched Arrowhead Heritage Preserve can be a good place to look for songbirds during migration. Bunched arrowhead is a species of small swamp wildflower, and the preserve protects one of the few remaining undisturbed areas containing the federally endangered plant. Walk the 1.3-mile loop trail clockwise. The trail takes you through mixed hardwood forest, fields, and swamp. The swamp that you reach within 0.1 mile of the parking lot can be excellent for migrating warblers and thrushes in spring and fall. During summer look for Acadian Flycatcher and Kentucky and Hooded Warblers. In the winter look for Winter Wren and Hermit Thrush.

Continue along the trail and after 0.6 mile you will see a couple grassy fields on the left side. During winter check the fields for sparrows, and in the summer check the fields and edges for breeding Yellow-breasted Chat, Blue Grosbeak, Indigo Bunting, and Field Sparrow. At the fields the main trail takes a sharp right, and in less than 100 feet you will see a small wetland on the left. Check the wetland for migrating waterfowl and shorebirds. In the winter the grassy area surrounding the wetland often contains numerous Swamp and Song Sparrows, with

View from Bunched Arrowhead Heritage Preserve parking lot, facing south with Paris Mountain in the background

lesser numbers of Fox and White-crowned Sparrows. It is also possible to find Lincoln's Sparrow in the wetland, but they are not to be expected. At dawn and dusk during winter, you may hear American Woodcock displaying in the farmland surrounding the preserve.

Paris Mountain State Park contains 1,540 acres of hardwood and mixed pine forest high in the hills just north of Greenville. The park has more than 12 miles of trails that lead through the forests and around several small lakes. Paris Mountain is at its best during spring and fall migration, when you can find flocks of migrating warblers, vireos, thrushes, tanagers, and other songbirds. Hairy Woodpecker and Brown-headed and White-breasted Nuthatches can all be found here year-round. The state park's close proximity to Greenville makes it a prime location for a fall birding trip if you can only spare a couple hours.

The park has many trails, but one of the best is the Sulphur Springs Trail, a 3.8-mile loop. From the Sulphur Springs picnic area, follow the trail clockwise around the loop. For the first 0.4 mile, the trail is a fairly easy hike as it follows Mountain Creek up to Mountain Lake. The lush, green forest along the banks of Mountain Creek is one of the best spots in the park to look for migrating songbirds. Once you pass Mountain Lake, the trail will continue to follow Mountain Creek for another 0.6 mile, but it becomes significantly steeper. During summer look for Wood Thrush, Hooded and Black-and-white Warblers, Ovenbird, and Scarlet Tanager.

If you are tired of climbing by the time you reach the Old Firetower Trail, you can follow this flat bike trail all the way to the east side of the Sulphur Springs Trail loop. As you hike along the ridge, listen for Red-breasted Nuthatch, which can be found in the pines during winter. From the ridge you will descend more than 500 feet on your way back to the Sulphur Springs picnic area. During spring and summer listen for Whip-poor-will at dusk along the park roads.

Lake Conestee Nature Park is a good place for a wide range of species, including many migrating songbirds. The park was opened to the public in 2006, and new trails and facilities are still being developed. Some 158 bird species have already been observed in the park, including 30 species of warblers. Before you get started, pick up a trail map from the kiosk in the parking lot. Begin by following the paved trail downhill. The early successional habitat along the upper part of the paved trail can be good for Indigo Bunting, Blue Grosbeak, and Orchard Oriole in summer. Look for Field and Song Sparrows year-round. During spring and fall the paved trail is one of the best areas in the park to look for migrating songbirds.

Follow the short connector path to the White Trail. The White Trail contains a wet, swampy area with a couple boardwalks, which is another good place to look for migrating songbirds. Follow the White Trail north until you reach the Yellow Trail and the bridge that crosses the northern section of the wetland. In the winter look for Swamp Sparrow and Rusty Blackbird from the bridge. During spring and fall look for Northern Waterthrush and other migrating songbirds. Once you reach the other side of the bridge, follow the Blue Trail clockwise until you reach the Reedy River. As the trail meanders along the bank of the river, keep an eye out for Spotted Sandpiper and migrating songbirds in spring and fall.

Continuing along the Blue Trail, you will pass through a beautiful hardwood forest with an open, grassy floor. This area was formerly a part of Lake Conestee and was completely underwater. An observation platform along the southern end of the Blue Trail provides a good view of the beaver pond. Permanent residents at the pond include Wood Duck, Red-shouldered Hawk, and Red-headed Woodpecker. Watch for shorebirds such as Solitary Sandpiper in spring and late summer and Wilson's Snipe during winter. In the summer look for Acadian and Great Crested Flycatchers, Red-eyed Vireo, Prothonotary Warbler, and Indigo Bunting.

For a good view of Lake Conestee, return to Fork Shoals Road and turn left. After 0.8 mile bear left on Conestee Road. Follow Conestee Road for 0.7 mile and turn left on Spanco Drive, a one-way street. Pull off the side of Spanco Drive and park. Scan the lake for American Bittern and waterfowl in winter. During spring watch for large flocks of swallows over the lake, including Purple Martin and Barn, Northern Rough-winged, and Tree Swallows.

General Information

Bunched Arrowhead Heritage Preserve is open daily from 8:00 a.m. to 6:00 p.m. during winter and 7:30 a.m. to 7:30 p.m. in the summer. Paris Mountain State Park is open daily from 8:00 a.m. to 6:00 p.m. during winter and 8:00 a.m. to 9:00 p.m. in the summer. Lake Conestee Nature Park is open year-round from dawn to dusk.

DeLorme atlas: Bunched Arrowhead Heritage Preserve, page 18, F1; Paris Mountain State Park, page 18, F1; Lake Conestee Nature Park, page 24, A2.

Elevation: 900 to 1,700 feet.

Hazards: Venomous snakes, ticks, poison ivy.

Nearest food, gas, lodging: Greenville.

Camping: Paris Mountain State Park.

For more information: Bunched Arrowhead Heritage Preserve; Paris Mountain State Park; Lake Conestee Nature Park.

37 Townville

Habitats: Farmland, pond, lake, mixed pine-hardwood forest.

Specialty birds: *Resident*—Wood Duck, Bald Eagle, Eurasian Collared-Dove, Horned Lark. *Summer*—Yellow-crowned Night-Heron, Black Rail, Cliff Swallow, Yellow Warbler, Field and Grasshopper Sparrows, Dickcissel. *Winter*—Common Loon; Horned Grebe; American Bittern; Greater White-fronted Goose; Sandhill Crane; Wilson's Snipe; Bonaparte's Gull; Winter Wren; American Pipit; White-crowned, Lincoln's, and Vesper Sparrows; Lapland Long-spur; Eastern Meadowlark; Brewer's Blackbird.

Best times to bird: November through March.

Directions: From exit 11 on Interstate 85, drive north on Highway 24. After 1.6 miles turn left on Fred Dobbins Road.

The Birding

Townville is an excellent place to look for winter rarities in South Carolina. One of the best locations for birding in this area is the **Dobbins Cattle Farm.** The farm is private property, so please confine all birding to the roadsides in this area. To reach the farm, follow the directions above and drive 1.7 miles to McAdams Road. Turn left on McAdams Road and drive 0.3 mile, until you see two ponds on the right. Pull off the road, and get out and scan the fields and ponds. *Do not* park in front of the feed troughs, because if you do, you will be in the way of the farmers.

In the winter the fields often have Wilson's Snipe, American Pipit, Horned Lark, and Savannah and Vesper Sparrows. Rarities such as Snow, Ross's, and Greater White-fronted Geese; Sandhill Crane; Short-eared Owl; Lapland Long-spur; and Brewer's Blackbird have all been found here in winter. Check the ponds for waterfowl and shorebirds during winter and migration. On a good day you can expect to find Northern Shoveler, Mallard, Green-winged Teal, Gadwall, Buffle-head, Ruddy Duck, Hooded Merganser, and Greater Yellowlegs, but keep an eye out for the occasional Northern Pintail, Redhead, or Upland Sandpiper. Year-round look for Eurasian Collared-Dove, Horned Lark, Field Sparrow, and Eastern Meadowlark. During summer you can often find several Grasshopper Sparrows singing in the fields and perhaps a Dickcissel if you are lucky.

Continue down McAdams Road for 0.5 mile and turn left onto a gated dirt road that leads into **Beaverdam Creek Wildlife Management Area.** Park along the side of the road without blocking the gate and walk into the WMA. The area contains agricultural fields that are flooded in winter to provide good waterfowl habitat. Besides waterfowl, this can be a good spot for American Bittern, sparrows, and other winter songbirds. Black Rails have occasionally been

American Pipit on a fence at Dobbins Cattle Farm

heard calling here at night during the summer. Also in the summer look for Yellow-crowned Night-Heron.

Head back to your car and backtrack 0.3 mile on McAdams Road to Gaines Road and turn right. The small wetlands at 0.4 mile on Gaines Road can be good for Swamp Sparrow and, if you are really lucky, you might find a Marsh or Sedge Wren. Continue another 0.4 mile and you will come to a stop sign at Fork School Road. If you continue straight across Fork School Road, you can park and walk the gated road into another section of Beaverdam Creek WMA. Before taking the road into the WMA, walk down Fork School Road to the bridge. In the summer the marsh here can occasionally produce Yellow Warbler or Least Bittern. During winter look for White-crowned, White-throated, and Swamp Sparrows (and perhaps Lincoln's Sparrow, but don't expect this one). The gated road into the WMA leads to a pond that can be good for waterfowl in winter.

Turn right (north) on Fork School Road and follow it 0.6 mile back to Fred Dobbins Road. The weedy fields along this section of Fork School Road are another good spot to look for breeding Dickcissels.

Lake Hartwell can be good for Common Loon, Horned Grebe, Bald Eagle, and Bonaparte's Gull in winter. Keep an eye out for rare birds; even Long-tailed Duck and Black or Surf Scoter are possible during migration. In the spring and summer, you should be able to find Cliff Swallows flying around the lake. Three boat ramps along Highway 24 near Townville provide easy access to view the lake: Camp Creek Access, Townville Recreation Area, and Coneross Access.

Follow Fred Dobbins Road east to Highway 24 and turn left. After 0.9 mile turn right on Oneal Ferry Road and follow signs to the Camp Creek Access. Continue another 1.1 miles west on Highway 24 and turn right on Coneross Road to reach the Townville Recreation Area. Go another 2.3 miles west on Highway 24 and turn right on Coneross Creek Road to reach the Coneross Access. All three boat ramps are well signed from Highway 24 and are denoted by boat ramp symbols in the DeLorme atlas.

General Information

Dobbins Cattle Farm is private property and should not be trespassed upon. Please confine all birding to roadsides only in the Dobbins Farm area. Parts of Beaverdam Creek WMA are closed from November 1 to February 1 to protect the wintering waterfowl.

DeLorme atlas: Page 22, E5.

Elevation: 680 to 760 feet.

Hazards: Poison ivy, ticks.

Nearest food, gas, lodging: Anderson.

Camping: Lake Hartwell State Recreation Area.

For more information: SCDNR Wildlife and Freshwater Fisheries Division.

Mountains

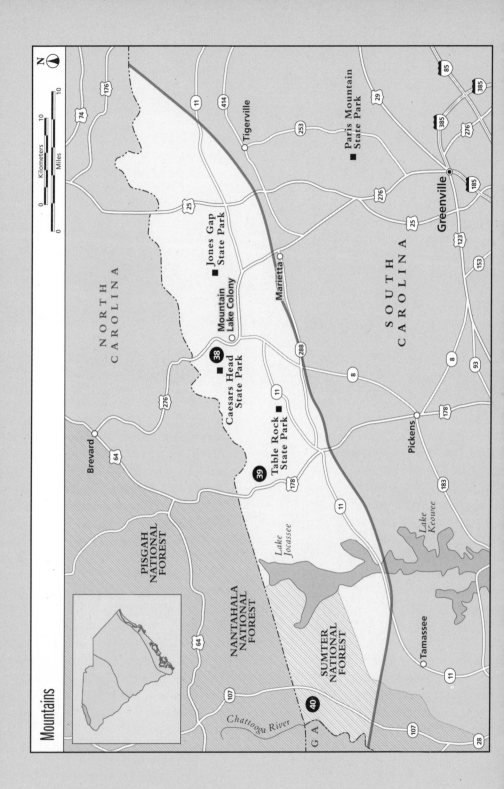

Mountains

38 Mountain Bridge Wilderness

Habitats: Field, hardwood forest, mixed pine-hardwood forest, stream, lake.

Specialty birds: *Resident*—Peregrine Falcon, Ruffed Grouse, American Woodcock, Common Raven, White-breasted Nuthatch, Dark-eyed Junco. *Summer*—Broad-winged Hawk; Eastern Phoebe; Acadian Flycatcher; Red-eyed and Blue-headed Vireos; Tree Swallow; Wood Thrush; Yellow, Black-throated Green, Black-throated Blue, Black-and-white, Chestnut-sided, and Worm-eating Warblers; American Redstart; Ovenbird; Louisiana Waterthrush; Scarlet Tanager. *Winter*—Bufflehead, Hooded Merganser, Red-breasted Nuthatch, Brown Creeper, Golden-crowned and Ruby-crowned Kinglets, Purple Finch, Pine Siskin. *Migration*—Cerulean Warbler, Rose-breasted Grosbeak.

Best times to bird: April through October.

Directions: To reach Jones Gap State Park from the intersection of Highway 288 and U.S. Highway 276 in Marietta, drive west on US 276 toward Cleveland. After 4.5 miles turn right on River Falls Road and follow it for 3.8 miles. At the fork in the road, bear left on Jones Gap Road and follow it 1.5 miles to the park entrance for Jones Gap State Park. To reach Caesars Head State Park from the intersection of Highway 11 and US 276 near Mountain Lake Colony, drive north on US 276. After 7.3 miles turn left into the parking lot for the Caesars Head State Park visitor center. To reach Table Rock State Park from the intersection of US 276 and Highway 11 (Cherokee Foothills Scenic Highway) near Mountain Lake Colony, drive west on Highway 11. After 5.3 miles turn left onto East Ellison Lane, which leads to the Table Rock State Park visitor center.

The Birding

The Mountain Bridge Wilderness is a narrow, 45-mile corridor that runs along the South Carolina–North Carolina border. The wilderness contains two of South Carolina's most popular state parks: Caesars Head and Jones Gap. Just 7 miles southwest of the Mountain Bridge Wilderness lies another popular area, Table Rock State Park. These parks are not only good for birding, but they also have some of the most scenic hiking trails in the state.

Jones Gap State Park is a good area to look for breeding songbirds in the summer, though the noise from streams can make it difficult to hear the birds. Swainson's Warbler can be found in the rhododendron thickets that border the trails. The Middle Saluda River, which runs through the park, is excellent for breeding Eastern Phoebe and Louisiana Waterthrush. Phoebe nests can often be found under the bridges near the visitor center. Other common breeding birds include Acadian Flycatcher, Red-eyed and Blue-headed Vireos, Wood Thrush, and Black-throated Green Warbler. Keep an eye out for American Woodcock in the damp areas near small streams.

There are several trails in the park that you can choose to hike. The Jones Gap Trail follows the Middle Saluda River for 5.3 miles to Caesars Head State Park. Although the trail ascends nearly 2,000 feet from start to finish, the climb is

View of Table Rock Mountain from the Table Rock State Park visitor center

gradual, making this the easiest trail for birding in the park. For a more challenging hike, try the Rim-of-the-Gap Trail, which starts a few hundred feet from the Jones Gap Trail trailhead. The very strenuous 5.2-mile hike offers ridgetop views of Jones Gap and the chance to escape from the roaring Middle Saluda River. As you leave Jones Gap State Park on River Falls Road, keep an ear out for singing Yellow Warblers along the shrubby edges of farm fields.

Caesars Head State Park has the most accessible peak in the Mountain Bridge Wilderness, since you can drive all the way to the top. Stop at the visitor center for trail maps and other information. One of the main attractions of the park is the view from the top of Caesars Head, at the north end of the parking lot near the water tower. From late August through October, the rocky outcrop is the best location in the state to see migrating raptors. If you visit during mid-September, you may see hundreds or even thousands of Broad-winged Hawks. Other raptors commonly seen from the hawk watch include Bald Eagle; Osprey; Cooper's, Sharp-shinned, and Red-tailed Hawks; and Peregrine Falcon. Golden Eagle, Merlin, and Mississippi Kite are usually sighted a couple times each year. Several knowledgeable volunteers, also known as "Caesars Head Wing Nuts," are often available to help point out hawks and assist in identification. Half of the fun is learning the hawk-watching lingo, such as "line out," "kettle," or "kiting." To see the annual species totals from the hawk watch, check out www.hmana.org/watches.php.

You have a good chance year-round of seeing Common Ravens and Peregrine Falcons, which nest on the cliffs of Table Rock Mountain. The Peregrine Falcons often like to perch just out of sight beneath Caesars Head, but you may catch them coming or going if you are patient. The Peregrines seem to have a particular hatred for the local Red-tailed Hawks and can perform an amazing aerial show for the lucky observer. During summer the lookout is the best spot in South Carolina to look for breeding Chestnut-sided Warblers, but even here you will need to get lucky to find one. Dark-eyed Juncos are a common sight year-round on the rocks, and the forest atop Caesars Head can be good for migrating warblers and other songbirds during spring and fall. In the winter keep an eye out for Purple Finch, Pine Siskin, and perhaps even Red Crossbill, which have nested here.

An excellent trail for birding and scenery within Caesars Head State Park is the **Raven Cliff Falls Trail.** To reach the trailhead, continue north on US 276 for 2.2 miles, then turn right into the parking lot. The trail starts on the opposite side of US 276 from the parking lot and follows the ridge 1.7 miles to the intersection with the Gum Gap Trail. This is a very flat, easy hike, as the trail follows the ridge, while having the added benefit of a great view. During spring and fall you can often find migrating warblers, tanagers, grosbeaks, and orioles feeding in the tops of trees along the trail. Since you are atop the ridge, many of these treetop foraging birds can be seen at eye level by looking downslope. In the summer this is a great area to see Black-throated Green, Black-throated Blue, Black-and-white, and Worm-eating Warblers; American Redstart; Ovenbird; and Scarlet Tanager. If you follow the trail to its end, about 0.5 mile beyond the intersection with the Gum Gap Trail, you will come to an observation platform with a good view of Raven Cliff Falls. Watch for Common Ravens nesting on the cliff near the waterfall during the summer months.

Table Rock State Park offers some of the most impressive scenery in South Carolina and good high-elevation birding as well. The visitor center has maps available for the more than 12 miles of trails within the park. Before you leave the visitor center parking lot, you may want to walk down to the lake and scan for waterfowl during winter. Bufflehead and Hooded Merganser are the most commonly observed, but every now and then you may find a Ring-necked or Ruddy Duck. During spring and fall scan the trees along the lakeshore for flocks of migrating warblers and other songbirds. In the summer Tree Swallows can often be found nesting in the boxes along the lawn.

The big attraction at the park is the **Table Rock Mountain Trail,** which has some of the finest views in the park. Be sure to arrive early if you want to beat the crowds. The 3.6-mile trail can be quite steep in places and involves an overall elevation gain of nearly 2,000 feet. The first 0.6 mile of the hike is on the Carrick Creek Trail. During summer look for Black-throated Green Warbler in hemlocks along the Carrick Creek Trail. Blue-headed Vireo, Black-and-white and Worm-eating Warblers, Ovenbird, and Scarlet Tanager are often easy to find during

Hawk-watchers on lookout at Caesars Head State Park. JEFF CATLIN PHOTO

summer as you climb to the summit along the Table Rock Mountain Trail. In the winter you can often find Yellow-bellied Sapsucker and Golden-crowned and Ruby-crowned Kinglets along the trail, and maybe even a Brown Creeper, Red-breasted Nuthatch, Purple Finch, or Pine Siskin. The rocky outcroppings at the top have a fantastic view and are a great place to look for Common Raven and Peregrine Falcon year-round.

General Information

Both Jones Gap State Park and Caesars Head State Park are open daily from 9:00 a.m. to 6:00 p.m. during winter and 9:00 a.m. to 9:00 p.m. in the summer. Table Rock State Park is open daily from 7:00 a.m. to 7:00 p.m. during winter and 7:00 a.m. to 9:00 p.m. in the summer. The entrance fee is $2 for adults at all three parks.

DeLorme atlas: Jones Gap State Park, page 17, C9; Caesars Head State Park, page 17, D8; Table Rock State Park, page 17, E7.

Elevation: 1,200 to 3,200 feet.

Hazards: Venomous snakes, ticks, poison ivy.

Nearest food, gas, lodging: Greenville.

Camping: Table Rock State Park.

For more information: Jones Gap State Park; Caesars Head State Park; Table Rock State Park.

39 Jocassee Gorges

Habitats: Stream, hardwood forest, mixed pine-hardwood forest, early successional.

Specialty birds: *Resident*—Wild Turkey, Ruffed Grouse, American Woodcock, Great Horned Owl, Hairy and Pileated Woodpeckers, White-breasted Nuthatch, Dark-eyed Junco. *Summer*—Broad-winged Hawk; Wood Thrush; Red-eyed and Blue-headed Vireos; Northern Parula; Swainson's, Kentucky, Hooded, Worm-eating, Black-and-white, Black-throated Blue, and Black-throated Green Warblers; Ovenbird; Louisiana Waterthrush; Scarlet Tanager. *Winter*—Red-breasted Nuthatch, Golden-crowned Kinglet, Brown Creeper, Winter Wren.

Best times to bird: April through October.

Directions: To reach Sassafras Mountain from the intersection of Highway 11 (Cherokee Foothills Scenic Highway) and U.S. Highway 178, drive north on US 178. After 7.2 miles turn right on F. Van Clayton Highway, but don't let the name fool you, because this is no highway.

The Birding

Jocassee Gorges contains roughly 43,500 acres of mountain wilderness owned by the South Carolina Department of Natural Resources. According to Native American legend, *Jocassee* means "Place of the Lost One," and it is easy to see how the area got its name. The other part of this area's name is derived from a series of rugged gorges created over time by fast-flowing streams heading toward Lake Jocassee.

Follow F. Van Clayton Highway as the small road winds its way up the steep slopes of **Sassafras Mountain** into the Jim Timmerman Natural Resource Area. Sassafras Mountain is the highest mountain in South Carolina and is excellent for high-elevation birds such as Ruffed Grouse, Common Raven, and Black-throated Blue Warbler. In the summer listen for Swainson's Warbler in the dense rhododendron bushes that border F. Van Clayton Highway, but beware, because Louisiana Waterthrush and Hooded Warbler, which can sound similar, are commonly heard along the roadsides as well.

Take F. Van Clayton Highway 1.3 miles to Chimney Top Gap, where you will find a trail crossing for the Foothills Trail. Pull off the road and walk either direction on the trail, listening for Worm-eating, Hooded, Black-throated Green, and Black-and-white Warblers during summer. In the spring and fall, keep an eye out for flocks of migrating warblers, thrushes, tanagers, and other songbirds. If there is no room to park alongside the road, you can park in the lot 500 feet down the road on the left.

Continue up the highway for 3.2 miles and the road will dead-end at a parking lot. The parking lot at the top is a good spot to look for migrating warblers and thrushes in the spring and fall. Hike the trails from the parking lot in summer and you should be able to find Red-eyed and Blue-headed Vireos; Wood Thrush; Black-throated Green, Black-throated Blue, Black-and-white, Worm-eating, and

Hooded Warblers; Ovenbird; and Scarlet Tanager. Cerulean, Chestnut-sided, Canada, and Blackburnian Warblers have also occasionally been found on Sassafras Mountain in summer.

The Foothills Trail crosses the top of Sassafras Mountain, and there are two hikes that you can take from the parking lot. If you follow the Foothills Trail uphill from the parking lot along the paved road, after 0.1 mile you will reach the summit of Sassafras Mountain. The views from the top are not nearly as spectacular as the view from Table Rock Mountain or Caesars Head, but you do get the satisfaction of having been atop the highest point in South Carolina. From the summit, the trail descends down the western slope of the mountain and after 0.4 mile you will intersect with F. Van Clayton Highway. Turn left and follow the road 0.3 mile back to the parking lot.

For a longer hike, you can follow the Foothills Trail downhill from the parking lot toward Hickorynut Mountain. This section is a good spot to look for Ruffed Grouse year-round, and you may be able to find Canada Warbler in the rhododendron during the summer. The grouse are most easily detected when the males are drumming in March and early April. The trail remains relatively flat as it runs along the ridge, which makes for easier birding. After 1.8 miles you will reach Hickorynut Mountain and the trail will begin a steep descent as it heads toward Emory Gap. If you follow the trail 3.5 miles beyond Hickorynut Mountain, it leads to Pinnacle Mountain, just inside the western border of Table Rock State Park.

Once you are finished birding Sassafras Mountain, return to US 178 and turn right. In 0.9 mile you will cross a small bridge over Eastatoe Creek. After crossing the bridge, turn left on Laurel Valley and take the upper gravel road, not the paved road. Follow the windy gravel road 0.2 mile uphill to the parking lot for the Foothills Trail and **Eastatoe Creek Heritage Preserve.** Though the preserve does not have many of the high-elevation specialty birds found at Sassafras Mountain, it does offer good opportunities to look for Swainson's Warbler during summer and migrating songbirds in the spring and fall.

From the parking lot, follow the gravel road on foot 0.1 mile to an old logging road with a red gate on the left. The logging road is the start of the trail. The first 1.5 miles of the hike are relatively flat and offer easy birding as you follow the ridge. Rhododendron bushes and regenerating clear-cuts along this section offer excellent breeding habitat for Swainson's and Kentucky Warblers. During spring and fall you will likely encounter large flocks of migrating warblers and other songbirds. The last 0.8 mile of the trail descends nearly 500 feet to the beautiful gorges of Eastatoe Creek. During summer scan the creek for Louisiana Waterthrush and Eastern Phoebe. The primitive campground along the creek frequently hosts a pair of Great Horned Owls. In the winter the campground is often a good area to look for Red-breasted Nuthatch, Brown Creeper, and Golden-crowned Kinglet.

General Information

The parking lot and trails in Jocassee Gorges are open year-round twenty-four hours a day. There are no facilities at Sassafras Mountain.

DeLorme atlas: Page 17, D7.

Elevation: 1,350 to 3,554 feet.

Hazards: Venomous snakes, poison ivy, ticks.

Nearest food, gas, lodging: Gas and food in Sunset; lodging in Easley.

Camping: Table Rock State Park.

For more information: Jim Timmerman Natural Resource Area; SCDNR Wildlife and Freshwater Fisheries Division.

40 Sumter National Forest—Andrew Pickens District

Habitats: Stream, river, pine forest, hardwood forest.

Specialty birds: *Resident*—Hairy and Pileated Woodpeckers, Eastern Phoebe, White-breasted and Red-breasted Nuthatches, Golden-crowned Kinglet, Brown Creeper, Red Crossbill. *Summer*—Acadian Flycatcher; Wood Thrush; Red-eyed and Blue-headed Vireos; Northern Parula; Black-throated Green, Black-throated Blue, Yellow-throated, Black-and-white, Worm-eating, and Hooded Warblers; American Redstart; Ovenbird; Louisiana Water-thrush; Scarlet Tanager; Dark-eyed Junco. *Winter*—Northern Saw-whet Owl, Winter Wren, Purple Finch, Pine Siskin.

Best times to bird: April through October.

Directions: To reach Burrell's Ford from the intersection of Highway 28 and Highway 107 near Mountain Rest, drive north on Highway 107. After 10.2 miles turn left on Burrell's Ford Road (FS Road 708). To reach Walhalla State Fish Hatchery from the intersection of Highway 28 and Highway 107 near Mountain Rest, drive north on Highway 107. After 11.7 miles turn left at the entrance to the fish hatchery.

The Birding

One of the best spots in South Carolina to find Red-breasted Nuthatch, Brown Creeper, and perhaps even Red Crossbill is **Burrell's Ford,** which lies along the banks of the beautiful Chattooga River in the Ellicott Rock Wilderness. Follow Burrell's Ford Road as it heads downhill toward the Chattooga River. The road parallels a stream surrounded by rhododendron bushes, which is good habitat to listen for singing Canada Warblers in spring. During winter try driving the road at night and listening for Northern Saw-whet Owls. They aren't easy to find, but this is one of the best areas in the state.

After 2.2 miles you will come to a parking area on the left. There are numerous trails in this area, and if you have the time, you could spend the entire day hiking. The Foothills Trail crosses FS Road 708 about 50 feet uphill from the parking lot. To hike a 2.7-mile loop, follow the Foothills Trail north from the parking lot toward the Walhalla State Fish Hatchery. The trail zigzags its way uphill through a mix of white pines and hemlock. Search the pine and hemlock trees year-round for Hairy Woodpecker, Brown Creeper, Red-breasted Nuthatch, and Golden-crowned Kinglet. If you are lucky, you may find Red Crossbill, but don't count on it. In the summer you should be able to find Blue-headed Vireo; Wood Thrush; Black-and-white, Black-throated Green, and Worm-eating Warblers; and Ovenbird. During winter keep an eye out for Purple Finch and Pine Siskin.

At 0.6 mile from the parking lot, you will come to a fork in the path. Bear left at the fork, following signs for the Chattooga Trail. Follow this small path

Chattooga River near Burrell's Ford

downhill for 1.1 miles, where you will come to an intersection with the Chattooga Trail. The intersection of the two trails has some nice large hemlocks and pines, which are often a good place to look for Golden-crowned Kinglet, Brown Creeper, and Red-breasted Nuthatch year-round. The relatively flat Chattooga Trail follows the eastern bank of the cool, clear Chattooga River. Turn left on the trail and follow it 0.8 mile back to Burrell's Ford Road. The Chattooga Trail is excellent for migrating songbirds during spring and fall. In the summer look for Acadian Flycatcher; Wood Thrush; Northern Parula; Black-throated Green, Black-throated Blue, Yellow-throated, and Hooded Warblers; Ovenbird; and Louisiana Waterthrush. Return to the parking lot by turning left on Burrell's Ford Road and following it 0.3 mile uphill. You can also park along the road near the Chattooga Trail if you prefer to hike only that section of the loop.

The **Walhalla State Fish Hatchery** is one of the best places in the entire state to visit for migrating songbirds. During spring and summer you should have no trouble finding American Redstart; Ovenbird; Louisiana Waterthrush; and Black-throated Green, Black-throated Blue, Hooded, and Black-and-white Warblers. After following the entrance road 0.2 mile, you will see a trail crossing for the Foothills Trail. Following the trail in either direction you should be able to find Black-and-white and Worm-eating Warblers, Ovenbird, and Scarlet Tanager during summer.

Continue on the entrance road, which winds its way downhill to the fish hatchery, and take advantage of several small pullouts where you can get off the road and listen for birds. After 1.5 miles you will see a small parking area on the right. There is a short, 0.2-mile loop trail at the end of the parking lot that passes by a small pond. The tall hemlocks that surround the parking lot offer good potential for Blackburnian Warbler during migration and perhaps even summer. The rhododendron bushes around the lot often contain Black-throated Blue and Hooded Warblers in summer.

Continue down the entrance road 0.2 mile to the parking lot near the fish hatchery. From the parking lot, you can walk the trail through the picnic area or walk along the entrance road. The massive hemlock trees in the picnic area are great for breeding Black-throated Green Warblers, and some are even bold enough to nest just above the picnic tables! You may even be able to find a few breeding Golden-crowned Kinglets or Dark-eyed Juncos. During winter you may hear Northern Saw-whet Owls at night if you are lucky. The East Fork Trail used to start at the end of the picnic area, but there is no longer a bridge across East Fork Creek. If you wish to hike the trail, you may have to get your feet wet or wait for a new bridge to be built. Walking along the creek, you can often find Eastern Phoebe, Acadian Flycatcher, and Louisiana Waterthrush in the summer.

General Information

Burrell's Ford is open year-round twenty-four hours a day. The roads and trails at the Walhalla State Fish Hatchery are open year-round from sunrise to sunset.

DeLorme atlas: Burrell's Ford, page 16, F3; Walhalla Fish Hatchery, page 16, F3.

Elevation: 2,000 to 3,000 feet.

Hazards: Venomous snakes, poison ivy, ticks.

Nearest food, gas, lodging: Food and gas in Walhalla; lodging in Seneca.

Camping: Oconee State Park or primitive camping at Burrell's Ford.

For more information: Oconee State Park; Sumter National Forest—Andrew Pickens District; Walhalla State Fish Hatchery.

Appendix A: Pelagic Birding in South Carolina

Pelagic birding in South Carolina may not be quite as good as the trips you can take out of Hatteras, North Carolina, but you can still get good looks at some of the more common species for a low fare. In Charleston you can take a trip aboard the *Thunderstar*. Late May through early August offers the highest diversity of pelagic birds, but check Appendix D if you are hoping to see a particular species.

Day trips take you within about 15 miles of the Gulf Stream, where you can usually find Cory's, Greater, and Audubon's Shearwaters; Black-capped Petrel; Wilson's Storm-Petrel; Red-necked and Red Phalaropes; and Sooty and Bridled Terns in the appropriate season. Magnificent Frigatebird, White-tailed Tropicbird, Northern Fulmar, Manx and Sooty Shearwaters, Leach's and Band-rumped Storm-Petrels, Roseate and Arctic Terns, and Brown Noddy are all seen occasionally but are not to be expected. Also keep an eye out for other interesting creatures such as flying fish, sharks, swordfish, dolphins, whales, and sea turtles.

Pelagic trips are unpredictable, so don't get discouraged if you have a bad day. You will nearly always see something, but it may take hours of searching to find a couple species. Sometimes it is worth paying the extra money to fish, just in case the birding is slow.

For more information and current prices, visit www.thunderstarfishing.com or call (843) 881-2792 or (843) 884-7586. As of this writing, costs were $80 to fish and $40 for non-fishing passengers. For the truly adventurous, the *Thunderstar* offers overnight trips, which will take you out into the Gulf Stream and improve your chances of finding some of the pelagic birds. There are also a number of charter, or "head," boats that leave out of Murrells Inlet near Georgetown. For information about pelagic trips out of Murrells Inlet, contact Captain Dick's Marina at (866) 577-FISH or visit www.captdicks.com.

Appendix B: South Carolina Birding Calendar

This appendix will help you determine where you should focus your birding for each month of the year. It will help answer questions such as: Where should I go birding in December? When is the best time to catch the fall hawk migration? When do the Wood Storks begin nesting? When should I go on a pelagic trip? When is the peak of shorebird migration at the Orangeburg Super Sod farm? The birding calendar will ensure that you don't miss any of the major birding events that occur throughout the year in South Carolina. Some people may tell you there are slow times of the year for birding, but if you look hard enough, there is nearly always something about which to get excited.

January: Wintering waterfowl reach their peak numbers and this is the best month to look for them. Many of the good sites to look for waterfowl are closed, but there are a few good areas open such as Huntington Beach State Park, Cape Romain National Wildlife Refuge, Savannah NWR, Santee NWR, Magnolia Plantation, and Dobbins Farm. Bald Eagles, Great Horned Owls, and Great Blue Herons begin nesting. Toward the end of the month, Barred Owls and Eastern Screech-Owls will begin courtship, which can be a good time to listen for them. Short-eared Owls are not easy to find, but look for them at dusk flying over the salt marsh at Folly Beach or Cape Romain NWR or over the fields at Dobbins Farm.

    February: Bear Island Wildlife Management Area, Donnelley WMA, and Broad River Waterfowl Management Area reopen to public use in February, so get out there and look for waterfowl before they are gone. Waterfowl begin migrating toward the end of the month, so you never know when or where rarities such as Common Goldeneye, White-winged Scoter, or Common Merganser may show up. Keep an eye out for the first Purple Martins, which can begin to arrive early in the month. Many resident songbirds such as Carolina Wren, Tufted Titmouse, Brown Thrasher, Pine Warbler, and Northern Cardinal will begin singing more frequently in February. If you are trying to learn bird songs, this is a great month to start practicing. If you wait until March or April, the number of species that are singing may overwhelm you. Fish Crows return to the piedmont in the middle of the month. Uncommon winter resident songbirds such as White-eyed Vireo, Blue-gray Gnatcatcher, Yellow-throated Warbler, and Common Yellowthroat will begin singing toward the end of the month.

    March: Spring is so close that you can almost taste it. Trees are starting to leaf out, resident songbirds are singing, and daytime temperatures can reach 80 degrees Fahrenheit. Some of the early migrating songbirds such as Northern Parula, Prothonotary Warbler, and Louisiana Waterthrush begin to show up in March. Congaree National Park, Congaree Bluffs Heritage Preserve, and Francis Beidler Forest Audubon Sanctuary are usually good areas to look for the early migrants.

Wood Storks, Great Egrets, and Anhingas all begin gathering in their large breeding rookeries during the latter half of the month. Dungannon Heritage Preserve, Magnolia Plantation, Donnelley WMA, Sea Pines Forest Preserve, and Pinckney Island NWR often provide good views of wading-bird rookeries. It is a real treat to watch the birds in full breeding plumage as they perform elaborate courtship displays and try to find the perfect stick for their nests.

Tree Swallows are abundant in early March, and by the end of the month the other swallow species begin to arrive. Bear Island WMA, Santee Coastal Reserve, and Cape Romain NWR are usually good places to look for large numbers of the migrating swallows. Toward the middle of the month, migrating shorebirds and seabirds start to show up, such as Greater and Lesser Yellowlegs, Black-necked Stilt, Wilson's Plover, Royal Tern, and Black Skimmer.

April: This is the month when spring really comes alive. At the beginning of April, songbird migrants are starting to trickle in, but by the end of the month, songbird migration is at its peak. The best places to see migrating warblers and thrushes are in the mountains and piedmont. Try visiting Walhalla State Fish Hatchery, Sassafras Mountain, Table Rock State Park, Caesars Head State Park, Lake Conestee Nature Park, Edwin M. Griffin Nature Preserve, Croft State Natural Area, Landsford Canal State Park, Lynch's Woods Park, and Saluda Shoals Park. A good spot to see migrant and breeding warblers, especially Prothonotary Warbler, not too far from the coast is the Francis Beidler Forest Audubon Sanctuary. A great way to learn more about the birds of Francis Beidler Forest is to take a guided tour during their Wine & Warblers event held this month.

Seabirds such as Least, Gull-billed, and Sandwich Terns begin showing up during the middle of the month. Most of the specialty breeding birds, such as Swallow-tailed and Mississippi Kites, Purple Gallinule, Swainson's Warbler, and Painted Bunting, will have returned by the middle of April and will become more and more numerous later in the month. Bachman's Sparrows begin singing at the beginning of the month, which makes them much easier to find. At the end of the month, many of the smaller egrets and herons will begin nesting in large rookeries. The best views of rookeries can be found at Dungannon Heritage Preserve, Magnolia Plantation, Donnelley WMA, and Pinckney Island NWR. During late April you will have your best chance of finding migrating Whimbrel and White-rumped Sandpipers.

May: This is my favorite month of the year for birding. You can find more bird species in late April and early May than any other time of year in South Carolina. A weeklong trip in early May that includes areas on the coast and in the mountains should tally up a list of over 160 species of birds! Early in the month is the peak of spring songbird migration in South Carolina, and to really experience it, you should visit sites in the piedmont and mountains. To look for migrating songbirds, try the same areas mentioned above in April.

While you can find some songbird migrants in the coastal region, the main attraction there is shorebird migration. At the beginning of the month, you should be able to find at least six species of terns and over twenty species of shorebirds. May is a great time to photograph shorebirds, as most are in their more attractive breeding plumage. Male Yellow-breasted Chats can be found performing song-flight displays, an interesting behavior that the male uses to attract a female and defend his territory. Young Barred Owls begin fledging and can be seen flying around with their parents begging for food, even in daylight hours. By the end of the month, early breeding songbirds such as White-eyed Vireo, Northern Parula, and Yellow-throated and Pine Warblers will start fledging their young too. This is a good month for a pelagic trip out of Charleston or Murrells Inlet to look for shearwaters and storm-petrels. (See Appendix A for more information about these trips.)

Honestly, the only negative thing that can be said about May is that mosquitoes and other biting flies start to make their presence known, especially in the salt marsh habitats.

June: This is a good month to look for some of the breeding birds that you might have missed in May, such as Swallow-tailed Kite, Purple Gallinule, Swainson's and Kentucky Warblers, Painted Bunting, and Bachman's Sparrow. Most of the migrating shorebirds will have passed through South Carolina by early June, and the remainder of the month is pretty slow for shorebirds. The end of the month is a great time to look for young songbirds and shorebirds. Keep an eye out for adult songbirds with insects in their bills, as they are probably headed back to a nest to feed their young. Likewise, adult terns and skimmers can often be seen flying back to their nests with fish. If you find a Purple Gallinule, keep an eye out for the small, black, downy chicks that are often not too far behind.

July: Songbird activity decreases dramatically this month, and many of the breeding species become much more difficult to locate. So the best thing to do is focus your attention on the shorebirds, which start returning from their breeding grounds in the Arctic during the middle of July. Toward the end of the month you may want to try a visit to the Orangeburg Super Sod farm to look for Upland and Pectoral Sandpipers.

The last half of the month is the best time to look for large foraging flocks of Swallow-tailed and Mississippi Kites as they prepare to migrate south. Flock sizes vary, but occasionally you can see more than a hundred kites in a single flock. The largest flocks of kites are often found catching insects around hay fields and old rice fields at such sites as Santee Delta WMA, Savannah NWR, and Caw Caw County Park.

A visit to Cape Romain NWR will often produce good numbers of Reddish Egrets, but you can also find them at Huntington Beach State Park, Pitt Street Bridge, and Fish Haul Creek Park. Hundreds of thousands of Purple Martins begin roosting on Bomb Island in Lake Murray this month in what is perhaps the largest martin roost in the country. South Carolina Wildlife Federation organizes a boat tour of Bomb Island and the martin roost around mid-July. Visit www.scwf .org or call (803) 256-0670 for more information.

August: Shorebird migration is in full swing, with the peak of fall migration around the middle of the month. Expect to see large flocks of Marbled Godwit, Red Knot, Short-billed Dowitcher, Western Sandpiper, and Semipalmated Plover. Large concentrations of terns gather on the beaches, including Least, Black, Common, Forster's, Royal, Caspian, Sandwich, and Gull-billed Terns. Some good places to look for the shorebirds and terns are Huntington Beach State Park, Cape Romain NWR, Folly Beach, and Hunting Island State Park.

During the beginning of the month, you may still be able to find large foraging flocks of Swallow-tailed and Mississippi Kites (see July for best sites). Early songbird migration is under way, with birds such as Yellow, Prairie, Cerulean, and Worm-eating Warblers; Northern Parula; and Louisiana Waterthrush all beginning to move. This is probably the best month for finding Roseate Spoonbill at Cape Romain NWR (also check Bear Island WMA or South Tibwin Plantation). Reddish Egrets can often be found at Cape Romain NWR, Huntington Beach State Park, and Hilton Head Island. August is also the best month to look for Upland Sandpipers at the Orangeburg Super Sod farm.

The beginning of the month is a good time to visit the Kathwood Ponds at Silver Bluff Audubon Sanctuary to look for Wood Storks. Be sure to call ahead to arrange a tour, as the ponds are often closed to protect the storks. Silver Bluff Audubon Sanctuary hosts a festival this month called Storks & Corks, which is an excellent way to see the storks and sample some good wine. This is also a good month to try a pelagic trip onboard the *Thunderstar* or a head boat out of Murrells Inlet. You have good chances of seeing Cory's, Greater, and Audubon's Shearwaters; Wilson's Storm-Petrel; and Sooty and Bridled Terns.

Late August is peak hurricane season along the South Carolina coast, and should one hit, you will definitely want to evacuate. The days following a hurricane or tropical storm can often be very productive for birding. Keep an eye out for pelagic birds such as Magnificent Frigatebird, Wilson's Storm-Petrel, and Sooty Tern that can get blown in close to shore or even as far inland as Lake Murray.

September: The beginning of the month is the peak of shorebird migration at the Orangeburg Super Sod farm and the best time to look for Buff-breasted Sandpiper. Common Nighthawks can be seen flying in large migratory flocks, sometimes numbering in the hundreds early in the month. September is probably the best month for fall warbler migration, which is at its peak in the latter half of the month. Thrushes, tanagers, and grosbeaks often gather in large flocks in dogwood trees and fruiting shrubs to feast on berries. Keep an eye on the weather forecast for any cold fronts moving into South Carolina. The migrating warblers and other birds will often show up in big numbers the morning after a cold front moves through the area. Some good sites to observe the fall warblers and other migrating songbirds are Patriots Point, James Island County Park, Folly Beach, Cape Romain NWR, Myrtle Beach State Park, Sea Pines Forest Preserve, Santee NWR, Carolina Sandhills NWR, Lynch's Woods Park, Saluda Shoals Park, Landsford Canal State Park, Lake Conestee Nature Park, Paris Mountain State Park, Caesars Head State Park, Walhalla State Fish Hatchery, Burrell's Ford, and Sassafras Mountain.

The last half of the month is excellent for observing hundreds of Broad-winged Hawks as they pass through South Carolina on their way to their wintering grounds in Central and South America. The best site to observe the hawks is from the hawk watch at Caesars Head State Park, but you can also see them at Congaree Bluffs Heritage Preserve and along the edge of the coast at sites such as South Tibwin Plantation, Fort Johnson, and Fish Haul Creek Park. On an exceptional day at Caesars Head, you may see more than a thousand Broad-winged Hawks. Also look for other migrating raptors, such as Sharp-shinned and Cooper's Hawks, Bald Eagle, Peregrine Falcon, and Merlin.

October: This is an excellent month for songbird migration. Expect good fall-outs of warblers when a cold front passes through, especially American Redstart and Black-throated Blue and Palm Warblers. Look for migrating songbirds in the same areas mentioned above in September. October is another good month to observe hawk migration. Watch for Bald Eagle, American Kestrel, Merlin, Peregrine Falcon, Osprey, and Sharp-shinned and Cooper's Hawks. Again, look for migrating hawks and other raptors in the same areas mentioned for September.

Shorebird migration at the Orangeburg Super Sod farm begins winding down in October, but you have good chances of finding American Golden-Plover. Wintering songbirds such as Yellow-bellied Sapsucker, Eastern Phoebe, Hermit Thrush, Yellow-rumped Warbler, Ruby-crowned Kinglet, and White-throated Sparrow begin to show up in small numbers throughout the state. Many important waterfowl areas (Bear Island WMA, Donnelley WMA, Broad River Waterfowl Management Area) close to the public in early October and do not reopen until February. It is best to call ahead and make sure the area is open before you start your trip.

November: Expect large numbers of wintering songbirds to arrive with each cold front. This is a great month for sparrow migration, and you may even find rarities such as White-crowned, Lincoln's, LeConte's, or Henslow's Sparrows. The best areas to look for sparrows are Lewis Ocean Bay Heritage Preserve, Lynchburg Savanna Heritage Preserve, Townville, Santee NWR, Saluda Shoals Park, and Folly Beach. Look for large numbers of Saltmarsh and Nelson's Sharp-tailed Sparrows at Huntington Beach State Park, Folly Beach, and Pitt Street Bridge. Gray Catbirds can still be seen in large numbers at the beginning of the month. Waterfowl such as Northern Shoveler and Ring-necked and Ruddy Ducks begin to show up in small numbers during November. Try visiting

Townville, Santee NWR, Cape Romain NWR, or Huntington Beach State Park to look for the early waterfowl.

December: Most of the wintering waterfowl species have now returned, and numbers will continue to build throughout the month. Thousands of Canada Geese can be seen in the fields at Santee NWR, and Snow, Ross's, and Greater White-fronted Geese can occasionally be found with them. Some other good sites to see waterfowl are Cape Romain NWR, Savannah NWR, Huntington Beach State Park, Townville, and Folly Beach. Other winter residents such as Common and Red-throated Loons, Horned Grebe, Northern Gannet, and Purple Sandpiper have returned as well. The hardwood swamps at Congaree National Park and Francis Beidler Forest Audubon Sanctuary are good places to look for winter resident songbirds such as Brown Creeper, Hermit Thrush, Winter Wren, Golden-crowned Kinglet, and Fox Sparrow. You may also be able to find a few overwintering White-eyed Vireos and Black-and-white or Yellow-throated Warblers in the swamps.

Christmas Birds Counts are conducted all over the state in the latter half of the month. These counts can be a great way for novices to team up with experienced birders to learn more about birding areas. Be sure to check the reports for any rare birds that may have been sighted on the Christmas Bird Counts.

Appendix C: Specialty Birds of South Carolina

This appendix contains detailed information on where to locate more than 175 of South Carolina's bird species. Many of these species are among the most sought-after by out-of-state birders, such as Swallow-tailed Kite, Purple Gallinule, Red-cockaded Woodpecker, and Painted Bunting. Other species are birds that are the most sought-after by in-state birders, such as Red-throated Loon, Red-breasted Nuthatch, and Vesper Sparrow. Some species such as Golden Eagle, Short-eared Owl, and Lapland Longspur are very difficult to locate in South Carolina, and birders will increase their chances of finding one of these rare birds if they are in the right place at the right time.

Species that were not included in this appendix are either common, with a widespread distribution throughout South Carolina, or are considered to be so rare in the state that you have very little likelihood of ever finding one. The bar graphs and list of accidental species in Appendix D will help you understand why certain species were not included here.

For each species in this appendix, listed in taxonomic order, you will find the bird's seasonal abundance, its habitat preference, and the best areas to search for the bird. *Winter* refers to November through March, *spring* refers to April through May, *summer* refers to June through August, and *fall* refers to September through

Common Loon

Wilson's Storm-Petrel

October. The habitats listed for each species, such as salt marsh, rock jetty, or large inland lake, are the habitats in which you are most likely to encounter the species. They are not, however, the only habitats in which you will find the species, especially during migration, when birds often show up in unexpected places. The *key sites* are the best areas in the state to find the species, but they do not always include all the areas where you might encounter it.

Red-throated Loon: Fairly common winter resident of tidal creeks and the ocean. *Key sites:* Huntington Beach State Park, Myrtle Beach State Park, Folly Island, Hunting Island State Park, and Fish Haul Creek Park.

Common Loon: Common winter resident of large inland lakes, tidal creeks, and the ocean. *Key sites:* Huntington Beach State Park, Myrtle Beach State Park, Pitt Street Bridge, Fort Johnson, Folly Island, Hunting Island State Park, Fish Haul Creek Park, Lake Hartwell, J. Strom Thurmond Dam, Lake Murray Dam Park, and Dreher Island State Park.

Horned Grebe: Common winter resident of large inland lakes, tidal creeks, and the ocean. *Key sites:* Huntington Beach State Park, Myrtle Beach State Park, Pitt Street Bridge, Fort Johnson, Folly Island, Port Royal Boardwalk Park, Fish Haul Creek Park, Lake Hartwell, and Dreher Island State Park.

Eared Grebe: Occasional winter resident of ponds and lakes.

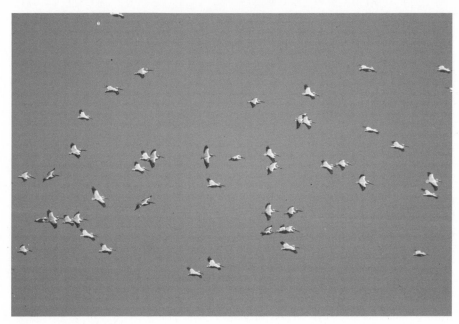

American White Pelican

Shearwaters, petrels, and other pelagic birds: In order to see these species, you will need to go on a pelagic bird or fishing trip, as most of these birds are rarely seen from land in South Carolina. Most commonly seen species are Black-capped Petrel; Greater, Audubon's, and Cory's Shearwaters; Wilson's Storm-Petrel; Red and Red-necked Phalaropes; and Sooty and Bridled Terns. Also possible, but not to be expected, are Northern Fulmar, Manx and Sooty Shearwaters, Leach's and Band-rumped Storm-Petrels, White-tailed Tropicbird, Roseate and Arctic Terns, and Brown Noddy. The best time to go on a pelagic trip is mid-May to mid-June or mid-August to mid-September, when the diversity of pelagic birds is at its peak.

Northern Gannet: Fairly common winter resident of the ocean. *Key sites:* Huntington Beach State Park, Myrtle Beach State Park, Cape Romain National Wildlife Refuge, Folly Island, and Hunting Island State Park.

American White Pelican: Uncommon permanent resident of coastal marshes and barrier islands. *Key sites:* Bear Island Wildlife Management Area is best especially in winter, but also try Donnelley WMA, Cape Romain NWR, and ACE Basin NWR.

Great Cormorant: Uncommon winter resident of rock jetties along the coast. *Key sites:* Huntington Beach State Park is best, but also try Folly Island and Breach Inlet.

Anhinga: Common permanent resident of freshwater marshes and swamps. Harder to find in winter. *Key sites:* Magnolia Gardens, Caw Caw County Park,

Savannah NWR, Donnelley WMA, Bear Island WMA, ACE Basin NWR, Francis Marion National Forest, and Santee NWR.

American Bittern: Uncommon winter resident of freshwater marshes. *Key sites:* Huntington Beach State Park, Magnolia Plantation, ACE Basin NWR, Bear Island WMA, Donnelley WMA, Savannah NWR, Carolina Sandhills NWR, Forty Acre Rock Heritage Preserve, and Lake Conestee Nature Park.

Least Bittern: Fairly common summer resident of freshwater marshes. *Key sites:* Bear Island WMA, Hunting Island State Park, Savannah NWR, Cape Romain NWR, ACE Basin NWR, Santee Coastal Reserve, Magnolia Gardens, and Caw Caw County Park.

Little Blue Heron: Common permanent resident of ponds, lakes, and marshes. *Key sites:* Rookeries at Magnolia Plantation and Pinckney Island NWR. Also try Donnelley WMA, Bear Island WMA, Savannah NWR, Huntington Beach State Park, Caw Caw County Park, Hunting Island State Park, Cape Romain NWR, and ACE Basin NWR.

Tricolored Heron: Common permanent resident of coastal salt marshes. *Key sites:* Rookeries at Magnolia Plantation and Pinckney Island NWR. Also try Huntington Beach State Park, Savannah NWR, Caw Caw County Park, Donnelley WMA, Bear Island WMA, Hunting Island State Park, Cape Romain NWR, and ACE Basin NWR.

Reddish Egret: Uncommon summer resident of coastal beaches. *Key sites:* Cape Romain NWR is best, but also try Huntington Beach State Park, Pitt Street Bridge, and Fish Haul Creek Park.

Anhinga

White Ibis

Yellow-crowned Night-Heron: Uncommon summer resident of hardwood swamps and coastal salt marshes. *Key sites:* Easiest to find at Francis Beidler Forest Audubon Sanctuary, Congaree National Park, and Francis Marion National Forest, but also try Huntington Beach State Park, Fort Johnson, Caw Caw County Park, Hunting Island State Park, Cape Romain NWR, Donnelley WMA, ACE Basin NWR, and Townville.

Black-crowned Night-Heron: Fairly common permanent resident of freshwater and coastal salt marshes. *Key sites:* Magnolia Plantation, Donnelley WMA, Bear Island WMA, Cape Romain NWR, ACE Basin NWR, and Dungannon Heritage Preserve.

White Ibis: Common permanent resident of coastal marshes and swamps. *Key sites:* Pinckney Island NWR, Cape Romain NWR, Caw Caw County Park, South Tibwin Plantation, Magnolia Plantation, Donnelley WMA, Bear Island WMA, Hunting Island State Park, Francis Beidler Forest Audubon Sanctuary, ACE Basin NWR, and Savannah NWR.

Glossy Ibis: Fairly common permanent resident of coastal marshes. Difficult to find in winter. *Key sites:* South Tibwin Plantation, Cape Romain NWR, Bear Island WMA, ACE Basin NWR, and Savannah NWR.

Roseate Spoonbill: Uncommon visitor in late summer in coastal salt marshes. *Key sites:* Cape Romain NWR is best, but also try Bear Island WMA, South Tibwin Plantation, and Silver Bluff Audubon Sanctuary.

Wood Stork: Fairly common permanent resident in coastal salt marshes and cypress swamps. Harder to find in winter. *Key sites:* Breeding colonies at Dungannon Heritage Preserve, Donnelley WMA, and Santee Coastal Reserve, but also found at Savannah NWR, Bear Island WMA, ACE Basin NWR, Caw Caw County Park, South Tibwin Plantation, Cape Romain NWR, Huntington Beach State Park, and Silver Bluff Audubon Sanctuary.

Winter waterfowl: The best time to look for waterfowl is December through February. Most commonly observed waterfowl are Gadwall, American Wigeon, Blue-winged and Green-winged Teals, Northern Shoveler, Northern Pintail, Ring-necked and Ruddy Ducks, Lesser Scaup, and Bufflehead. *Key sites:* Huntington Beach State Park, Savannah NWR, Santee NWR, Bear Island WMA, Santee Coastal Reserve, Broad River Waterfowl Management Area, and Townville.

Black-bellied Whistling-Duck: Uncommon summer resident of old rice fields along the coast. *Key sites:* Donnelley WMA is best, but also try Bear Island WMA, Magnolia Plantation, and Savannah NWR.

Greater White-fronted Goose: Occasional winter visitor to farm fields. *Key sites:* Santee NWR and Townville.

Snow Goose: Uncommon winter resident of farm fields. *Key sites:* Santee NWR and Townville.

Ross's Goose: Rare winter resident of farm fields. *Key sites:* Santee NWR and Townville.

Mottled Duck

Tundra Swan: Fairly common winter resident of shallow ponds, lakes, and marshes. *Key sites:* Bear Island WMA is best, but also try Cape Romain NWR and Santee NWR.

American Black Duck: Uncommon winter resident of ponds and marshes throughout the state. *Key sites:* Cape Romain NWR, Huntington Beach State Park, Bear Island WMA, Santee Coastal Reserve, and Carolina Sandhills NWR.

Mottled Duck: Fairly common permanent resident of coastal marshes. *Key sites:* Bear Island WMA, South Tibwin Plantation, Cape Romain NWR, and Santee Coastal Reserve.

Canvasback: Uncommon winter resident of ponds and lakes. *Key sites:* Savannah NWR, Cape Romain NWR, Huntington Beach State Park, Santee Coastal Reserve, and Santee NWR.

Redhead: Uncommon winter resident of ponds and lakes. *Key sites:* Cape Romain NWR, Huntington Beach State Park, Hunting Island State Park, Santee NWR, Lake Murray Dam Park, and J. Strom Thurmond Dam.

Greater Scaup: Uncommon winter resident of the ocean. Beware of confusion with the much more common Lesser Scaup, which can also be found in the same habitat. *Key sites:* Huntington Beach State Park, Cape Romain NWR, and Folly Island.

Common Eider: Occasional winter resident along rock jetties and piers. *Key sites:* Huntington Beach State Park is best, but also try Myrtle Beach State Park and Folly Island.

Black, Surf, and White-winged Scoters: Winter residents of the ocean. Black is fairly common, Surf and White-winged are uncommon. *Key sites:* Huntington Beach State Park is best, but also try Myrtle Beach State Park, Cape Romain NWR, Folly Island, Edisto Island, and Hunting Island State Park.

Long-tailed Duck: Occasional winter resident of the ocean and large inland lakes. *Key sites:* Huntington Beach State Park is best, but also try Myrtle Beach State Park and Folly Island. On rare occasions this bird can be found on the large inland lakes such as Lake Hartwell and Lake Murray.

Common Goldeneye: Occasional winter resident of the ocean, lakes, and rivers. *Key sites:* Cape Romain NWR, Huntington Beach State Park, Santee NWR, and Bear Island WMA.

Hooded Merganser: Common winter resident of lakes, ponds, and rivers. *Key sites:* Huntington Beach State Park, Santee Coastal Reserve, Pitt Street Bridge, Hunting Island State Park, Cape Romain NWR, Silver Bluff Audubon Sanctuary, Carolina Sandhills NWR, and Townville.

Red-breasted Merganser: Fairly common winter resident in the ocean and tidal creeks. *Key sites:* Huntington Beach State Park, Myrtle Beach State Park, Cape Romain NWR, Pitt Street Bridge, Fort Johnson, Folly Island, and Hunting Island State Park.

Swallow-tailed Kite

Common Merganser: Rare winter resident of large inland lakes and the ocean. *Key sites:* Cape Romain NWR, Huntington Beach State Park, Dreher Island State Park, Lake Murray Dam Park, and J. Strom Thurmond Dam.

Mississippi Kite: Fairly common summer resident of old rice fields, swamps, forests, and farmland. *Key sites:* Caw Caw County Park, South Tibwin Plantation, ACE Basin NWR, Santee Coastal Reserve, Donnelley WMA, Webb WMA, Silver Bluff Audubon Sanctuary, Santee NWR, Orangeburg Super Sod farm, Congaree National Park, and Congaree Bluffs Heritage Preserve.

Swallow-tailed Kite: Uncommon summer resident of rivers, swamps, and old rice fields. Large groups of feeding kites, anywhere from ten to a hundred, can occur during late July. *Key sites:* During spring and early summer, try Francis Marion National Forest, Caw Caw County Park, ACE Basin NWR, Francis Beidler Forest Audubon Sanctuary, and Santee Coastal Reserve. A canoe or kayak trip along the Edisto River from Givhan's Ferry State Park to Willtown Bluff Landing is a great way to see kites from April through June. The best areas for large flocks in late July are Santee Delta WMA, Savannah NWR, and the hay fields near Allendale. In late July 2007 one hay field near the small town of Millett, about 17 miles northwest of Allendale, produced a Swallow-tailed Kite flock in excess of 110 birds!

Bald Eagle: Fairly common permanent resident of coastal marshes, large inland lakes, and rivers. *Key sites:* Savannah NWR, Bear Island WMA, Donnelley

Broad-winged Hawk

WMA, ACE Basin NWR, Santee Coastal Reserve, Huntington Beach State Park, Santee NWR, Silver Bluff Audubon Sanctuary, Dreher Island State Park, and Lake Hartwell.

Red-shouldered Hawk: Fairly common permanent resident of moist mixed pine-deciduous forests, swamps, and marshes. *Key sites:* Savannah NWR, Donnelley WMA, ACE Basin NWR, Magnolia Plantation, Francis Beidler Forest Audubon Sanctuary, Santee NWR, Congaree Bluffs Heritage Preserve, Congaree National Park, Saluda Shoals Park, Forty Acre Rock Heritage Preserve, and Townville.

Broad-winged Hawk: Uncommon spring migrant and common fall migrant throughout the state. Uncommon summer resident of forests in the piedmont and mountains. *Key sites:* Caesars Head State Park, Table Rock State Park, Sassafras Mountain, Walhalla State Fish Hatchery, and Poinsett State Park.

Golden Eagle: Occasional winter visitor of open fields and marshes. *Key sites:* Caesars Head State Park, Huntington Beach State Park, Cape Romain NWR, Bear Island WMA, and Sandhills NWR.

Merlin: Uncommon winter resident of coastal salt marshes. Best time to find them is during fall migration in October. *Key sites:* Cape Romain NWR, South Tibwin Plantation, Huntington Beach State Park, Santee Coastal Reserve, Bear Island WMA, Pitt Street Bridge, Folly Island, and Fish Haul Creek Park.

Peregrine Falcon: Uncommon permanent resident in the mountains. Uncommon winter resident of coastal salt marshes. *Key sites:* Caesars Head State Park, Table Rock State Park. During winter, Huntington Beach State Park, Folly Island, Cape Romain NWR, Santee Coastal Reserve, and Fish Haul Creek Park.

Ruffed Grouse: Occasional permanent resident in the deciduous forests of the mountains. *Key sites:* Best bets are Sassafras Mountain and Caesars Head State Park, but also try Walhalla State Fish Hatchery and Burrell's Ford.

Northern Bobwhite: Fairly common permanent resident of brushy clear-cuts and open woodlands. Easiest to find during the summer, when they call frequently. *Key sites:* Santee NWR, Landsford Canal State Park, Lynchburg Savanna Heritage Preserve, Longleaf Pine Heritage Preserve, Bunched Arrowhead Heritage Preserve, Carolina Sandhills NWR, and Enoree River Waterfowl Management Area.

Black Rail: Occasional permanent resident of marshes and wet meadows throughout the state. *Key sites:* Bear Island WMA, Santee Coastal Reserve, Santee NWR, and Townville.

King Rail: Uncommon permanent resident of freshwater marshes. *Key sites:* Caw Caw County Park, Magnolia Plantation, Bear Island WMA, Savannah NWR, and ACE Basin NWR.

Virginia Rail: Fairly common winter resident of rice fields and freshwater and salt marshes. *Key sites:* Cape Romain NWR, Caw Caw County Park, Magnolia Plantation, Pinckney Island NWR, Huntington Beach State Park, Donnelley WMA, and Savannah NWR.

Sora: Fairly common winter resident of rice fields and freshwater and salt marshes. *Key sites:* Cape Romain NWR, Bear Island WMA, Pinckney Island NWR, Caw Caw County Park, Magnolia Plantation, Donnelley WMA, and Savannah NWR.

Purple Gallinule: Fairly common summer resident of lily pad–covered ponds. *Key sites:* Savannah NWR is the best bet, but also try Donnelley WMA, South Tibwin Plantation, and Webb WMA.

Sandhill Crane: Uncommon winter visitor to farm fields. *Key sites:* Santee NWR is best, but also try Townville and the Orangeburg Super Sod farm.

Whooping Crane: Rare winter resident of coastal marshes. From 2005 to 2007 several Whooping Cranes spent the winter in the ACE Basin. It remains to be seen whether or not they will continue to winter in South Carolina. If you do happen to see these federally endangered birds, please do not approach them, because it is vital to the survival of the Whooping Crane that they maintain a healthy fear of humans.

Migrating shorebirds: Most common migrants are Black-bellied and Semi-palmated Plovers; Greater and Lesser Yellowlegs; Spotted Sandpiper; Ruddy Turnstone; Sanderling; Semipalmated, Western, and Least Sandpipers; Dunlin; and

Short-billed Dowitcher. *Key sites:* Huntington Beach State Park, Santee Coastal Reserve, Cape Romain NWR, Fish Haul Creek Park, Bear Island WMA, Donnelley WMA, and Folly Island.

American Golden-Plover: Uncommon migrant in fall and occasional in spring to sod and turf farms. *Key sites:* Orangeburg Super Sod farm.

Wilson's Plover: Fairly common summer resident of coastal beaches and mudflats. Occasional in winter. *Key sites:* Huntington Beach State Park, Cape Romain NWR, Folly Island, and Hunting Island State Park.

Piping Plover: Uncommon winter resident of coastal beaches. *Key sites:* Huntington Beach State Park, Folly Island, Hunting Island State Park, Cape Romain NWR, and Fish Haul Creek Park.

American Oystercatcher: Common permanent resident of coastal mudflats, beaches, and oyster beds. It is estimated that over 35 percent of the entire Atlantic population of oystercatchers winter in South Carolina. *Key sites:* A sure bet in any season is Cape Romain NWR. Also try Fort Johnson, Pitt Street Bridge, Port Royal Boardwalk, Hunting Island State Park, and Huntington Beach State Park.

Black-necked Stilt: Fairly common summer resident of coastal marshes, ponds, and rice fields. *Key sites:* Bear Island WMA, Huntington Beach State Park, Savannah NWR, Cape Romain NWR, and ACE Basin NWR.

American Avocet: Uncommon migrant and occasional winter visitor of coastal marshes, ponds, and rice fields. *Key sites:* Huntington Beach State Park, Bear Island WMA, and Santee Coastal Reserve.

Dunlin

Piping Plovers fighting

Solitary Sandpiper: Fairly common migrant in spring and fall of ponds and marshes. *Key sites:* Lake Conestee Nature Park, Forty Acre Rock Heritage Preserve, Edwin M. Griffin Nature Preserve, Orangeburg Super Sod farm, and Silver Bluff Audubon Sanctuary.

Upland Sandpiper: Uncommon migrant in late summer at sod and turf farms. *Key sites:* Orangeburg Super Sod farm.

Whimbrel: Fairly common migrant in spring and uncommon in fall to coastal mudflats and salt marshes. Occasional winter resident. *Key sites:* Edisto Beach State Park, Folly Island, Hunting Island State Park, Fish Haul Creek Park, Huntington Beach State Park, and Cape Romain NWR.

Long-billed Curlew: Occasional winter resident of mudflats along the coast. *Key sites:* Cape Island on Cape Romain NWR.

Marbled Godwit: Fairly common winter resident of coastal mudflats and salt marshes. *Key sites:* Fish Haul Creek Park, Pitt Street Bridge, Cape Romain NWR, and Huntington Beach State Park.

Red Knot: Common migrant in spring and fall of sandy beaches and mudflats along the coast. Uncommon winter resident. *Key sites:* Huntington Beach State Park, Cape Romain NWR, Breach Inlet, Folly Island, Hunting Island State Park, and Fish Haul Creek Park.

White-rumped Sandpiper: Uncommon migrant in spring and occasional in fall to mudflats along the coast. *Key sites:* Huntington Beach State Park, Cape

Romain NWR, Donnelley WMA, Bear Island WMA, and Santee Coastal Reserve.

Pectoral Sandpiper: Uncommon migrant in spring and fairly common in fall to sod and turf farms and coastal mudflats. *Key sites:* Orangeburg Super Sod farm, Santee Coastal Reserve, Bear Island WMA, and Silver Bluff Audubon Sanctuary.

Purple Sandpiper: Fairly common winter resident of rock jetties along the coast. *Key sites:* Huntington Beach State Park is best, but also try Fort Moultrie.

Stilt Sandpiper: Occasional migrant in spring and fall of coastal salt marshes and rice fields. *Key sites:* Bear Island WMA, Cape Romain NWR, Santee Coastal Reserve, and Huntington Beach State Park.

Buff-breasted Sandpiper: Uncommon migrant in late summer at sod and turf farms. *Key sites:* The Orangeburg Super Sod farm is the best bet, but also try Huntington Beach State Park.

Long-billed Dowitcher: Uncommon migrant and winter resident in impoundments or ponds with muddy bottoms. *Key sites:* Santee Coastal Reserve, Cape Romain NWR, and Donnelley WMA.

American Woodcock: Uncommon permanent resident of woodland thickets with moist soil, often near open grassy fields. *Key sites:* Sassafras Mountain, Francis Marion National Forest, Francis Beidler Forest Audubon Sanctuary, Silver Bluff Audubon Sanctuary, Jones Gap State Park, Enoree River Waterfowl Management Area, Lynch's Woods Park, and Bunched Arrowhead Heritage Preserve.

Wilson's Snipe: Fairly common winter resident of wet farm fields and fresh-water marshes. *Key sites:* Donnelley WMA, Santee NWR, Orangeburg Super Sod farm, Townville, and Lake Conestee Nature Park.

Wilson's Phalarope: Occasional migrant in spring and late summer of shallow pools of water and mudflats. *Key sites:* Cape Romain NWR and Orangeburg Super Sod farm.

Bonaparte's Gull: Fairly common winter resident of large inland lakes and coastal beaches. *Key sites:* Bear Island WMA, Huntington Beach State Park, Myrtle Beach State Park, Lake Hartwell, Lake Murray Dam Park, J. Strom Thurmond Dam, and Dreher Island State Park.

Lesser Black-backed Gull: Uncommon winter visitor of coastal beaches. *Key sites:* Fish Haul Creek Park, Folly Island, Cape Romain NWR, and Huntington Beach State Park.

Great Black-backed Gull: Fairly common winter resident of coastal beaches. Occasional in summer. *Key sites:* Huntington Beach State Park is best, but also try Folly Island, Fort Johnson, and Cape Romain NWR.

Gull-billed Tern: Uncommon summer resident of salt marshes along the coast. *Key sites:* South Tibwin Plantation, Cape Romain NWR, Bear Island WMA, Fort Johnson, Folly Island Patriots Point, and Pitt Street Bridge.

Sandwich Tern

Sandwich Tern: Fairly common summer resident along coastal beaches. *Key sites:* Cape Romain NWR, Huntington Beach State Park, Hunting Island State Park, Fish Haul Creek Park, Fort Johnson, and Pitt Street Bridge.

Least Tern: Fairly common summer resident of coastal rivers and beaches. *Key sites:* Huntington Beach State Park, Cape Romain NWR, Pitt Street Bridge, Fort Johnson, Edisto Beach State Park, Bear Island WMA, Hunting Island State Park, and Fish Haul Creek Park.

Sooty Tern: Uncommon offshore pelagic in summer. Can occasionally be seen on barrier islands in summer, but be careful not to confuse with Black Tern. *Key sites:* Cape Romain NWR.

Black Tern: Fairly common visitor in late summer to coastal beaches, lakes, and ponds. *Key sites:* Cape Romain NWR, Bear Island WMA, Huntington Beach State Park, Folly Island, Hunting Island State Park, Silver Bluff Audubon Sanctuary, and J. Strom Thurmond Dam.

Black Skimmer: Common summer resident of coastal marshes and beaches. Uncommon in winter. *Key sites:* Fish Haul Creek Park, Hunting Island State Park, Bear Island WMA, ACE Basin NWR, Edisto Beach State Park, Fort Johnson, Folly Island, Pitt Street Bridge, Cape Romain NWR, and Huntington Beach State Park.

Razorbill: Occasional winter visitor offshore and sometimes seen from land. *Key sites:* Huntington Beach State Park is best, but also try Myrtle Beach State Park.

Black Tern

Eurasian Collared-Dove: Fairly common permanent resident of residential areas. *Key sites:* Bear Island WMA, Folly Island, Fort Moultrie, Orangeburg Super Sod farm, and Townville.

White-winged Dove: Occasional visitor year-round to residential areas along the coast. *Key sites:* Folly Island and Bear Island WMA.

Common Ground-Dove: Uncommon permanent resident of dry, brushy areas with sandy soils. *Key sites:* Fort Moultrie, Pitt Street Bridge, Fort Johnson, Cape Romain NWR, Huntington Beach State Park, Webb WMA, and Orangeburg Super Sod farm.

Barn Owl: Uncommon permanent resident of marshes and open fields. *Key sites:* Santee Coastal Reserve, Bear Island WMA, Savannah NWR, Cape Romain NWR, and Carolina Sandhills NWR.

Eastern Screech-Owl: Fairly common permanent resident of pine and mixed pine forests. *Key sites:* Francis Marion National Forest, Congaree Bluffs Heritage Preserve, Silver Bluff Audubon Sanctuary, Carolina Sandhills NWR, and Table Rock State Park.

Barred Owl: Common permanent resident of moist forests, often in swamps. *Key sites:* Francis Beidler Forest Audubon Sanctuary, Dungannon Heritage Preserve, Caw Caw County Park, Francis Marion National Forest, Hunting Island State Park, Silver Bluff Audubon Sanctuary, Congaree National Park, Congaree Creek Heritage Preserve, and ACE Basin NWR.

Black Skimmer

Northern Saw-whet Owl: Rare winter resident of high-elevation mixed pine-hardwood forests. *Key sites:* Walhalla State Fish Hatchery and Burrell's Ford.

Short-eared Owl: Occasional winter visitor to salt marshes and weedy fields. *Key sites:* Huntington Beach State Park, Cape Romain NWR, Folly Island, and Townville.

Common Nighthawk: Uncommon summer resident of large cities and open, scrubby forests with sandy soil. *Key sites:* Carolina Sandhills NWR, Bear Island WMA, Folly Island, and Lynch's Woods Park.

Chuck-will's-widow: Common summer resident of dry pine and deciduous forests adjacent to fields and open areas. *Key sites:* Francis Marion National Forest, Donnelley WMA, Hunting Island State Park, Silver Bluff Audubon Sanctuary, Carolina Sandhills NWR, ACE Basin NWR, Broad River Waterfowl Management Area, and Enoree River Waterfowl Management Area.

Whip-poor-will: Fairly common summer resident of upland deciduous and mixed forests adjacent to fields and open areas. *Key sites:* Silver Bluff Audubon Sanctuary, Francis Marion National Forest, Broad River Waterfowl Management Area, Enoree River Waterfowl Management Area, Paris Mountain State Park, and Table Rock State Park.

Ruby-throated Hummingbird: Fairly common summer resident of moist deciduous forests and residential areas. Common migrant in spring and fall throughout the state. *Key sites:* ACE Basin NWR, Caw Caw County Park,

Patriots Point, Silver Bluff Audubon Sanctuary, Francis Beidler Forest Audubon Sanctuary, Congaree National Park, Congaree Bluffs Heritage Preserve, and Santee NWR.

Overwintering hummingbirds: It is not uncommon to have hummingbirds spend the entire winter at hummingbird feeders in South Carolina. The most common overwintering species is the Rufous Hummingbird, but Ruby-throated, Black-chinned, Calliope, and Buff-bellied Hummingbirds have also been documented.

Red-headed Woodpecker: Uncommon permanent resident of open woods, swamps, and groves. Easiest to find during summer months. *Key sites:* ACE Basin NWR, Donnelley WMA, Silver Bluff Audubon Sanctuary, Carolina Sandhills NWR, Congaree National Park, Santee Coastal Reserve, South Tibwin Plantation, Longleaf Pine Heritage Preserve, Enoree River Waterfowl Management Area, Lake Conestee Nature Park, and Saluda Shoals Park.

Hairy Woodpecker: Fairly common permanent resident of mature forests. *Key sites:* Donnelley WMA, Francis Beidler Forest Audubon Sanctuary, Congaree National Park, Paris Mountain State Park, Caesars Head State Park, Burrell's Ford, and Sassafras Mountain.

Red-cockaded Woodpecker: Uncommon permanent resident of mature longleaf pine forests. Easiest to find at a colony (look for trees marked with white paint rings) around dawn or dusk. The best times to look for the woodpeckers are during the breeding season (May to July), when they are more active around the nesting colonies. *Key sites:* Francis Marion National Forest, Webb WMA, Carolina Sandhills NWR, Santee Coastal Reserve, Longleaf Pine Heritage Preserve, and Lewis Ocean Bay Heritage Preserve.

Pileated Woodpecker: Fairly common permanent resident of large, mature forests. *Key sites:* Dungannon Heritage Preserve, Congaree National Park, Francis Beidler Forest Audubon Sanctuary, Donnelley WMA, Magnolia Plantation, Webb WMA, Caesars Head State Park, Burrell's Ford, and Santee NWR.

Eastern Wood-Pewee: Fairly common summer resident of dry, open, mature forests. *Key sites:* Francis Marion National Forest, Donnelley WMA, Edisto Beach State Park, Carolina Sandhills NWR, Silver Bluff Audubon Sanctuary, Longleaf Pine Heritage Preserve, and Kings Mountain.

Acadian Flycatcher: Fairly common summer resident of deciduous forests near swamps and streams. *Key sites:* Congaree National Park, Congaree Creek Heritage Preserve, Francis Marion National Forest, Caw Caw County Park, Donnelley WMA, Dungannon Heritage Preserve, Hunting Island State Park, Silver Bluff Audubon Sanctuary, Carolina Sandhills NWR, and ACE Basin NWR.

Western Kingbird: Occasional winter visitor to open areas. Often found perched on telephone wires and fences. *Key sites:* Folly Island and Cape Romain NWR.

Gray Kingbird: Occasional summer visitor to open areas along the coast. *Key sites:* Folly Island and Cape Romain NWR.

Scissor-tailed Flycatcher: Occasional summer and fall visitor to farm fields, roadsides, and other open areas. Often found perched on telephone wires and fences. *Key sites:* Folly Island.

Loggerhead Shrike: Fairly common permanent resident of farm fields. *Key sites:* Bear Island WMA, Donnelley WMA, Folly Island, Cape Romain NWR, Silver Bluff Audubon Sanctuary, Carolina Sandhills NWR, Francis Beidler Forest Audubon Sanctuary, Orangeburg Super Sod farm, and Townville.

White-eyed Vireo: Common summer resident of dense thickets, especially near water. Uncommon winter resident in the understory of hardwood swamps. *Key sites:* Donnelley WMA, Caw Caw County Park, Francis Marion National Forest, Santee Coastal Reserve, Francis Beidler Forest Audubon Sanctuary, Congaree National Park, Saluda Shoals Park, Enoree River Waterfowl Management Area, and Croft State Natural Area.

Yellow-throated Vireo: Fairly common summer resident of mature deciduous forests and hardwood swamps. *Key sites:* Donnelley WMA, Dungannon Heritage Preserve, Silver Bluff Audubon Sanctuary, Congaree National Park, Poinsett State Park, Enoree River Waterfowl Management Area, Croft State Natural Area, and Francis Beidler Forest Audubon Sanctuary.

Blue-headed Vireo: Fairly common summer resident of high-elevation forests. Fairly common winter resident along coast and coastal plain. *Key sites:* During summer, Walhalla Fish Hatchery, Burrell's Ford, Sassafras Mountain, Table Rock State Park, Caesars Head State Park, and Enoree River Waterfowl Management Area. In the winter, Congaree National Park, Carolina Sandhills NWR, Francis Marion National Forest, Saluda Shoals Park, Donnelley WMA, Edisto Beach State Park, and Francis Beidler Forest Audubon Sanctuary.

Warbling Vireo: Rare migrant in spring and occasional in fall. *Key sites:* Patriots Point, Santee NWR, Saluda Shoals Park, and Lynch's Woods Park.

Philadelphia Vireo: Rare migrant in spring and occasional in fall in the coastal plain and piedmont. *Key sites:* Saluda Shoals Park, Lynch's Woods Park, Santee NWR, and Landsford Canal State Park.

Common Raven: Uncommon permanent resident in the mountains. *Key sites:* Best bet is Table Rock State Park or Caesars Head State Park, but also try Sassafras Mountain, Walhalla State Fish Hatchery, and Jones Gap State Park.

Horned Lark: Fairly common permanent resident of farm fields. Easier to find in winter. *Key sites:* Orangeburg Super Sod farm and Townville.

Cliff Swallow: Fairly common summer resident under bridges in the piedmont. *Key sites:* Dreher Island State Park, Landsford Canal State Park, and Lake Hartwell.

Cave Swallow: Occasional migrant and winter visitor in marshes along the coast. *Key sites:* Huntington Beach State Park and Bear Island WMA.

Brown-headed Nuthatch

Red-breasted Nuthatch: Uncommon winter resident in pine and mixed pine forests. Occasional summer resident in pine/hemlock forests above 3,000 feet. *Key sites:* Walhalla State Fish Hatchery and Burrell's Ford.

Brown-headed Nuthatch: Common permanent resident in pine forests. *Key sites:* Francis Marion National Forest, Carolina Sandhills NWR, Webb WMA, Santee Coastal Reserve, Longleaf Pine Heritage Preserve, Lynchburg Savanna Heritage Preserve, Paris Mountain State Park, Bunched Arrowhead Heritage Preserve, Hunting Island State Park, Silver Bluff Audubon Sanctuary, and ACE Basin NWR.

Winter Wren: Fairly common winter resident in hardwood swamps and damp forests with fallen logs. *Key sites:* Congaree National Park, Francis Beidler Forest Audubon Sanctuary, Bunched Arrowhead Heritage Preserve, Saluda Shoals Park, Lynch's Woods Park, Forty Acre Rock Heritage Preserve, Landsford Canal State Park, and Beaverdam Creek WMA.

Sedge Wren: Uncommon winter resident of grassy meadows and marshes. *Key sites:* Santee NWR is best, but also try Pinckney Island NWR, Savannah NWR, Bear Island WMA, ACE Basin NWR, Caw Caw County Park, Magnolia Plantation, Cape Romain NWR, and Huntington Beach State Park.

Veery, Swainson's, Gray-cheeked, and Bicknell's Thrushes: *Catharus* thrushes are fairly common to uncommon migrants during spring and fall. Veery and Swainson's Thrush are fairly common, while Gray-cheeked Thrush is uncommon. Bicknell's Thrush is possible, but the only reliable way to distinguish it from a Gray-cheeked Thrush is by call. *Key sites:* Caesars Head State Park, Lake Conestee Nature Park, Bunched Arrowhead Heritage Preserve, Croft State Natural Area, Cottonwood Nature Trail, Landsford Canal State Park, Lynch's Woods Park, Saluda Shoals Park, Congaree National Park, Francis Beidler Forest Audubon Sanctuary, and Patriots Point.

Hermit Thrush: Common winter resident in swamps and a wide variety of forests. *Key sites:* Congaree National Park, Francis Beidler Forest Audubon Sanctuary, Santee NWR, Dungannon Heritage Preserve, Bunched Arrowhead Heritage Preserve, Lynch's Woods Park, Landsford Canal State Park, and Saluda Shoals Park.

Wood Thrush: Fairly common summer resident in mature deciduous forests. *Key sites:* Poinsett State Park, Kings Mountain, Santee NWR, Congaree National Park, Congaree Creek Heritage Preserve, Walhalla State Fish Hatchery, Burrell's Ford, Table Rock State Park, Caesars Head State Park, and Sassafras Mountain.

American Pipit: Fairly common winter resident of farm fields throughout the state. *Key sites:* Donnelley WMA, Bear Island WMA, Orangeburg Super Sod farm, Santee NWR, Silver Bluff Audubon Sanctuary, and Townville.

Migrating warblers: In the spring the bulk of migrants come through between mid-April and mid-May, while during fall it is from early September to late October. Songbird migration is often much better in the piedmont than along the coast. Spring migration along the coast is generally pretty poor. Migrants typically seen in South Carolina include Magnolia, Chestnut-sided, Blue-winged,

Tennessee Warbler

Tennessee, Blackburnian, Canada, Cape May, Bay-breasted, and Blackpoll Warblers and Northern Waterthrush. Less commonly seen are Nashville, Mourning, Connecticut, Wilson's, Golden-winged, and Cerulean Warblers. *Key sites:* In the spring the best places to look for warblers are Landsford Canal State Park, Saluda Shoals Park, Lynch's Woods Park, Croft State Natural Area, Edwin M. Griffin Nature Preserve, Lake Conestee Nature Park, Congaree National Park, Walhalla State Fish Hatchery, Burrell's Ford, Caesars Head State Park, and Sassafras Mountain. In the fall try the same areas as in spring, plus migrant traps such as Patriots Point, Folly Island, James Island County Park, Sea Pines Forest Reserve, Cape Romain NWR, and Myrtle Beach State Park.

Orange-crowned Warbler: Fairly common winter resident of wax myrtle thickets and live oak forests. *Key sites:* Savannah NWR, Donnelley WMA, Edisto Beach State Park, Folly Island, Cape Romain NWR, South Tibwin Plantation, Huntington Beach State Park, Aiken State Natural Area, and Congaree National Park.

Northern Parula: Common summer resident of swamps and mature, moist forests with Spanish moss. *Key sites:* Donnelley WMA, Edisto Beach State Park, Dungannon Heritage Preserve, Francis Marion National Forest, Francis Beidler Forest Audubon Sanctuary, Congaree National Park, and Poinsett State Park.

Yellow Warbler: Occasional summer resident of wet, brushy areas in the piedmont. Uncommon migrant in spring; common in fall, especially along the coast. *Key sites:* During summer try Townville and along River Falls Road near Jones Gap State Park.

Chestnut-sided Warbler: Rare summer resident in mountains. Uncommon migrant in spring and fairly common in fall in mountains and piedmont. *Key sites:* During summer try Caesars Head State Park and Sassafras Mountain.

Black-throated Blue Warbler: Summer resident of shady understory within the deciduous and mixed pine forests of the mountains. Fairly common migrant throughout the state. *Key sites:* During summer try Caesars Head State Park, Sassafras Mountain, and Walhalla State Fish Hatchery.

Black-throated Green Warbler: Common summer resident of mature pine and mixed pine forests in the mountains. Rare summer resident in coastal swamps. *Key sites:* Walhalla State Fish Hatchery, Burrell's Ford, Sassafras Mountain, Caesars Head State Park, Table Rock State Park, and Francis Marion National Forest.

Yellow-throated Warbler: Common summer resident of hardwood swamps and pine forests. Uncommon winter resident in swamps. *Key sites:* In summer, Hunting Island State Park, Donnelley WMA, ACE Basin NWR, Francis Marion National Forest, Silver Bluff Audubon Sanctuary, Congaree National Park, Francis Beidler Forest Audubon Sanctuary, Poinsett State Park, and Carolina Sandhills NWR. In winter, Savannah NWR, Webb WMA, Francis Beidler Forest Audubon Sanctuary, and perhaps Santee NWR or Congaree National Park.

Pine Warbler: Common permanent resident of pine forests. *Key sites:* Carolina Sandhills NWR, Lynchburg Savanna and Longleaf Pine Heritage Preserves, Forty Acre Rock Heritage Preserve, Silver Bluff Audubon Sanctuary, Francis Marion National Forest, Lewis Ocean Bay Heritage Preserve, and Edisto Beach State Park.

Prairie Warbler: Common summer resident of early successional pine forests. *Key sites:* Francis Marion National Forest, Forty Acre Rock Heritage Preserve, Congaree Bluffs Heritage Preserve, Lynchburg Savanna Heritage Preserve, Lewis Ocean Bay Heritage Preserve, and Carolina Sandhills NWR.

Palm Warbler: Fairly common migrant and uncommon winter resident of clear-cuts, brushy fields, marshes, sand dunes, and forest edges. *Key sites:* Santee NWR, Hunting Island State Park, James Island County Park, Bear Island WMA, Donnelly WMA, Savannah NWR, and Silver Bluff Audubon Sanctuary.

Cerulean Warbler: Occasional migrant and rare summer resident of mature hardwood forests with little understory on steep slopes in the mountains. *Key sites:* During summer, Caesars Head State Park, Walhalla State Fish Hatchery, and Sassafras Mountain.

Black-and-white Warbler: Fairly common summer resident in the mature deciduous and mixed pine forests of the mountains and piedmont. Uncommon winter resident of hardwood swamps. *Key sites:* In summer, Sassafras Mountain, Caesars Head State Park, Table Rock State Park, Burrell's Ford, Enoree River Waterfowl Management Area, Kings Mountain, Forty Acre Rock Heritage Preserve, and Landsford Canal State Park. In winter, Congaree National Park, Francis Beidler Forest Audubon Sanctuary, Savannah NWR, and Webb WMA.

American Redstart: Fairly common summer resident of deciduous forests, especially near water. Common migrant in spring and fall throughout the state. *Key sites:* In summer, Caesars Head State Park, Walhalla State Fish Hatchery, Sassafras Mountain, Landsford Canal State Park, and Forty Acre Rock Heritage Preserve.

Prothonotary Warbler: Common summer resident of swamps, rivers, and ponds. *Key sites:* Francis Beidler Forest Audubon Sanctuary, Congaree National Park, Francis Marion National Forest, Donnelley WMA, Dungannon Heritage Preserve, Magnolia Plantation, Caw Caw County Park, Santee NWR, Silver Bluff Audubon Sanctuary, Landsford Canal State Park, Forty Acre Rock Heritage Preserve, and Enoree River Waterfowl Management Area.

Worm-eating Warbler: Fairly common summer resident of densely wooded slopes in the mountains and evergreen shrub bogs in the coastal plain. Fairly common fall migrant throughout the state. *Key sites:* Sassafras Mountain, Eastatoe Creek Heritage Preserve, Caesars Head State Park, Table Rock State Park, Walhalla State Fish Hatchery, and Burrell's Ford, but also try Lewis Ocean Bay Heritage Preserve, and Francis Marion National Forest.

Swainson's Warbler: Fairly common summer resident of floodplain forests in the coastal plain and dense rhododendron thickets in the mountains. *Key sites:* Francis Marion National Forest, Congaree Creek Heritage Preserve, Congaree National Park, Francis Beidler Forest Audubon Sanctuary, Sassafras Mountain, Eastatoe Creek Heritage Preserve, Jones Gap State Park, Walhalla State Fish Hatchery, and Burrell's Ford.

Ovenbird: Common summer resident of semi-open mature deciduous forests in the mountains and piedmont. Fairly common migrant throughout the rest of the state. *Key sites:* Sassafras Mountain, Caesars Head State Park, Table Rock State Park, Burrell's Ford, Kings Mountain, Forty Acre Rock Heritage Preserve, and Landsford Canal State Park.

Louisiana Waterthrush: Fairly common summer resident of rocky, fast-flowing streams in the mountains and Piedmont. *Key sites:* Walhalla State Fish Hatchery, Burrell's Ford, Sassafras Mountain, Eastatoe Creek Heritage Preserve, Jones Gap State Park, Table Rock State Park, Landsford Canal State Park, and Poinsett State Park.

Kentucky Warbler: Uncommon summer resident of dense understory within mature deciduous forests. *Key sites:* Francis Marion National Forest, Congaree National Park, Congaree Bluffs Heritage Preserve, Congaree Creek Heritage Preserve, Enoree River Waterfowl Management Area, Forty Acre Rock Heritage Preserve, Landsford Canal State Park, and Eastatoe Creek Heritage Preserve.

Common Yellowthroat: Common permanent resident of freshwater marshes and wet fields. Easiest to find in summer. *Key sites:* Santee Coastal Reserve, Forty

Common Yellowthroat

Summer Tanager

Acre Rock Heritage Preserve, Santee NWR, Bear Island WMA, ACE Basin NWR, Saluda Shoals Park, and Edwin M. Griffin Nature Preserve.

Hooded Warbler: Fairly common summer resident in understory of mature deciduous forests and swamps. *Key sites:* Sassafras Mountain, Walhalla State Fish Hatchery, Burrell's Ford, Caesars Head State Park, Table Rock State Park, Congaree Bluffs Heritage Preserve, Congaree National Park, Silver Bluff Audubon Sanctuary, Carolina Sandhills NWR, Francis Marion National Forest, and Edisto Beach State Park.

Yellow-breasted Chat: Fairly common summer resident of shrubby, early successional forests and open pine forests. Rare winter resident. *Key sites:* Bear Island WMA, Francis Marion National Forest, Silver Bluff Audubon Sanctuary, Congaree Bluffs Heritage Preserve, Carolina Sandhills NWR, Lynchburg Savanna Heritage Preserve, Longleaf Pine Heritage Preserve, and Enoree River Waterfowl Management Area.

Summer Tanager: Common summer resident of mixed pine forests. *Key sites:* Edisto Beach State Park, Francis Marion National Forest, Cape Romain NWR, Silver Bluff Audubon Sanctuary, Carolina Sandhills NWR, Congaree National Park, Saluda Shoals Park, Dreher Island State Park, and Enoree River Waterfowl Management Area.

Scarlet Tanager: Fairly common summer resident of deciduous forests in the mountains. During migration, fairly common in piedmont and uncommon in

Scarlet Tanager

coastal plain. *Key sites:* Walhalla State Fish Hatchery, Sassafras Mountain, Caesars Head State Park, and Table Rock State Park.

Bachman's Sparrow: Fairly common permanent resident of open pine forests. Present in winter but often extremely difficult to find. *Key sites:* Francis Marion National Forest, Santee Coastal Reserve, Webb WMA, Carolina Sandhills NWR, Lynchburg Savanna Heritage Preserve, Longleaf Pine Heritage Preserve, ACE Basin NWR, and Silver Bluff Audubon Sanctuary.

Clay-colored Sparrow: Occasional migrant in fall to open brushy areas interspersed with grass. *Key sites:* Patriots Point, Folly Island, and Cape Romain NWR.

Field Sparrow: Fairly common permanent resident of weedy fields. *Key sites:* In winter, Saluda Shoals Park, Lynch's Woods Park, Santee NWR, and Broad River Waterfowl Management Area. In summer, Bunched Arrowhead Heritage Preserve, Enoree River Waterfowl Management Area, Townville, and farmlands near Landsford Canal State Park.

Vesper Sparrow: Uncommon winter resident of farmland. *Key sites:* Bear Island WMA, Donnelley WMA, Santee NWR, Townville, and Orangeburg Super Sod farm.

Grasshopper Sparrow: Uncommon summer resident of grassy fields. Occasional winter resident of grassy fields and power line rights-of-way. *Key sites:* In winter, Santee NWR, Francis Marion National Forest, ACE Basin NWR, Lynchburg Savanna Heritage Preserve, and Lewis Ocean Bay Heritage Preserve. In summer, Townville and Landsford Canal State Park.

Henslow's Sparrow: Occasional winter resident of wet, grassy pine forests or along power line rights-of-way. *Key sites:* Santee NWR, Francis Marion National Forest, Lynchburg Savanna Heritage Preserve, Longleaf Pine Heritage Preserve, and Lewis Ocean Bay Heritage Preserve.

LeConte's Sparrow: Occasional winter resident of grassy fields and power line rights-of-way. *Key sites:* Santee NWR, Lynchburg Savanna Heritage Preserve, and Francis Marion National Forest.

Saltmarsh and Nelson's Sharp-tailed Sparrows: Saltmarsh is a fairly common winter resident of coastal salt marshes. Nelson's is found in the same habitat, but is an uncommon winter resident. The best time to look for these secretive birds is at high tide, when they have less cover available. Both species of sharp-tailed sparrows often move about the salt marsh in small flocks with Seaside Sparrows. *Key sites:* Huntington Beach State Park is best, but also try Folly Island, Pitt Street Bridge, Hunting Island State Park, Cape Romain NWR, South Tibwin Plantation, and Santee Coastal Reserve.

Seaside Sparrow: Fairly common permanent resident of coastal salt marshes. Easiest to find during the spring and early summer, when males often perch atop the salt marsh grass and sing. *Key sites:* Bear Island WMA, Huntington Beach State Park, Cape Romain NWR, South Tibwin Plantation, Santee Coastal Reserve, Pitt Street Bridge, and Hunting Island State Park.

Fox Sparrow: Fairly common winter resident of brushy thickets within forests. *Key sites:* Congaree National Park, Saluda Shoals Park, Francis Beidler Forest Audubon Sanctuary, Bunched Arrowhead Heritage Preserve, Aiken State Natural Area, Carolina Sandhills NWR, Donnelley WMA, Santee Coastal Reserve, and Edisto Beach State Park.

White-crowned Sparrow: Uncommon winter resident of brushy and weedy areas of fields. *Key sites:* Townville, Bunched Arrowhead Heritage Preserve, and Carolina Sandhills NWR.

Lincoln's Sparrow: Uncommon winter resident of brushy areas along streams, ponds, and marshes. *Key sites:* Townville, Bunched Arrowhead Heritage Preserve, Lynchburg Savanna Heritage Preserve, and Santee NWR.

Rose-breasted Grosbeak: Fairly common migrant in mature deciduous forests. *Key sites:* Caesars Head State Park, Sassafras Mountain, Walhalla State Fish Hatchery, Silver Bluff Audubon Sanctuary, Landsford Canal State Park, and Lake Conestee Nature Park.

Blue Grosbeak: Fairly common summer resident of open, brushy, and weedy fields. *Key sites:* Francis Marion National Forest, Santee NWR, Donnelley WMA, Bear Island WMA, ACE Basin NWR, Cape Romain NWR, Silver Bluff Audubon Sanctuary, Lynchburg Savanna Heritage Preserve, Longleaf Pine Heritage Preserve, Enoree River Waterfowl Management Area, and Congaree Bluffs Heritage Preserve.

Painted Bunting

Indigo Bunting: Common summer resident of open, brushy areas and pine forests. *Key sites:* ACE Basin NWR, Donnelley WMA, Hunting Island State Park, Francis Marion National Forest, Silver Bluff Audubon Sanctuary, Carolina Sandhills NWR, Table Rock State Park, Congaree National Park, Congaree Bluffs Heritage Preserve, Lynchburg Savanna Heritage Preserve, Longleaf Pine Heritage Preserve, and Santee NWR.

Painted Bunting: Fairly common summer resident of forest edges near marshes, ponds, and wet areas. Occasional in winter at backyard bird feeders. *Key sites:* Hunting Island State Park, Pinckney Island NWR, Bear Island WMA, Donnelley WMA, Edisto Beach State Park, Caw Caw County Park, Folly Island, South Tibwin Plantation, Cape Romain NWR, Huntington Beach State Park, Webb WMA, and Santee NWR.

Dickcissel: Uncommon summer resident of weedy fields. Occasional visitor during fall and early winter. *Key sites:* Townville.

Bobolink: Uncommon migrant in spring and fairly common in fall to farm fields and rice fields. *Key sites:* Bear Island WMA, Caw Caw County Park, Magnolia Plantation, Silver Bluff Audubon Sanctuary, Santee NWR, and Townville.

Lapland Longspur: Occasional winter resident of farm fields and coastal beaches. *Key sites:* The Orangeburg Super Sod farm and Townville are best, but also try Cape Romain NWR and Huntington Beach State Park.

Rusty Blackbird: Fairly common winter resident of swamps. *Key sites:* Donnelley WMA, Magnolia Plantation, Caw Caw County Park, Congaree Creek

Heritage Preserve, Santee NWR, Lake Conestee Nature Park, and Edwin M. Griffin Nature Preserve.

Brewer's Blackbird: Occasional winter resident of farmland. *Key sites:* Townville and Santee NWR.

Shiny Cowbird: Occasional summer resident of lawns and roadsides in suburban areas along the coast. *Key site:* Folly Island.

Baltimore Oriole: Uncommon migrant in spring and fall to open deciduous forests, often near water. Occasional winter resident in backyards with bird feeders, especially along the coast. *Key sites:* In the winter try Magnolia Plantation. During migration try Caesars Head State Park, Edwin M. Griffin Nature Preserve, Landsford Canal State Park, Lynch's Woods Park, and Saluda Shoals Park.

Orchard Oriole: Common summer resident of shrubby, early successional farmland. *Key sites:* Bear Island WMA, Donnelley WMA, Edisto Beach State Park, ACE Basin NWR, Santee NWR, Carolina Sandhills NWR, and Lynchburg Savanna Heritage Preserve.

Red Crossbill: Occasional permanent resident of hemlock/white pine forests. *Key sites:* Burrell's Ford, Walhalla State Fish Hatchery, and Caesars Head State Park.

Purple Finch: Irregular, uncommon winter resident of pine and hardwood forests, mainly in the piedmont and mountains. *Key sites:* Burrell's Ford, Walhalla State Fish Hatchery, and Kings Mountain.

Pine Siskin: Irregular, uncommon winter resident of pine and hardwood forests, mainly in the piedmont and mountains. *Key sites:* Burrell's Ford and Walhalla State Fish Hatchery.

Appendix D: Status and Distribution Chart

The chart below contains bar graphs for 349 bird species that are known to occur in South Carolina. Species that are considered to be extremely rare or accidental are not included in the chart, but are listed at the end of this appendix. The graphs will help you to determine what time of year and in which region(s) you are most likely to find each species. It is important to note that the graphs indicate your likelihood of observing at least one individual of the species within the appropriate habitat, but they do not reflect the overall abundance of each species.

For example, although Bald Eagle and Blue-winged Teal are both listed as fairly common winter residents, it does not mean that you will see the same number of Bald Eagles as you will Blue-winged Teal. You will, however, have a high likelihood of finding both Blue-winged Teal and Bald Eagle if you are in the appropriate habitat. "Appropriate habitat" can be defined as the habitat type and birding areas in which the species is most often encountered. See Appendix C to learn more about the habitats and birding-area preferences for more than 175 of South Carolina's birds.

There are several factors that can influence the likelihood of observing certain species, such as knowledge of the observer, weather, and irruptions. Knowledgeable birders will often have an easier time finding many of these species because they have a search image and are already familiar with the bird's vocalizations and behavior. Weather can either increase or decrease the likelihood of finding certain species. Windy and rainy days often make for poor conditions to look for songbirds. However, a strong east wind during winter may bring gannets and sea ducks closer to the coast and make them easier to observe. During fall pay particularly close attention to cold fronts. The day after a cold front moves through you can expect to see large flocks of migrating songbirds and your likelihood of observing many species will increase. Some species such as Red-breasted Nuthatch, Purple Finch, Red Crossbill, and Pine Siskin are irruptive and during most years they will be scarce. However, every once in a blue moon they will "irrupt," in other words, descend in masses into South Carolina, and your chances of observing them will be greatly increased.

These graphs are the first of their kind for South Carolina. They were created using a variety of sources, including information from Will Post and Sid Gauthreaux's *Status and Distribution of South Carolina Birds,* bird checklists from parks and refuges throughout the state, sightings posted on the CarolinaBirds Listserv, and my own personal observations.

Descriptions of the four regions—Coast (Co), Coastal Plain (Cp), Piedmont (Pi), and Mountains (Mo)—can be found in the "Climate and Topography" section of the introduction. *Pelagic* denotes birds that are only found many miles out in the deep ocean, while *Statewide* denotes birds that are found throughout all four of South Carolina's regions. The following definitions correspond to the width of the lines in the graphs:

Keys

▬▬ Common: Seen on 75 to 100 percent of trips in appropriate habitat.
━━ Fairly common: Seen on 25 to 75 percent of trips in appropriate habitat.
═══ Uncommon: Seen on 10 to 25 percent of trips in appropriate habitat.
─── Occasional: Seen on less than 10 percent of trips, but usually seen at least once every year.
- - - - Rare: Not seen every year, but known to occur in South Carolina.

Co = Coast
Cp = Coastal Plain
Pi = Piedmont
Mo = Mountains

Bird Species	Region	Month of Occurrence (J F M A M J J A S O N D)
GAVIIDAE: LOONS		
☐ Red-throated Loon	Co	
☐ Common Loon	Co	
	Cp/Pi	
PODICIPEDIDAE: GREBES		
☐ Pied-billed Grebe	Co/Cp	
	Pi	
☐ Horned Grebe	Co/Cp	
	Pi	
☐ Red-necked Grebe	Co	
☐ Eared Grebe	Co/Cp	
PROCELLARIIDAE: SHEARWATERS and PETRELS		
☐ Northern Fulmar	Pelagic	
☐ Black-capped Petrel	Pelagic	
☐ Cory's Shearwater	Pelagic	
☐ Greater Shearwater	Pelagic	
☐ Sooty Shearwater	Pelagic	
☐ Manx Shearwater	Pelagic	
☐ Audubon's Shearwater	Pelagic	
HYDROBATIDAE: STORM-PETRELS		
☐ Wilson's Storm-Petrel	Pelagic	
☐ Leach's Storm-Petrel	Pelagic	
☐ Band-rumped Storm-Petrel	Pelagic	
PHAETHONTIDAE: TROPICBIRDS		
☐ White-tailed Tropicbird	Pelagic	
SULIDAE: BOOBIES and GANNETS		
☐ Masked Booby	Pelagic	
☐ Northern Gannet	Co	

Month of Occurrence

Bird Species	Region	J F M A M J J A S O N D
PELECANIDAE: PELICANS		
☐ American White Pelican	Co	
☐ Brown Pelican	Co	
PHALACROCORACIDAE: CORMORANTS		
☐ Double-crested Cormorant	Co/Cp	
	Pi	
☐ Great Cormorant	Co	
ANHINGIDAE: DARTERS		
☐ Anhinga	Co/Cp	
FREGATIDAE: FRIGATEBIRDS		
☐ Magnificent Frigatebird	Pelagic	
ARDEIDAE: BITTERNS and HERONS		
☐ American Bittern	Co/Cp	
	Pi	
☐ Least Bittern	Co/Cp	
	Pi	
☐ Great Blue Heron	Co/Cp	
	Pi	
☐ Great Egret	Co/Cp	
	Pi	
☐ Snowy Egret	Co	
	Cp/Pi	
☐ Little Blue Heron	Co	
	Cp	
	Pi	
☐ Tricolored Heron	Co	
	Cp/Pi	
☐ Reddish Egret	Co	
☐ Cattle Egret	Co/Cp	
	Pi	
☐ Green Heron	Co	
	Cp/Pi	
☐ Black-crowned Night-Heron	Co	
	Cp	
☐ Yellow-crowned Night-Heron	Co/Cp	
	Pi	
THRESKIORNITHIDAE: IBISES and SPOONBILLS		
☐ White Ibis	Co	
	Cp	
	Pi	
☐ Glossy Ibis	Co	
	Cp/Pi	
☐ Roseate Spoonbill	Co	
	Cp	
CICONIIDAE: STORKS		
☐ Wood Stork	Co	
	Cp	
	Pi	

Bird Species	Region	J F M A M J J A S O N D
CATHARTIDAE: AMERICAN VULTURES		
☐ Black Vulture	Co/Cp	
	Pi	
	Mo	
☐ Turkey Vulture	Statewide	
ANATIDAE: SWANS, GEESE, and DUCKS		
☐ Black-bellied Whistling-Duck	Co	
☐ Fulvous Whistling-Duck	Co	
☐ Greater White-fronted Goose	Cp/Pi	
☐ Snow Goose	Cp/Pi	
☐ Ross's Goose	Cp/Pi	
☐ Canada Goose	Statewide	
☐ Brant	Co	
☐ Tundra Swan	Co/Cp	
☐ Mute Swan	Statewide	
☐ Wood Duck	Statewide	
☐ Gadwall	Co	
	Cp/Pi	
☐ American Wigeon	Co/Cp	
	Pi	
☐ American Black Duck	Statewide	
☐ Mallard	Statewide	
☐ Mottled Duck	Co	
☐ Blue-winged Teal	Co/Cp	
	Pi	
☐ Northern Shoveler	Co/Cp	
	Pi	
☐ Northern Pintail	Co/Cp	
	Pi	
☐ Green-winged Teal	Co/Cp	
	Pi	
☐ Canvasback	Co	
	Cp/Pi	
☐ Redhead	Statewide	
☐ Ring-necked Duck	Statewide	
☐ Greater Scaup	Co	
☐ Lesser Scaup	Co	
	Cp	
	Pi	
☐ Common Eider	Co	
☐ Surf Scoter	Co	
	Cp/Pi	
☐ White-winged Scoter	Co	
	Cp/Pi	
☐ Black Scoter	Co	
	Cp/Pi	

Bird Species	Region	J	F	M	A	M	J	J	A	S	O	N	D

ANATIDAE: SWANS, GEESE, and DUCKS (continued)

☐ Long-tailed Duck — Co / Cp/Pi

☐ Bufflehead — Co/Cp / Pi

☐ Common Goldeneye — Statewide

☐ Hooded Merganser — Co/Cp / Pi

☐ Common Merganser — Statewide

☐ Red-breasted Merganser — Co / Cp/Pi

☐ Ruddy Duck — Co / Cp/Pi

ACCIPITRIDAE: KITES, HAWKS, EAGLES, and ALLIES

☐ Osprey — Co/Cp / Pi / Mo

☐ Swallow-tailed Kite — Co/Cp / Pi

☐ Mississippi Kite — Co/Cp / Pi

☐ Bald Eagle — Statewide

☐ Northern Harrier — Statewide

☐ Sharp-shinned Hawk — Co/Cp/Pi / Mo

☐ Cooper's Hawk — Statewide

☐ Red-shouldered Hawk — Statewide

☐ Broad-winged Hawk — Co/Cp / Pi/Mo

☐ Red-tailed Hawk — Statewide

☐ Golden Eagle — Co/Cp / Pi/Mo

FALCONIDAE: FALCONS

☐ American Kestrel — Statewide

☐ Merlin — Co / Cp/Pi/Mo

☐ Peregrine Falcon — Co / Mo

PHASIANIDAE: GROUSE and TURKEY

☐ Ruffed Grouse — Mo

☐ Wild Turkey — Statewide

ODONTOPHORIDAE: NEW WORLD QUAIL

☐ Northern Bobwhite — Statewide

Bird Species	Region	J	F	M	A	M	J	J	A	S	O	N	D

RALLIDAE: RAILS, GALLINULES, and COOTS

Bird Species	Region
☐ Yellow Rail	Co
☐ Black Rail	Co
	Cp
	Pi
☐ Clapper Rail	Co
☐ King Rail	Co
	Cp
	Pi
☐ Virginia Rail	Co/Cp
	Pi
☐ Sora	Co
	Cp/Pi
☐ Purple Gallinule	Co
☐ Common Moorhen	Co
	Cp
	Pi
☐ American Coot	Statewide

GRUIDAE: CRANES

Bird Species	Region
☐ Sandhill Crane	Statewide
☐ Whooping Crane	Co

CHARADRIIDAE: PLOVERS

Bird Species	Region
☐ Black-bellied Plover	Co
	Cp/Pi
☐ American Golden-Plover	Co
	Cp
☐ Snowy Plover	Co
☐ Wilson's Plover	Co
☐ Semipalmated Plover	Co
	Cp/Pi
☐ Piping Plover	Co
☐ Killdeer	Statewide

HAEMATOPODIDAE: OYSTERCATCHERS

Bird Species	Region
☐ American Oystercatcher	Co

RECURVIROSTRIDAE: STILTS and AVOCETS

Bird Species	Region
☐ Black-necked Stilt	Co
☐ American Avocet	Co

SCOLOPACIDAE: SANDPIPERS, PHALAROPES, and ALLIES

Bird Species	Region
☐ Greater Yellowlegs	Co
	Cp
	Pi
☐ Lesser Yellowlegs	Co
	Cp
	Pi
☐ Solitary Sandpiper	Statewide
☐ Willet	Co

Bird Species	Region	J F M A M J J A S O N D
SCOLOPACIDAE: SANDPIPERS, PHALAROPES, and ALLIES (continued)		
☐ Spotted Sandpiper	Statewide	
☐ Upland Sandpiper	Statewide	
☐ Whimbrel	Co	
☐ Long-billed Curlew	Co	
☐ Marbled Godwit	Co	
☐ Ruddy Turnstone	Co	
☐ Red Knot	Co	
☐ Sanderling	Co	
☐ Semipalmated Sandpiper	Co	
	Cp/Pi	
☐ Western Sandpiper	Co	
	Cp/Pi	
☐ Least Sandpiper	Co	
	Cp	
	Pi	
☐ White-rumped Sandpiper	Co	
	Cp/Pi	
☐ Baird's Sandpiper	Co/Cp/Pi	
☐ Pectoral Sandpiper	Co	
	Cp	
☐ Purple Sandpiper	Co	
☐ Dunlin	Co	
	Cp/Pi	
☐ Stilt Sandpiper	Co	
	Cp	
☐ Buff-breasted Sandpiper	Cp	
☐ Short-billed Dowitcher	Co	
	Cp/Pi	
☐ Long-billed Dowitcher	Co	
	Cp/Pi	
☐ Wilson's Snipe	Statewide	
☐ American Woodcock	Statewide	
☐ Wilson's Phalarope	Co/Cp	
☐ Red-necked Phalarope	Pelagic	
	Co/Cp	
	Pi	
☐ Red Phalarope	Pelagic	
LARIDAE: JAEGERS and SKUAS		
☐ Pomarine Jaeger	Pelagic	
☐ Parasitic Jaeger	Pelagic	
LARIDAE: GULLS, TERNS, and SKIMMERS		
☐ Laughing Gull	Co	
	Cp	
	Pi	

Bird Species	Region	Month of Occurrence
		J F M A M J J A S O N D

LARIDAE: GULLS, TERNS, and SKIMMERS (continued)

☐ Franklin's Gull — Co
☐ Bonaparte's Gull — Co/Cp/Pi
☐ Ring-billed Gull — Co
    Cp/Pi
☐ Herring Gull — Co
    Cp/Pi
☐ Iceland Gull — Co
☐ Lesser Black-backed Gull — Co
☐ Glaucous Gull — Co
☐ Great Black-backed Gull — Co
☐ Sabine's Gull — Pelagic
☐ Black-legged Kittiwake — Pelagic
☐ Gull-billed Tern — Co
☐ Caspian Tern — Co
    Cp
    Pi
☐ Royal Tern — Co
☐ Sandwich Tern — Co
☐ Common Tern — Co
☐ Arctic Tern — Pelagic
☐ Forster's Tern — Co
    Cp/Pi
☐ Least Tern — Co
    Cp
☐ Bridled Tern — Pelagic
☐ Sooty Tern — Pelagic
☐ Black Tern — Co
    Cp
    Pi
☐ Brown Noddy — Pelagic
☐ Black Skimmer — Co

ALCIDAE: AUKS and MURRES

☐ Razorbill — Co

COLUMBIDAE: PIGEONS and DOVES

☐ Rock Pigeon — Statewide
☐ Eurasian Collared-Dove — Statewide
☐ White-winged Dove — Co
    Cp
☐ Mourning Dove — Statewide
☐ Common Ground-Dove — Co/Cp

CUCULIDAE: CUCKOOS

☐ Black-billed Cuckoo — Co/Cp
    Pi/Mo
☐ Yellow-billed Cuckoo — Statewide

Month of Occurrence

Bird Species	Region	J F M A M J J A S O N D

TYTONIDAE: BARN OWLS
- ☐ Barn Owl — Statewide

STRIGIDAE: TYPICAL OWLS
- ☐ Eastern Screech-Owl — Statewide
- ☐ Great Horned Owl — Statewide
- ☐ Barred Owl — Co/Cp, Pi/Mo
- ☐ Short-eared Owl — Co/Cp, Pi
- ☐ Northern Saw-whet Owl — Statewide

CAPRIMULGIDAE: GOATSUCKERS
- ☐ Common Nighthawk — Statewide
- ☐ Chuck-will's-widow — Co/Cp/Pi, Mo
- ☐ Whip-poor-will — Co, Cp/Pi, Mo

APODIDAE: SWIFTS
- ☐ Chimney Swift — Statewide

TROCHILIDAE: HUMMINGBIRDS
- ☐ Ruby-throated Hummingbird — Statewide
- ☐ Black-chinned Hummingbird — Co/Cp
- ☐ Rufous Hummingbird — Statewide

ALCEDINIDAE: KINGFISHERS
- ☐ Belted Kingfisher — Statewide

PICIDAE: WOODPECKERS
- ☐ Red-headed Woodpecker — Statewide
- ☐ Red-bellied Woodpecker — Statewide
- ☐ Yellow-bellied Sapsucker — Co/Cp/Pi, Mo
- ☐ Downy Woodpecker — Statewide
- ☐ Hairy Woodpecker — Co/Cp, Pi/Mo
- ☐ Red-cockaded Woodpecker — Co/Cp
- ☐ Northern Flicker — Statewide
- ☐ Pileated Woodpecker — Statewide

TYRANNIDAE: TYRANT FLYCATCHERS
- ☐ Olive-sided Flycatcher — Statewide
- ☐ Eastern Wood-Pewee — Co/Cp, Pi, Mo
- ☐ Yellow-bellied Flycatcher — Co/Cp
- ☐ Acadian Flycatcher — Co/Cp, Pi/Mo
- ☐ Willow Flycatcher — Statewide
- ☐ Least Flycatcher — Statewide

Bird Species	Region	Month of Occurrence J F M A M J J A S O N D

TYRANNIDAE: TYRANT FLYCATCHERS (continued)

Bird Species	Region
☐ Eastern Phoebe	Co/Cp
	Pi/Mo
☐ Great Crested Flycatcher	Statewide
☐ Western Kingbird	Co
	Cp/Pi
☐ Eastern Kingbird	Statewide
☐ Gray Kingbird	Co
	Cp
☐ Scissor-tailed Flycatcher	Co
	Cp/Pi
	Mo

LANIIDAE: SHRIKES

☐ Loggerhead Shrike	Co/Cp

VIREONIDAE: VIREOS

☐ White-eyed Vireo	Co/Cp
	Pi
	Mo
☐ Yellow-throated Vireo	Statewide
☐ Blue-headed Vireo	Co/Cp
	Pi/Mo
☐ Warbling Vireo	Statewide
☐ Philadelphia Vireo	Co
	Cp/Pi
☐ Red-eyed Vireo	Statewide

CORVIDAE: JAYS and CROWS

☐ Blue Jay	Statewide
☐ American Crow	Statewide
☐ Fish Crow	Co
	Cp
	Pi
☐ Common Raven	Pi
	Mo

ALAUDIDAE: LARKS

☐ Horned Lark	Co
	Cp
	Pi

HIRUNDINIDAE: SWALLOWS

☐ Purple Martin	Statewide
☐ Tree Swallow	Co/Cp
	Pi
☐ Northern Rough-winged Swallow	Statewide
☐ Bank Swallow	Statewide
☐ Cliff Swallow	Co
	Cp
	Pi

Month of Occurrence

Bird Species	Region	J F M A M J J A S O N D
HIRUNDINIDAE: SWALLOWS (continued)		
☐ Cave Swallow	Co	
☐ Barn Swallow	Co	
	Cp/Pi	
PARIDAE: TITMICE		
☐ Carolina Chickadee	Statewide	
☐ Tufted Titmouse	Statewide	
SITTIDAE: NUTHATCHES		
☐ Red-breasted Nuthatch	Co	
	Cp/Pi	
	Mo	
☐ White-breasted Nuthatch	Co/Cp	
	Pi	
	Mo	
☐ Brown-headed Nuthatch	Co/Cp/Pi	
	Mo	
CERTHIIDAE: CREEPERS		
☐ Brown Creeper	Co/Cp/Pi	
	Mo	
TROGLODYTIDAE: WRENS		
☐ Carolina Wren	Statewide	
☐ House Wren	Co/Cp	
	Pi	
☐ Winter Wren	Statewide	
☐ Sedge Wren	Co/Cp	
	Pi	
☐ Marsh Wren	Co	
	Cp	
	Pi	
REGULIDAE: KINGLETS		
☐ Golden-crowned Kinglet	Co/Cp	
	Pi	
	Mo	
☐ Ruby-crowned Kinglet	Statewide	
SYLVIIDAE: GNATCATCHERS		
☐ Blue-gray Gnatcatcher	Co/Cp	
	Pi/Mo	
TURDIDAE: THRUSHES		
☐ Eastern Bluebird	Statewide	
☐ Veery	Co/Cp	
	Pi/Mo	
☐ Gray-cheeked Thrush	Co/Cp	
	Pi/Mo	
☐ Swainson's Thrush	Co/Cp	
	Pi/Mo	
☐ Hermit Thrush	Statewide	

Bird Species	Region	Month of Occurrence J F M A M J J A S O N D
TURDIDAE: THRUSHES (continued)		
☐ Wood Thrush	Co	
	Cp/Pi/Mo	
☐ American Robin	Co/Cp	
	Pi/Mo	
MIMIDAE: MIMIC THRUSHES		
☐ Gray Catbird	Co/Cp	
	Pi/Mo	
☐ Northern Mockingbird	Statewide	
☐ Brown Thrasher	Statewide	
STURNIDAE: STARLINGS		
☐ European Starling	Statewide	
MOTACILLIDAE: PIPITS		
☐ American Pipit	Statewide	
BOMBYCILLIDAE: WAXWINGS		
☐ Cedar Waxwing	Co/Cp	
	Pi/Mo	
PARULIDAE: WOOD-WARBLERS		
☐ Blue-winged Warbler	Co/Cp	
	Pi/Mo	
☐ Golden-winged Warbler	Co/Cp	
	Pi/Mo	
☐ Tennessee Warbler	Co/Cp	
	Pi/Mo	
☐ Orange-crowned Warbler	Co	
	Cp	
	Pi/Mo	
☐ Nashville Warbler	Co/Cp	
	Pi/Mo	
☐ Northern Parula	Co/Cp	
	Pi/Mo	
☐ Yellow Warbler	Co/Cp	
	Pi/Mo	
☐ Chestnut-sided Warbler	Co	
	Cp	
	Pi	
	Mo	
☐ Magnolia Warbler	Co/Cp	
	Pi/Mo	
☐ Cape May Warbler	Co	
	Cp/Pi/Mo	
☐ Black-throated Blue Warbler	Co	
	Cp/Pi	
	Mo	
☐ Yellow-rumped Warbler	Statewide	

Month of Occurrence

Bird Species	Region	J	F	M	A	M	J	J	A	S	O	N	D

PARULIDAE: **WOOD-WARBLERS (continued)**

- Black-throated Green Warbler — Co, Cp/Pi, Mo
- Blackburnian Warbler — Co, Cp/Pi, Mo
- Yellow-throated Warbler — Co/Cp, Pi, Mo
- Pine Warbler — Co/Cp/Pi, Mo
- Prairie Warbler — Co/Cp, Pi/Mo
- Palm Warbler — Co/Cp, Pi
- Bay-breasted Warbler — Co/Cp, Pi/Mo
- Blackpoll Warbler — Co/Cp, Pi/Mo
- Cerulean Warbler — Co/Cp/Pi, Mo
- Black-and-white Warbler — Co, Cp, Pi, Mo
- American Redstart — Co, Cp, Pi, Mo
- Prothonotary Warbler — Co/Cp, Pi
- Worm-eating Warbler — Co/Cp, Pi, Mo
- Swainson's Warbler — Co/Cp, Pi, Mo
- Ovenbird — Co/Cp, Pi, Mo
- Northern Waterthrush — Co, Cp/Pi
- Louisiana Waterthrush — Co, Cp/Pi, Mo

Bird Species	Region	J F M A M J J A S O N D
PARULIDAE: WOOD-WARBLERS (continued)		
☐ Kentucky Warbler	Statewide	
☐ Connecticut Warbler	Co/Cp	
	Pi/Mo	
☐ Mourning Warbler	Statewide	
☐ Common Yellowthroat	Co/Cp	
	Pi	
	Mo	
☐ Hooded Warbler	Statewide	
☐ Wilson's Warbler	Statewide	
☐ Canada Warbler	Co/Cp/Pi	
	Mo	
☐ Yellow-breasted Chat	Co/Cp	
	Pi	
	Mo	
THRAUPIDAE: TANAGERS		
☐ Summer Tanager	Co/Cp/Pi	
☐ Scarlet Tanager	Co	
	Cp	
	Pi/Mo	
☐ Western Tanager	Co/Cp	
EMBERIZIDAE: TOWHEES, SPARROWS, and ALLIES		
☐ Eastern Towhee	Statewide	
☐ Bachman's Sparrow	Co/Cp	
	Pi	
☐ Chipping Sparrow	Co/Cp	
	Pi	
	Mo	
☐ Clay-colored Sparrow	Co	
	Cp/Pi/Mo	
☐ Field Sparrow	Co	
	Cp	
	Pi	
	Mo	
☐ Vesper Sparrow	Co/Cp	
	Pi	
☐ Lark Sparrow	Statewide	
☐ Savannah Sparrow	Statewide	
☐ Grasshopper Sparrow	Co	
	Cp/Pi	
☐ Henslow's Sparrow	Co/Cp	
	Pi	
☐ LeConte's Sparrow	Co/Cp	
	Pi	
☐ Nelson's Sharp-tailed Sparrow	Co	
☐ Saltmarsh Sharp-tailed Sparrow	Co	

Bird Species	Region	J F M A M J J A S O N D

EMBERIZIDAE: TOWHEES, SPARROWS, and ALLIES (continued)

Bird Species	Region	Month of Occurrence
☐ Seaside Sparrow	Co	
☐ Fox Sparrow	Statewide	
☐ Song Sparrow	Co/Cp	
	Pi/Mo	
☐ Lincoln's Sparrow	Co	
	Cp	
	Pi	
☐ Swamp Sparrow	Statewide	
☐ White-throated Sparrow	Statewide	
☐ White-crowned Sparrow	Co/Cp	
	Pi	
☐ Dark-eyed Junco	Co	
	Cp/Pi	
	Mo	
☐ Lapland Longspur	Statewide	

CARDINALIDAE: CARDINALS, GROSBEAKS, and ALLIES

Bird Species	Region	Month of Occurrence
☐ Northern Cardinal	Statewide	
☐ Rose-breasted Grosbeak	Co/Cp	
	Pi/Mo	
☐ Blue Grosbeak	Co	
	Cp/Pi	
	Mo	
☐ Indigo Bunting	Statewide	
☐ Painted Bunting	Co	
	Cp	
	Pi	
☐ Dickcissel	Co	
	Cp/Pi	
	Mo	

ICTERIDAE: BLACKBIRDS and ORIOLES

Bird Species	Region	Month of Occurrence
☐ Bobolink	Co/Cp/Pi	
☐ Red-winged Blackbird	Statewide	
☐ Eastern Meadowlark	Co/Cp	
	Pi/Mo	
☐ Yellow-headed Blackbird	Co	
	Cp/Pi	
☐ Rusty Blackbird	Co/Cp/Pi	
☐ Brewer's Blackbird	Co/Cp/Pi	
☐ Common Grackle	Statewide	
☐ Boat-tailed Grackle	Co	
	Cp	
☐ Shiny Cowbird	Co	

Bird Species	Region	Month of Occurrence J F M A M J J A S O N D

Month of Occurrence

ICTERIDAE: BLACKBIRDS *and* ORIOLES (continued)

Bird Species	Region
☐ Brown-headed Cowbird	Co/Cp/Pi
	Mo
☐ Orchard Oriole	Statewide
☐ Baltimore Oriole	Co/Cp
	Pi/Mo

FRINGILLIDAE: FINCHES

Bird Species	Region
☐ Purple Finch	Co/Cp
	Pi/Mo
☐ House Finch	Statewide
☐ Red Crossbill	Co/Cp/Pi
	Mo
☐ Pine Siskin	Co/Cp
	Pi/Mo
☐ American Goldfinch	Co/Cp
	Pi/Mo
☐ Evening Grosbeak	

PASSERIDAE: OLD WORLD SPARROWS

Bird Species	Region
☐ House Sparrow	Statewide

Unexpected Birds

Species that are very rare in South Carolina, are accidentals, or are extirpated (denoted by *E*).

Eurasian Wigeon
Cinnamon Teal
King Eider
Harlequin Duck
Pacific Loon
Western Grebe
Little Shearwater
Red-billed Tropicbird
Brown Booby
Red-footed Booby
Snail Kite
Northern Goshawk
Swainson's Hawk
Rough-legged Hawk
Limpkin
Northern Lapwing
Eskimo Curlew (E)
Hudsonian Godwit
Red-necked Stint
Sharp-tailed Sandpiper
Curlew Sandpiper
Ruff
South Polar Skua
Little Gull
Black-headed Gull
White-winged Tern
Long-tailed Jaeger
Dovekie
Common Murre
Thick-billed Murre
Black Guillemot
Long-billed Murrelet
Band-tailed Pigeon
Passenger Pigeon (E)
Carolina Parakeet (E)
Smooth-billed Ani

Groove-billed Ani
Snowy Owl
Burrowing Owl
Long-eared Owl
Say's Phoebe
Vermilion Flycatcher
Fork-tailed Flycatcher
Broad-billed Hummingbird
Buff-bellied Hummingbird
Blue-throated Hummingbird
Calliope Hummingbird
Ivory-billed Woodpecker (E)
Bell's Vireo
Bewick's Wren
Townsend's Solitaire
Bicknell's Thrush
Varied Thrush
White Wagtail
Sprague's Pipit
Bachman's Warbler (E)
Black-throated Gray Warbler
Kirtland's Warbler
Green-tailed Towhee
Spotted Towhee
American Tree Sparrow
Lark Bunting
Harris's Sparrow
Golden-crowned Sparrow
Smith's Longspur
Snow Bunting
Black-headed Grosbeak
Lazuli Bunting
Western Meadowlark
Bullock's Oriole
Pine Grosbeak
Common Redpoll

Appendix E: Addresses and Phone Numbers

ACE Basin National Wildlife
Refuge
P.O. Box 848
Hollywood, SC 29449
(843) 889-3084
www.fws.gov/acebasin

Aiken State Natural Area
1145 State Park Road
Windsor, SC 29856
(803) 649-2857
www.southcarolinaparks.com

Andrew Jackson State Park
196 Andrew Jackson Park Road
Lancaster, SC 29720
(803) 285-3344
www.southcarolinaparks.com

Bear Island Wildlife Management
Area
585 Donnelley Drive
Green Pond, SC 29446
(843) 844-8957
www.dnr.sc.gov

Beaverdam Creek Wildlife
Management Area
1000 Assembly Street
Columbia, SC 29201
(803) 734-3886
www.dnr.sc.gov

Bunched Arrowhead Heritage
Preserve
153 Hopewell Road
Pendleton, SC 29670
(864) 654-6738, ext. 15
www.dnr.sc.gov

Caesars Head State Park
8155 Geer Highway
Cleveland, SC 29635
(864) 836-6115
www.southcarolinaparks.com

Cape Romain Bird Observatory
5801 Highway 17 North
Awendaw, SC 29429
(843) 928-3264
www.crbo.net

Carolina Sandhills National
Wildlife Refuge
23734 U.S. Highway 1
McBee, SC 29101
(843) 335-8401
www.fws.gov/carolinasandhills

Caw Caw County Park
5200 Savannah Highway
Ravenel, SC 29470
(843) 795-4386
www.ccprc.com

Cheraw State Park
100 State Park Road
Cheraw, SC 29520
(843) 537-9656
www.southcarolinaparks.com

Chester State Park
759 State Park Drive
Chester, SC 29706
(803) 385-2680
www.southcarolinaparks.com

Coastal Expeditions
Shem Creek Maritime Center
514-B Mill Street
Mt. Pleasant, SC 29464
(843) 884-7684
www.coastalexpeditions.com

Congaree National Park
1000 National Park Road
Hopkins, SC 29061
(803) 776-4396, ext. 0
www.nps.gov/cosw

Croft State Natural Area
450 Croft State Park Road
Spartanburg, SC 29302
(864) 585-1283
www.southcarolinaparks.com

Donnelley Wildlife Management Area
585 Donnelley Drive
Green Pond, SC 29446
(843) 844-8957
www.dnr.sc.gov

Dreher Island State Park
3677 State Park Road
Prosperity, SC 29127
(803) 364-4152
www.southcarolinaparks.com

Edisto Beach State Park
8377 State Cabin Road
Edisto Island, SC 29438
(843) 869-4425
www.southcarolinaparks.com

Edwin M. Griffin Nature Preserve
Spartanburg Area Conservancy
P.O. Box 18168
Spartanburg, SC 29318
(864) 948-0000

Folly Beach County Park
1100 West Ashley Avenue
Folly Beach, SC 29439
(843) 588-2426
www.ccprc.com

Folly Beach Fishing Pier
101 East Arctic Avenue
Folly Beach, SC 29439
(843) 588-3474
www.ccprc.com

Fort Sumter National Monument
1214 Middle Street
Sullivan's Island, SC 29482
(843) 883-3123
www.nps.gov/fosu

Francis Beidler Forest Audubon
Sanctuary
336 Sanctuary Road
Harleyville, SC 29448
(843) 462-2150
http://sc.audubon.org

Francis Marion National Forest
4931 Broad River Road
Columbia, SC 29212
(803) 561-4000
www.fs.fed.us/r8/fms

Givhans Ferry State Park
746 Givhans Ferry Road
Ridgeville, SC 29472
(843) 873-0692
www.southcarolinaparks.com

Hunting Island State Park
2555 Sea Island Parkway
Hunting Island, SC 29920
(843) 838-2011
www.southcarolinaparks.com

Huntington Beach State Park
16148 Ocean Highway
Murrells Inlet, SC 29576
(843) 237-4440
www.southcarolinaparks.com

James Island County Park
871 Riverland Drive
Charleston, SC 29412
(843) 795-7275
www.ccprc.com

Jim Timmerman Natural Resource
Area
206 Laurel Valley Road
Sunset, SC 29685
(864) 878-9071
www.dnr.sc.gov

Jones Gap State Park
303 Jones Gap Park Road
Marietta, SC 29661
(864) 836-3647
www.southcarolinaparks.com

J. Strom Thurmond Dam and Lake
510 Clarks Hill Highway
Clarks Hill, SC 29821
(864) 333-1100

Kings Mountain National Military
Park
2625 Park Road
Blacksburg, SC 29702
(864) 936-7921
www.nps.gov/kimo

Kings Mountain State Park
1277 Park Road
Blacksburg, SC 29702
(803) 222-3209
www.southcarolinaparks.com

Lake Conestee Nature Park
Conestee Foundation
P.O. Box 9111
Greenville, SC 29604
(864) 380-5233
www.consteepark.com

Lake Hartwell State Recreation Area
19138-A Highway 11 South
Fair Play, SC 29643
(864) 972-3352
www.southcarolinaparks.com

Landsford Canal State Park
2051 Park Drive
Catawba, SC 29704
(803) 789-5800
www.southcarolinaparks.com

Lee State Natural Area
487 Loop Road
Bishopville, SC 29010
(803) 428-5307
www.southcarolinaparks.com

Magnolia Plantation & Gardens
3350 Ashley River Road
Charleston, SC 29414
(800) 367-3517
www.magnoliaplantation.com

Myrtle Beach State Park
4401 South Kings Highway
Myrtle Beach, SC 29575
(843) 238-5325
www.southcarolinaparks.com

Newberry Soil & Water Conservation
District
USDA Service Center
719 Kendall Road
Newberry, SC 29108
(803) 276-1978, ext. 3

Oconee State Park
624 State Park Road
Mountain Rest, SC 29664
(864) 638-5353
www.southcarolinaparks.com

Paris Mountain State Park
2401 State Park Road
Greenville, SC 29609
(864) 244-5565
www.southcarolinaparks.com

Pinckney Island National Wildlife
Refuge
1000 Business Center Drive
Parkway Business Center, Suite 10
Savannah, GA 31405
(912) 652-4415
www.fws.gov/pinckneyisland

Poinsett State Park
6660 Poinsett Park Road
Wedgefield, SC 29168
(803) 494-8177
www.southcarolinaparks.com

Rocky Branch Campground
Enoree Ranger District,
Enoree Office
20 Work Center Road
Whitmire, SC 29178
(803) 276-4810
www.fs.fed.us/r8/fms

Saluda Shoals Park
5605 Bush River Road
Columbia, SC 29212
(803) 772-1218
www.icrc.net/saludashoals

Santee Coastal Reserve
P.O. Box 37
McClellanville, SC 29458
(843) 546-8665
www.dnr.sc.gov

Santee National Wildlife Refuge
2125 Fort Watson Road
Summerton, SC 29148
(803) 478-2314
www.fws.gov/santee

Santee State Park
251 State Park Road
Santee, SC 29142
(803) 854-2408
www.southcarolinaparks.com

Savannah National Wildlife Refuge
1000 Business Center Drive
Parkway Business Center, Suite 10
Savannah, GA 31405
(912) 652-4415
www.fws.gov/savannah

SCDNR Marine Resource Division
217 Fort Johnson Road
Charleston, SC 29422
(843) 953-9300
www.dnr.sc.gov

SCDNR Wildlife and Freshwater
Fisheries Division
1000 Assembly Street
Columbia, SC 29201
(803) 734-3886
www.dnr.sc.gov

Sea Pines Forest Preserve Foundation
Community Services Associates Inc.
Hilton Head Island, SC 29928
(843) 671-7170

Sesquicentennial State Park
9564 Two Notch Road
Columbia, SC 29223
(803) 788-2706
www.southcarolinaparks.com

Sewee Visitor and Environmental
Education Center
5821 Highway 17 North
Awendaw, SC 29429
(843) 928-3368
www.fws.gov/seweecenter

Silver Bluff Audubon Sanctuary
4542 Silver Bluff Road
Jackson, SC 29831
(803) 471-0291
http://sc.audubon.org

Skidaway Island State Park
52 Diamond Causeway
Savannah, GA 31411
www.gastateparks.org

Sumter National Forest—Andrew
Pickens District
112 Andrew Pickens Circle
Mountain Rest, SC 29664
(864) 638-9568
www.fs.fed.us/r8/fms

Sumter National Forest—Enoree
District
Enoree Office
20 Work Center Road
Whitmire, SC 29178
(803) 276-4810
www.fs.fed.us/r8/fms

Super Sod
3086 Five Chop Road
Orangeburg, SC 29115
(803) 531-4443 or (800) 255-0928
www.super-sod.com

Table Rock State Park
158 East Ellison Lane
Pickens, SC 29671
(864) 878-9813
www.southcarolinaparks.com

Walhalla State Fish Hatchery
198 Fish Hatchery Road
Mountain Rest, SC 29664
(864) 638-2866
www.dnr.sc.gov

Webb Wildlife Management Area
1282 Webb Avenue
Garnett, SC 29922
(803) 625-3569
www.dnr.sc.gov

Appendix F: Additional Resources for Birding in South Carolina

South Carolina Nature Guides

Carter, Robin M. *Finding Birds in South Carolina*. Columbia, SC: University of South Carolina Press, 1993.

Clark, John, and John Dantzler. *Hiking South Carolina*. Helena, MT: Falcon Publishing, 1998.

Jerman, Patricia L. *South Carolina Nature Viewing Guide*. Columbia, SC: South Carolina Department of Natural Resources, 1998.

Birding Field Guides

Kaufman, Kenn. *Birds of North America*. New York: Houghton Mifflin, 2000.

National Geographic. *Field Guide to the Birds of North America*. 5th ed. Washington, DC: National Geographic, 2006.

Peterson, Roger Tory. *Birds of Eastern and Central North America*. New York: Houghton Mifflin, 2002.

Sibley, David A. *The Sibley Field Guide to Birds of Eastern North America*. New York: Alfred A. Knopf, 2003.

Rare Bird Alerts

North Carolina and South Carolina Statewide Rare Bird Alerts (RBA), (704) 332-2473.

CarolinaBirds Listserv: www.duke.edu/~cwcook/cbirds.html. Information on how to receive e-mails from this Listserv can be found at this Web site. This mailing list serves as a forum to discuss wild birds, birders, and birding in the Carolinas, including rare birds, bird finding, bird identification, bird behavior, backyard birding, trip reports, bird counts, and bird club information.

Birdingonthe.net: www.birdingonthe.net/mailinglists/CARO.html. If you don't want to sign up to receive e-mails from CarolinaBirds, you can always check the fifty most recent messages on this Web site, which contains recent postings from the Listserv.

CarolinaBirds archives: https://lists.duke.edu/sympa/arc/carolinabirds. The searchable archives of the CarolinaBirds Listserv can be very useful if you are hoping to see a particular species, such as Black Rail, Henslow's Sparrow, Dickcissel, or other rare birds.

Useful Internet Sites

Breeding Bird Atlas: www.dnr.sc.gov/wildlife/bbatlas/bba.html. Distribution maps for all of South Carolina's breeding bird species.

Cape Romain Bird Observatory: www.crbo.net. Birding information for coastal South Carolina and a list of events and field trips offered by the observatory.

Carolina Bird Club: www.carolinabirdclub.org. Birding information and maps for more than seventy sites in South Carolina.

Columbia Audubon Society: www.columbiaaudubon.org. A birding calendar for the state, birding site descriptions, and links to numerous birding checklists for both state and federal lands in South Carolina.

Google Maps: http://maps.google.com. Excellent, user-friendly maps to help you plan trips to all of the birding areas in this guide.

Hawk Migration Association of North America: www.hmana.org. Species totals, maps, and other valuable information for hawk watch sites in North America.

South Carolina Department of Natural Resources (SCDNR) Managed Lands: www.dnr.sc.gov/managed/index.html. Information on all lands managed by SCDNR, such as wildlife management areas and heritage preserves.

South Carolina State Parks: www.southcarolinaparks.com. Information on all state parks within South Carolina, including admission fees, hours of operation, and maps.

South Carolina State Trails Program: www.sctrails.net. Maps, directions, and descriptions for most of South Carolina's hiking, biking, and horse trails.

TopoZone: www.topozone.com. USGS topographic maps for the entire United States.

USGS Bird Checklists of South Carolina: www.npwrc.usgs.gov/resource/birds/chekbird/r4/45.htm. Seasonal abundance checklists for federally owned lands in South Carolina.

Appendix G: South Carolina Birding Organizations

Audubon South Carolina, the state office of the National Audubon Society, works hard to protect birds and their habitat throughout South Carolina. The state office is located at the Francis Beidler Forest Audubon Sanctuary near Harleyville. Since the sanctuary was acquired in 1973, Audubon has successfully preserved nearly 16,000 acres of land within Four Holes Swamp. Additionally, Audubon South Carolina's conservation efforts have lead to increased protection for nesting seabirds along the coast, high-quality foraging areas for post-breeding Wood Storks, the designation of more than forty Important Bird Areas (IBA) throughout the state, and much more. Audubon South Carolina is a nonprofit organization and operates largely on donations. If you would like to help make a difference for birds in South Carolina, please consider making a donation to Audubon South Carolina. Donations may be mailed to Audubon South Carolina, 336 Sanctuary Road, Harleyville, SC 29448. Call (843) 462-2150 or visit http://sc.audubon.org for more information.

The numerous Audubon chapters throughout the state can always use volunteer help with Christmas Bird Counts, Spring and Fall Migration Counts, and local conservation efforts. See the list below to locate the chapter nearest to you.

Augusta-Aiken Audubon Society, www.augustaaikenaudubon.org
Charleston Natural History Society, www.charlestonaudubon.org
Columbia Audubon Society, www.columbiaaudubon.org
Hilton Head Audubon Society, www.hiltonheadaudubon.org
Piedmont Audubon Society in Spartanburg, 385 South Spring Street, Spartanburg, SC 29306
Waccamaw Audubon Society in Myrtle Beach, http://ww2.coastal.edu/richard/audubon

Carolina Bird Club is a nonprofit educational and scientific organization that was founded in 1973. The club holds meetings three times each year in various locations throughout North and South Carolina. Often the highlights of these meetings are numerous field trips to some of the best bird-watching areas in the state. The club's quarterly bulletin, *The Chat,* frequently contains interesting scientific articles about the birds of the Carolinas. The club's Web site features maps and directions to many of the best bird-watching areas in North and South Carolina. For more information about the Carolina Bird Club, visit www.carolinabirdclub.org.

Greenville County Bird Club, founded in 2000, offers a regular program of monthly field trips led by friendly, knowledgeable birders. The club is also involved in a variety of community conservation projects, including the Reedy River Project, Lake Conestee Project, Caesars Head Hawk Watch, Spring and Fall Migration Counts, and the Christmas Bird Count. For more information about the Greenville County Bird Club, visit http://gcbirdclub.org.

Appendix H: References

American Ornithologists' Union. 1998. *Check-list of North American Birds.* 7th ed. Lawrence, KS: American Ornithologists' Union.

Carter, R. M. 1993. *Finding Birds in South Carolina.* Columbia, SC: University of South Carolina Press.

————. 1995. *Checklist of Birds of Congaree National Park.* Columbia, SC: U.S. Fish & Wildlife Service.

Cely, J. E. 2003. *The South Carolina Breeding Bird Atlas.* Columbia, SC: South Carolina Department of Natural Resources.

Cely, J. E., and A. J. Day. 2005. *Swallow-tailed Kite Investigations, South Carolina, 1998–2004.* Columbia, SC: South Carolina Department of Natural Resources.

Clark, J. F., and J. Dantzler. 1998. *Hiking South Carolina.* Helena, MT: Falcon Publishing.

Dodd, M. G., and T. M. Murphy. 1996. *The Status and Distribution of Wading Birds in South Carolina, 1988–1996.* Columbia, SC: South Carolina Department of Natural Resources.

Dodd, S. L., and M. D. Spinks. 2001. "Shorebird assemblages of the Cape Romain Region, South Carolina." *The Chat* 65: 45–67.

Dugas, G. C., Jr., A. Daniels, B. Lowes, and P. Mulhollan. 2002. *Birder's Guide to Hilton Head Island, S.C. and the Low Country.* 4th ed. Hilton Head, SC: Hilton Head Audubon Society.

Dunn, J. L., and K. L. Garrett. 1997. *A Field Guide to Warblers of North America.* New York: Houghton Mifflin.

Ferguson, L. M., P. G. Jodice, W. Post, and F. I. Sanders. 2005. "Reddish Egret Extends its Breeding Range along the North American Atlantic Coast into South Carolina." *Waterbirds* 28: 525–26.

Foothills Trail Conference. 1998. *Guide to the Foothills Trail.* 3rd ed. Greenville, SC: Foothills Trail Conference.

Forsythe, D. M. 2001. *Checklist of Birds of Coastal Carolina*. Charleston, SC: The Citadel.

Gibbons, J. W., and M. E. Dorcas. 2002. "Defensive behavior of Cottonmouths (*Agkistrodon piscivorus*) towards humans." *Copeia* (1): 195–98.

Hamel, P. B. 1992. *The Land Managers' Guide to the Birds of the South*. Chapel Hill, NC: The Nature Conservancy.

Jerman, P. L. 1998. *South Carolina Nature Viewing Guide*. Columbia, SC: South Carolina Department of Natural Resources.

Jodice, P. G., T. M. Murphy, F. J. Sanders, and L. M. Ferguson. 2007. "Long-term Trends in Nest Counts of Colonial Seabirds in South Carolina, USA." *Waterbirds* 30: 40–51.

Koehler, P. 2004. *Checklist of Birds of Silver Bluff Audubon Sanctuary*. Jackson, SC: Silver Bluff Audubon Sanctuary.

Langley, R. L. 2005. "Alligator attacks on humans in the United States." *Wilderness and Environmental Medicine* 16: 119–24.

McNair, D. B., and W. Post. 1993. *Supplement to Status and Distribution of South Carolina Birds*. Charleston, SC: The Charleston Museum.

National Audubon Society. 2002. *Field Notes: The 102nd Christmas Bird Count, 2001–02*. Vol. 56. New York: National Audubon Society.

National Audubon Society. 2003. *Field Notes: The 103rd Christmas Bird Count, 2002–03*. Vol. 57. New York: National Audubon Society.

National Audubon Society. 2004. *Field Notes: The 104th Christmas Bird Count, 2003–04*. Vol. 58. New York: National Audubon Society.

National Audubon Society. 2005. *Field Notes: The 105th Christmas Bird Count, 2004–05*. Vol. 59. New York: National Audubon Society.

National Audubon Society. 2006. *Field Notes: The 106th Christmas Bird Count, 2005–06*. Vol. 60. New York: National Audubon Society.

National Audubon Society. 2007. *Field Notes: The 107th Christmas Bird Count, 2006–07*. Vol. 61. New York: National Audubon Society.

Naturaland Trust. 1998. *Mountain Bridge Trails*. 3rd ed. Greenville, SC: Naturaland Trust.

Nugent, P. E. 2006. *Checklist of the Birds of Caw Caw Interpretive Center*. Ravenel, SC: Caw Caw County Park.

Peachey, J., P. Turner, and S. Turner. 2006. *Checklist of Birds of Huntington Beach State Park*. Murrells Inlet, SC: Huntington Beach State Park.

Pettingill, O. S., Jr. 1977. *A Guide to Bird Finding East of the Mississippi*. 2nd ed. Boston: Houghton Mifflin.

Post, W., and S. A. Gauthreaux, Jr. 1989. *Status and Distribution of South Carolina Birds*. Charleston, SC: The Charleston Museum.

Post, W., and P. E. Nugent. 1995. *Checklist of the Birds of Magnolia Plantation Wildlife Refuge*. Charleston, SC: Magnolia Plantation.

Price, J., S. Droege, and A. Price. 1995. *The Summer Atlas of North American Birds*. London and San Diego: Academic Press.

Shahid, A. 2005. *Checklist of Birds of Francis Beidler Forest Audubon Sanctuary*. Harleyville, SC: Audubon South Carolina.

Sprunt, A., Jr., and E. B. Chamberlain. 1949. *South Carolina Bird Life*. Charleston, SC: The Charleston Museum.

U.S. Fish and Wildlife Service. 2001. *Carolina Sandhills National Wildlife Refuge Bird List*. McBee, SC: Carolina Sandhills National Wildlife Refuge.

————. 2004. *Cape Romain National Wildlife Refuge Bird List*. Awendaw, SC: Cape Romain National Wildlife Refuge.

————. 2005. *ACE Basin National Wildlife Refuge Bird List*. Hollywood, SC: ACE Basin National Wildlife Refuge.

USDA Forest Service. 1984. *Checklist of Birds of the Francis Marion National Forest*. Columbia, SC: USDA Forest Service.

Vetter, R. S. 2005. "Arachnids submitted as suspected Brown Recluse Spiders (*Araneae Sicariidae*): *Loxosceles* spiders are virtually restricted to their known distributions but are perceived to exist throughout the U.S." *Journal of Medical Entomology* 42: 512–21.

Index

About the Author

Jeff Mollenhauer has a diverse background in ornithology, which includes behavioral research, mist-netting and bird banding, coastal bird management, and leading education programs. Jeff has been an avid birder for more than ten years and has traveled all over the United States in search of birds. His life list totals more than 500 bird species in the United States, with nearly 300 in South Carolina alone.

Though born and raised in New Jersey, Jeff has been a southern Yankee for more than seven years. He received his BS in wildlife biology at Penn State University in 2000, and in 2003 he received his MS in biology from the University of Southern Mississippi. His MS research led him all the way to northern Sweden, where he studied the migration of Bluethroats, a small type of thrush.

In 2004 Jeff and his wife, Meagan, moved to Charleston, South Carolina. After working for two years with saltwater fish at the South Carolina Department of Natural Resources, Jeff landed his dream job. In 2007 he began his new job as the Director of Bird Conservation for Audubon South Carolina at the Francis Beidler Forest Audubon Sanctuary.